Most Roads Led To 10 Regt

By
Brian (Harry) Clacy

Dedication

This book is dedicated to 24523379 Driver Paul K Bulman Royal Corps of Transport. Paul 'Geordie' Bulman was just 19 years old when, sadly, he was killed on the 19th of May 1981 whilst on Operations in South Armagh Northern Ireland.

When 'Geordie' arrived at 10 Regiment RCT in Bielefeld he was assigned to 17 Squadron RCT, the Squadron was already three weeks into their Northern Ireland training and 'Geordie' was devastated when the Officer Commanding told him he would be remaining with the Rear Party whilst the rest of the Squadron deployed to Ulster. Paul argued forcefully that he wanted to go with the Squadron but the OC would not be moved on the subject. Paul immediately requested a Commanding Officers interview so that he could plead his case with the highest authority within 10 Regiment RCT. On Commanding Officers Orders, Paul again appealed for permission to deploy with the rest of 17 Squadron, but the CO pointed out to him that he would be nearly three weeks behind everyone else in the training regime. The only way the Colonel would allow Paul to deploy was if he caught up with everyone else on their training and he passed every physical and written test that the Training Staff set him. Paul more than rose to the challenge and much to his delight the Commanding Officer gave authority for Paul to deploy out to Northern Ireland with the rest of 17 Squadron RCT.

Paul was an exceptionally keen soldier and Driver who had an infectious smile and a cheerful disposition, he wanted to be involved in everything. For instance, every time he drove a Saracen Armoured Personnel Carrier (APC) he always wanted to drive the lead vehicle. On that fateful day in May 1981 Paul left the Bessbrook location at 0700 hours and drove the lead Saracen on a two vehicle mobile patrol to check the road was safe for use by other vehicles. As his vehicle stopped to allow the Infantry to deploy and check a culvert, the IRA detonated a massive mine that had been buried under the road. The Saracen and its occupants were instantaneously obliterated. Driver Paul 'Geordie' Bulman RCT and four other soldiers from 1st Battalion the Royal Green Jackets (Riflemen Michael Bagshaw aged 24, Andrew Gavin aged 19, John King aged 29 and Lance Corporal Grenville Winstone aged 27) were all killed in the explosion. Paul died doing his duty, a soldier, amongst soldiers.

We will remember them.

Acknowledgements

Major (Retired) Terry Cavender is the author of one of the funniest books I have ever read, his RCT autobiography, 'A Boy from Nowhere', is nothing short of comic genius. I owe you so much Terry for everything you've done for me on this and my previous books, many, many thanks 'old son'.

Yet another huge debt of gratitude goes to Eric Hartley BA MA (Hons) MA and Reece Taylor of ELK Marketing in Beverley East Yorkshire, Eric and Reece designed and photographed this fantastic book cover.

I must also thank a few old RCT soldiers who have provided me with the photographs of participants in the book. Norman Sweetlove who supplied the photograph of Lance Corporal Roy Malkin, Roy Burrows for the picture of Staff Sergeant Derek 'Windy' Gale in a Mark III Millie, and Ted Medler who let me use his photograph of a SEAC Pack Air Despatch load. I would also like to wish Paul Rees lots of luck, he's another ex RCT soldier who has recently set out on a literary career, good luck old son. If I've missed out any other Trog's/Trogg's then I apologise unreservedly.

I must also give a massive thank you to Ken Blake and Titch Fry for their help on my dedication of this book to Driver Paul 'Geordie' Bulman RCT, Titch Fry was serving with 'Geordie' in Bessbrook location when he was killed.

I am so lucky to be married to one of the most gracious women on this planet, my beautiful wife Nicky has done a mass of typing, photograph placement, driving, map-reading, hotel booking and computer advising to help me write this book, and all with only the odd look of slight irritation. You really are an amazing women Nicky, thanks babes.

Harry Clacy

Contents

(All ranks listed are those held when discharged from the British Army)

23699240 Warrant Officer Class 1 (RSM) Derek Gale

24115820 Sergeant Seamus O'Callaghan

533840 Lieutenant Colonel Peter Shields MBE QGM

24212479 Sergeant Roy Malkin

24242832 Driver Vince Rollock

24267089 Lance Corporal Ray Ratcliffe

24274523 Warrant Officer Class II Ricky Lodge

24316562 Sergeant Bill Baker

24316568 Sergeant David Hand

24357695 Driver Ken Blake

24361322 Corporal George Redpath

24457567 Corporal Ric Spurr

24597487 Staff Sergeant Les Reed

24588230 Warrant Officer Class 1 (RSM) Bob Alexander QCVS

Ancestry of the British Army's transport formations

The Royal Waggoner's 1794 – 1795

The Royal Wagon Train 1799 – 1833

Land Transport Corps 1855 – 1857

The Military Train1857 – 1869

Army Service Corps 1869 – 1881

Commissariat and Transport Corps 1881 – 1886

Army Service Corps 1889 – 1918

Royal Army Service Corps 1918 – 1965

Royal Corps of Transport 1965 – 1993

Royal Logistic Corps 1993 - to date

Introduction

The British Army's Military Transport system has evolved over the years, I'd like to say it has matured like a fine wine but that would be bordering on the bleeding ridiculous. But it has definitely rolled with the punches that have been thrown at it since 1794 when the very first British Army Transport Organisation (**The Royal Waggoner's**) was thrown together. Those who have served in the Royal Corps of Transport (**RCT**) will know that it was the Duke of Marlborough who organised the very first British uniformed Transport formation, and he recruited the Drivers who filled its ranks with convicted felons and delinquents from prisons around the country. This really set the perceived standard impression of British Army Drivers throughout the subsequent history of our Corps. In the First World War the Army Service Corps (**ASC**) was referred to by other British Soldiers as '**A**nglais **S**an **C**ourage' (the English Without Courage) and **A**lly **S**loper's **C**avalry. In 1867 the first British cartoon character was included in a magazine, the character was a shifty and conniving ne'er-do-well who was always sloping down back alleys to avoid his creditors and this was how ASC Drivers were perceived by the rest of the British Army. In the Second World War things didn't get any better because the Corps successors, the Royal Army Service Corps (**RASC**) and their Drivers were nicknamed the, **R**un **A**way **S**omeone's **C**oming. Drivers in our Corps also dished it out to other Troops like the Royal Army Medical Corps (**RAMC**) medics who were labelled as the sort of men who would, **R**ob **A**ll **M**y **C**omrades (an insinuation that medics went through the pockets of defenceless battlefield casualties to steal their valuables), or they were more than likely to **R**un **A**way **M**atrons **C**oming. This macabre sense of humour is gradually impressed into every British soldier during their basic training, just as surely as the army supplies soldiers with a rifle and helmet.

The British Army is a complex military machine that is made up of many different facets and assets, so co-ordinating the Infantry, Armour, Artillery and Army Air Corps in battle must be like trying to herd a Regiment of cats - who'd be a General eh! Putting the different Teeth Arms to one side for a minute, just try to imagine what it must be like to try and sustain each Army, Corps, Division, Brigade, Regiment, Company, Platoon, Section, and Uncle Tom Cobley and all. Each army unit will place different supply demands on the rear echelons and if those requests for rations and medical supplies alone aren't met, then the life of the average Infantryman, Tankie, Gunner, and Air-Trooper of the Army Air Corps could become unbearable to say the least. They certainly wouldn't be able to defeat the enemy without tons of the right ammunition for their own particular weapon systems.

I do understand that for an Infantry soldier to engage with the enemy takes an awesome amount of courage. To kill another human-being by squeezing the trigger of a rifle or plunging a bayonet into his chest, and then to watch him die, is beyond the comprehension of most people. Thankfully most people don't have to deal with that sort of business in their everyday lives. But soldiers sometimes have to do these things because their Governments send them off to do the dirty work that they wouldn't have the guts to do themselves. 'Grunts' (Infantry), 'Tankies' (Armoured Units), 'Breech Creatures' (Royal Artillery) and 'Teeny Weeny Airways' (Army Air Corps) soldiers are the sort of men that have to carry out these appalling tasks because that is what they are trained to do. To a lesser degree the same can be said of every British Soldier, even army chefs have to be trained to fire a rifle before they're trained to fry a sausage. Every member of every Corps in the British Army is a soldier first, and a Tradesman second. The reality is that the so called REMF's (Rear Echelon Mother F***ers) can be just as tough and motivated as any of the Combatants from the fighting elements of the army. Incidentally, before the Falklands War started I briefly got to know the Army Catering Corps (**ACC**) Master Chef who was serving with 3 Para. During the Battle for Mount Longdon this older soldier ran up the mountain with heavy boxes of ammunition and returned carrying 3 Para casualties. He delivered these screaming and suffering soldiers to Captain 'Doc' Burgess RAMC who had based his Regimental Aid Post (RAP) just behind the attack start line on Mount Longdon. This **A**ndy **C**app **C**ommando then picked up more ammunition boxes and started yet another of many runs back up Mount Longdon that night. I can't remember the Warrant Officers name but he was awarded a Mentioned in Dispatches Oak Leaf for his outstanding courage under fire during the night of 11- 12 June 1982. Only a slop jockey? I don't fucking think so!

In regards to all army truck driving soldiers who support many army's around the world, it has to be said that they're usually regarded as second rate soldiers who aren't good enough to get into a combat branch of the Armed Forces. Unfortunately these truckies are usually too busy getting the right kit up to the right soldiers at the right time to get involved in front line action, but there are times when these 'D Day Dodgers' have had to show extraordinary valour supporting the combat troops, and in some historical cases they've dug them right out of the shit. At the battle of Waterloo in 1815, Corporal Brewster of the

Royal Wagon Train delivered some desperately needed ammunition to the 3rd Regiment of Foot Guards (now the Coldstream Guards), and at the Battle of Arnhem Bridge the RASC delivered some desperately needed ammunition to the surrounded and beleaguered British 2nd Parachute Battalion. I could also mention the D Day action at Port-en-Bessin where Captain Cousins of 47 Commando stormed ashore and captured a German held bunker with four of his fellow Royal Marines. This gallant RM Captain was killed during the attack and even today their Corps still believe he should have been awarded a Victoria Cross for his actions. Little is mentioned about the Drivers from 522 Company RASC who drove through Machine Gun and Tank fire to resupply these beleaguered Commando's, they were low on ammunition and would more than likely have been either killed or taken prisoner without the help of some British Army drivers.

Army truck drivers (both male and female) don't have the advantage of working in a close knit unit like an Infantry Platoon or Company. In these formations the Platoon Commander or Sergeant calls all of the shots and the Tom's (Privates) simply follow orders and do as instructed. Drivers on the other hand have to maintain a complicated piece of kit, be it an ambulance, staff car, Land Rover, fuel tanker, fork lift truck or a massive truck and trailer, and they have to get their load of ammunition, rations or fuel to the right place so the fighting elements can continue the battle, and hopefully help win the war. If Drivers are lucky enough they might have a co-driver to do the map reading who can also ride along as shotgun, if not, then they will have to read the map themselves to make sure that they're on the right road. And whilst doing that they'll also be looking out for enemy aircraft, mines and any behind the lines Special Forces who want to stop them from doing their job, i.e; ambush him. Drivers often have to work incredibly long hours whilst trying to avoid falling asleep at the wheel and crashing into a ditch at the side of the road. If they do have a problem with their vehicle, its load, or any Spetsnaz soldiers, they don't have the luxury of being able to shout out, "Sarge, what the fuck do I do now?" They simply have to rely on their own wits and courage to see the mission through on their lonesome.

For a fairly realistic view of what army divers have to suffer in war the reader is recommended to watch an American film called 'The Red Ball Express' which was made in 1952. The name comes from a US Priority Freight System that operated in the States and was adopted by US Army truck drivers after the D Day landings. The British, Canadian and American logistic lines where stretched to the limit by late August 1944, so the Yanks solved the problem of supplying Patton's lightning 3rd Army by utilising nearly six thousand trucks that ran day and night to keep his troops on the move. The US Army re-supply trucks were manned by at least 75% African-American drivers who were given priority on the one way Red Ball routes. These troops were deemed to be of a poor quality by their own army purely because of the colour of their skin. Each day these amazing soldiers shifted nearly 13,000 tons of food, ammunition and petrol from the Normandy Beaches up to the fighting troops, and they often removed the governor's on their engines to increase the speed of their trucks. Authors note: This was something quite a few RCT Drivers often did to their Mark III Millie's in the 1970's and with disastrous results. If I remember rightly, a certain Driver from 9 Squadron RCT (who shall remain nameless) was somewhat surprised when his pistons burst through the engine cover whilst driving along an autobahn at a speed of well over 70 mph, true story. The port of Antwerp was opened in mid-November 1944 and the Red Ball Express was no longer needed, which was good news because the majority of the trucks used had deteriorated to such a state they were even beyond the skills of a 'Kwik Fit Fitter.'

For anyone who would prefer a British version of a World War Two truck drivers' war then I wholly recommend a book called 'My War on Wheels.' Mike Holdsworth has published his fathers' war diary about his service as an RASC Driver during World War Two. Driver John A Holdsworth enlisted in 1939 and served in the Corps for five years and seven months. John's diary goes into detail about some of the gruesome loads he had to pick up from the US Army front line and the result of what happened to an RASC convoy after it was attacked by Luftwaffe aircraft, and the reality of how many Drivers were killed during one single strafe.

Meanwhile, back to the RCT. The Corps took over the British Army Transportation baton from the RASC on 15th July 1965, after the McLeod Report (named after General Sir Roderick McLeod who headed the committee) was published, its findings recommended that the duties covered by the RASC would be split up between the RCT, RAOC, REME and ACC. The newly formed RCT would be solely responsible for the Transport and Movement duties of the British Army. Let's take a brief look at just some of the trades and tasks for which the RCT was going to be exclusively accountable. The following synopsis and abbreviated accounts are just a few of the many that I could have extracted from our Corps history, and the order they're written in is not a reflection of each trade's importance and standing within the RCT.

Army Aviation

The RASC had had a finger in the aviation pie from the early days when its soldiers became Glider Pilots and Air Despatchers in the Second World War. When the RCT took over its mantle they retained some of its aviation tasks, the Corps reluctantly also agreed to take part in an MOD integration scheme where it would allow some of its Officers and NCO's to continue their military careers, but as helicopter and light aircraft pilots. These pilots would fly purely logistic sorties and the Army Air Corps pilots would deal with the reconnaissance side of army aviation, it was one way of keeping an RCT finger in the pie without losing some of its best soldiers. Before the integration scheme ceased, army aviation had twenty six commissioned Officers, one Warrant Officer and one Senior NCO from the RCT serving as qualified pilots alongside those of the Army Air Corps (AAC).

One such pilot was Captain JG Greenhalgh RCT (Later Colonel AAC) who was awarded the Distinguished Flying Cross for his gallant actions during the Falklands War. The citation for his award reads:

497429 Captain John Greenhalgh DFC

From the early hours of 28th May 1982, 2nd Battalion the Parachute Regiment was engaged in fierce fighting to take enemy positions in the area of the Goose Green settlement on the island of East Falkland. Throughout the day Captain Greenhalgh flew many missions in direct support of the battalions operations, continually exposing his helicopter to enemy artillery and mortar fire. Enemy observation posts were able to pinpoint his helicopter each time it landed and as a result the barrage always intensified on whichever landing site he chose. Regardless, he continued to fly to bring ammunition forward and to evacuate casualties. Later that night, several severely injured casualties still remained on the battlefield. Captain Greenhalgh was by then back at Brigade Headquarters, over 20 km away. On hearing the plight of the casualties Captain Greenhalgh volunteered to fly forward to pick them up. In doing so he was forced to fly into the vicinity of the enemy positions at Goose Green. He located the casualties in the darkness and successfully extricated them. Visibility throughout had been poor, with low cloud making flying particularly dangerous. It is without doubt that Captain Greenhalgh's brave pilotage saved the lives of these casualties. Later, during the battle for Wireless Ridge on the night of 13ᵗʰ June 1982 he again flew many missions in extremely bad conditions under very intense artillery fire. His flying skill, daring and outstanding bravery again saved many lives. Throughout, his conduct and courageous actions were most inspiring.

Air Despatch

The RASC Air Despatchers (AD) who supplied the British 1ˢᵗ Airborne landings on **'OPERATION MARKET GARDEN'** in September 1944 were incredibly brave men, so much so that these RASC soldier won the 'Dakota Formation Badge' that was worn on RCT Air Despatchers right and left uniform sleeves for many years. When the Dakota went out of service and was replaced by more modern and up to date aircraft, the older RASC Air Despatchers who had operated on the outgoing C47 Dakota were respectfully nicknamed 'Dak's.'

During **'OPERATION CORPORATE'** 47 AD Squadron RCT flew plenty of air re-supply missions from Ascension Island and down to the Task Force steaming towards Ajax Bay in the South Atlantic. The despatched loads ranged from soldier's mail to high priority stores and equipment urgently needed by the Royal Navy and SAS Special Forces. Some of the re-supply runs required the RAF C 130 Hercules aircraft to be In Flight Refuelled (IFR) twice before heading back to Ascension Island, and because the Hercules top speed couldn't even match the Victor Tankers stalling speed, it all had to be done whilst both aircraft were in a steep dive. For their distinguished conduct during many operations these RCT Air Despatchers received the following awards:

Warrant Officer Class 2 D Moore RCT – MBE.
Warrant Officer Class 2 P M Williams RCT – MBE.
Corporal C J Holdsworth RCT – Commander in Chiefs Task Force Commendation.
Driver G J Hunt RCT – Air Officer Commanding 38 Group Commendation.

Port and Maritime

What the RASC achieved through the Mulberry Harbour after D Day went beyond even Field Marshal Erwin Rommel's worst nightmares. It has to be said that the British designed and built snap-together military port had a huge part to play in the Allies winning the Second World War. Remnants of the Mulberry Harbour are still visible from Arromanches beach in Normandy today, but more importantly, the British brought the idea of a mobile port back with them and so was born 17 Port and Maritime Regiment RCT. Since its foundation in 1949,

17 Port and Maritime Regiment RASC/RCT/RLC has served with the British Army in Korea, the Malayan Emergency, Christmas Island, Suez, Tobruk, Borneo, Belize, the Falkland Islands, Bosnian, and the Wars in the Gulf and Afghanistan.

During the Falklands War back in 1982 Sergeant Derek Sydney Boultby RCT deployed with the Task Force on one of Her Majesty's Army Vessels (HMAV) and was awarded the Military Medal for his actions throughout the conflict. His citation reads:

Sergeant Boultby of 17 Port Regiment RCT was the NCO in charge of Mexeflote rafts throughout the Falkland Islands operations. At Ascension Island, during a massive re-stow operation he worked all hours under difficult conditions to move cargo quickly. In San Carlos Water, the Mexeflote rafts played a major part in the logistic landing of equipment to ensure the success of the fighting troops. From the exposed position, which such rafts offer, Sergeant Boultby worked continuously throughout daylight hours and in extreme weather conditions. The vulnerability of his position to constant enemy air attack did not deter him from his task and he was an inspiration to his crew and other RCT personnel. He was coxswain of the Mexeflote present at Fitzroy during the bombing of RFA Sir Galahad and RFA Sir Tristram, and repeatedly returned to the area of the stricken ships to rescue survivors and, with complete disregard for his own safety, dived into the sea to rescue a Chinese crewman. Sergeant Boultby's dedication to his tasks in dangerous conditions was outstanding.

In addition to the MM awarded to Sergeant Boultby and Captain J G Greenhalgh's DFC, twenty six other members of the RCT received awards during the Falklands War, including five MIDs, three CBEs, one OBE, five MBEs and a BEM.

Since the Falklands War the RCT continued to provide logistic support to the British Army wherever it was deployed and this included serving out in Iraq where two Junior NCO's and one Officer received substantial Gallantry awards. Captain (later Lieutenant Colonel) Peter Shield's career and Queens Gallantry Medal citation are covered in detail in his very own chapter within this book. Another Queens Gallantry Medal was awarded to Corporal M J Driscoll RCT who was attached to 24 Airmobile Field Ambulance RAMC, his citation reads:

Corporal MJ Driscoll QGM RCT

On 28th February 1991, Corporal Driscoll RCT was in the front of an ambulance on a joint convoy of medical vehicles made up from 142 Medical Company of the 429th Medical Battalion (US Army) and 24 Airmobile Field Ambulance RAMC. At approximately 1500 hours, during poor weather in a sandstorm, the convoy encountered perceived enemy fire. A medical officer had been killed following an explosion which appeared to have been as a result of a mine. Shortly afterwards, a second explosion was heard off the track near Corporal Driscoll's ambulance. In this instance, a young female medical assistant had sustained a traumatic amputation of a leg with a large open abdominal wound. Four other casualties had been taken, each lying off the track in what now appeared to be a minefield. Corporal Driscoll, despite having sustained a shrapnel wound to his thigh, set out to provide medical care for the wounded, having moved the injured female to a place of safety. He then subsequently directed the evacuation requirements and called for an air ambulance helicopter. After having his own wound dressed, he refused to board the aircraft until all the wounded had been boarded and, when satisfied, was persuaded to be evacuated to a forward hospital. Corporal Driscoll's actions in the rescue of the casualty, without hesitation and without regard to his own safety, showed uncommon bravery and was an inspiration to those around him. His subsequent command and control of an extremely confused situation ensured all casualties received prompt attention and were sustained until the arrival of the casualty evacuation helicopter. Corporal Driscoll showed great presence of mind and devotion to duty, and behaved in a manner above that expected of his rank.

Just over three years later the RCT handed over the British Army Transportation baton, which it had held for twenty eight years, to the Royal Logistic Corps (RLC) and along with that baton the RCT handed over to the new Corps the Drivers, NCO's and Officers from within its ranks. One of those Junior NCO's was Lance Corporal Darren George Dickson who was an RCT Territorial Army soldier serving with the Scottish Transport Regiment. Darren was 22 years old and had only been in the RCT for three years when he deployed out to Iraq, within five days of his first Operational Tour he was to be awarded a Military Cross with the following citation:

Lance Corporal Darren Dickson MC RLC

On 8th May 2004, at approximately 0640 hours, a section of low mobility water tankers, with escorts from 1st Cheshire Battle Group was ambushed in the city of Al Basrah. The ambush was initiated by a roadside bomb, followed by small arms fire and rocket-propelled grenades. Dickson a 22-year old Territorial Army soldier of only three years' military service, on his first operational tour and five days in theatre, was top cover sentry in the packet commanders' unarmoured Land Rover. His duty was to provide force protection to the convoy, a task for which he had only recently qualified.

The infantry escorts engaged the enemy from their armoured vehicles and were joined without hesitation by Dickson. In accordance with the accepted drill, the convoy pushed through the initial ambush and overcame an attempt by the enemy to dislocate the escorts from the water tankers. Thereafter, the convoy encountered a second, heavier ambush which once more caused Dickson to return fire from his exposed position. During this engagement Dickson was wounded by a rifle shot to his left shoulder causing him to collapse to the bottom of the vehicle. Despite heavy bleeding, he resumed his position as top cover and with no concern for his own safety continued to return fire against the insurgents. Although a heavy weight of rocket-propelled grenade and small arms fire continued against the convoy, the aggressive fire from Dickson was sufficient to ensure that the enemy's own fire was hasty and inaccurate, with rockets passing between the vehicles. During the engagement, the occupants of the section commander's vehicle, including the injured Dickson, dismounted and took up a defensive position in order to ensure the safety of the tankers and drivers. Having discharged his entire magazine of ammunition, he was only prevented from providing addition fire by the severity of his injuries which left him unable to reload. The enemy fire having been suppressed, the section commander was able to reorganise the convoy and lead it to the safety of the nearest coalition force base. It was only at this point that Dickson received medical attention, eventually being evacuated to the field hospital where he underwent surgery. It has been estimated that the series of ambushes involved up to 50 insurgent gunmen, and that several were killed or wounded by the heavy weight of the return fire. Dickson displayed remarkable fortitude and courage... his selfless disregard for his own safety and prompt action undoubtedly saved lives.

And so the Corps continues, albeit with another name, The Royal Logistic Corps who's Drivers have continued in the same gutsy and underestimated fashion as the Drivers of the Royal Corps of Transport. For years the RCT has quoted Sir Winston Churchill's, "War is like a flower and without transport as its stem, it could never blossom," this of course referred to the soldiers of the Army Service Corps and Royal Army Service Corps who served throughout the First and Second World Wars. The Royal Corps of Transport has successfully participated in every war from 1965 through to 1993, wars and conflicts like Aden, Cyprus, Northern Ireland, the Falkland Islands, Iraq and even the 'Cold War'. We who have served within the ranks of the Royal Corps of Transport should have signed off with another quote from another great soldier, this time from General Sir Peter de la Billiere who was Commander In Chief of British Forces during the First Gulf War. In a letter he addressed to the Corps' very last DGTM (Director General Transport and Movement) Major General J D MacDonald, Sir Peter praised the soldiers of the RCT and succinctly told our very own General, "No RCT – no war". Which brings me to the main role of the RCT, the role for which every army truck driver is renowned, driving vehicles of just about every shape and size.

In this book I have included the careers of RCT soldiers who have been Staff Car and General Transport Drivers, Air Despatchers, Corps and army boxers, Tank Transporter Drivers, re-fuelling specialists, Paratroopers and those who have made the transition from Territorial to Regular army Drivers. I have also included some of their distressing experiences on Operations in Aden, Northern Ireland and the Gulf War, and others that happened whilst taking part on routine Field Exercises in Belize, Canada and BAOR. The British Army ethos is that everyone in the army is a soldier first and a Tradesman second, in the RCT everyone was a Heavy Goods Driver first and a Hovercraft Operator, Railwayman, Clerk, Port Operator, Radio Operator, Air Despatcher, Crane Operator, Maritime Operator, Seaman, Tank Transporter Driver, Movement Controller, Stevedore, Paratrooper or Staff Car Driver second.

Harry Clacy

23699240 Warrant Officer Class 1 (RSM) Derek Gale
RASC and RCT 1959 - 1982

Derek Gale was born and raised in Gloucester so he speaks with a proper West Country burr, as did his dad Charlie who Derek describes as being "a strict but good man." Charlie Gale had been a Royal Artillery (RA) soldier in the Regular British Army for 28 years before being discharged in the late 1940's after achieving the rank of WO 1 RSM (Regimental Sergeant Major). He'd served in the 'Gunners' throughout the Second World War and had seen action in the Far East but, like most wartime soldiers, he never spoke about what he'd experienced.

WO1 (RSM) Charlie Gale RA being presented to Queen Elizabeth in 1945.

It was just before Christmas in 1958 that Derek told his dad he wanted to enlist into the Royal Army Service Corps (RASC). Charlie offered only a few words of advice about army life and simply told his son, "If you go into the army, you can only take it or leave it, but let me tell you this one thing, it's a hard life son." Derek wasn't deterred and neither were his brothers who also served as Drivers in the RASC later the RCT. Charlie Gale, the eldest brother, served for 3 years in the Royal Corps of Transport which included a tough stint with 63

(Parachute) Squadron RCT. During his two weeks Basic Training at Buller Barracks, Driver Derek Gale was unimaginatively bestowed with the nickname 'Windy' Gale by his fellow recruits, a tag that has remained securely attached to him over the years. After successfully completing his fortnight of square bashing in Aldershot, Derek was posted to 6 Training Battalion RASC in Yeovil to complete the rest of his Military and Trade Training. During his time at Yeovil Derek would learn about the bizarre practises of NCO's in the British Army, traditions and rituals that included taking a lot of hassle and, what at the time seemed to be, un-necessary aggravation from his Training NCO. Derek's Platoon was accommodated in a wooden spider hut and they were put in the charge of a Corporal who suffered from a severe stutter. With the usual cruel squaddie humour he was surreptitiously nicknamed 'Stuttering Sid', but no-one dared call him this to his face. Unfortunately when 'Stuttering Sid' heard an arrogant recruit from the Platoon mimicking his stutter behind his back, it spelt trouble for all of those recruits in the twelve man room.

When Corporal 'Stuttering Sid' carried out a room inspection the following day one of the recruits stamped on a large spider that was crawling across the floor, Sid spotted the incident and told everyone to get changed into their best boots and uniforms. After getting changed they were ordered to report to the Quartermaster Stores where each recruit had to sign for either a pick or shovel and they were then marched over to the training ground. Corporal 'Stuttering Stan' then halted the squad on a rough patch of ground and presented them with the dead spider, now laid out in a matchbox coffin. He snarled at his recruits, saying "This Platoon is responsible for the death of my pet spider and as a result you are all now going to give him the Regimental Funeral that he deserves. You will all dig a grave six feet long by six feet deep and two feet wide, you will then bury my spider in that grave. I'll be back in twenty minutes to make sure the grave is the right size." The recruits eventually buried the spider and as a result of their labours everyone's uniforms and boots were caked in mud and sweat. The recruits all had an idea why they were being punished and not one of them ever dared mock their corporal's stutter again. Derek was 17½ years old when he went home in uniform on his first furlough. He was as proud as punch when he strode into the Red Lion pub in King's Stanley near Gloucester and offered to buy his dad a drink. A grim faced Charlie was as strict as Derek's Training Corporal and he remonstrated with his son, "Go to the pub over the road and get yourself a pint in there my boy. Until you're legally old enough, I won't let you buy me a pint of beer!"

As Derek approached the end of his military training in Yeovil he automatically entered the Driver Training phase. This meant he had to pass a driving test in an Austin K9 truck, a 1 ton military vehicle that was an AWD (All Wheel Drive) vehicle, equipped with an un-dynamic 3995cc petrol engine. The K9 was the first Austin truck to be developed in Britain after the end of the Second World War. The British Army adapted the civilian Loadstar range for their own use and introduced it into the army in 1952. The Austin K9's were used as Water Carrier's, Radio Trucks, Ambulances and Royal Electrical and Mechanical Engineers (REME) recovery vehicles as well as General Service (GS) vehicles. The majority of these military lorry's had rifle racks, observation hatches, convoy lights and a trailer electrical circuit added as standard fittings for the army. This adaptable and very simple army truck had a below par cross country capability and was eventually replaced in the mid 1950's by the redoubtable Bedford RL three ton truck, but in some cases the Austin K9 continued to give over thirty years of reliable service. Derek took to driving like a duck takes to water and so he passed his trade and driving tests without a hitch.

On completion of his training, Derek was posted to 6 Training Battalion RASC's Permanent Staff and remained at Yeovil for the next three years. During that time he also passed his HGV 2 test driving an AEC Mk 1 Militant 10 ton truck (Millie) and his motorcycle test on the army's newly acquired BSA 350cc army motorbike. With his newly acquired licences Derek thought life was definitely on the up but when the Battalions' Commanding Officer also promoted him to the giddy heights of Lance Corporal, well, his cup runneth over. Unfortunately for Derek his delight was short-lived because the 'Redcaps' Royal Military Police (RMP) caught him urinating against the wall outside a local pub in Yeovil. Derek's Commanding Officer was so displeased with the reported incident that he took the Lance Corporal's stripe back off him. By 1963 Derek had regained his Lance Jack and he managed to refrain from publically pissing up against any other walls and hung on to his stripe this time.

At this time an uprising was taking place out in Aden and anti-British guerrilla groups like the Front for the Liberation of Occupied South Yemen (FLOSY) and the National Liberation Front (NLF) were pursuing a terrorist campaign against the British Army. These terrorist groups weren't only fighting the British Army they were also fighting each other, the main targets for both terrorist groups being off duty soldiers and policemen. In one particular attack at RAF Khormaksar a party of British children became an unintentional target of a grenade attack (the weapon of choice for these terrorist groups). This resulted in one child being killed and four others severely injured. Lance Corporal Derek Gale was just one of many servicemen despatched to Aden on an RAF VC 10 to combat the uprising. These extra troops were drafted in to secure the area and hopefully prevent any further attacks against British personnel and their families. In reality the experiences in Aden were to be an excellent training regime for the British Army's future involvement in Northern Ireland some six years later.

Initially Derek was sent to 90 Company RASC and during his tour he drove around in a fabulous army Ford Zephyr 6 Staff Car. In today's modern world this vehicle was comparable to a top of the range BMW 7 Series, the Zephyr 6 was a beast of a car in 1963. Every time Derek left the safety of a military camp he had to strap a 9mm Browning pistol onto his web belt. Aden was an incredibly dangerous place to be if you wore a British uniform and if it kicked off anywhere near him, Derek would have to defend whoever was travelling in the back of his Staff Car. His first incumbent was Brigadier Montenero, an ex-Royal Engineer officer who'd been involved in **'OPERATION FRANKTON'** (The 1942 Cockleshell Heroes mission) near Bordeaux in occupied France. Derek held this wartime officer in very high esteem. When Brigadier Montenero was posted out of Aden this high ranking officer was replaced by another wartime officer called Brigadier Kyte. The new Brigadier's Married Quarter was situated the other side of Aden and so Derek was moved out of 90 Company's crappy wooden huts and into RAF Steamer Point camp which had modern brick built accommodation. "It was absolute luxury" recalls Derek. "We had hot showers every day and the standard of food in the RAF restaurant, well, by rights you couldn't call it a cookhouse, it was like eating in an upper class bistro back home."

But life wasn't all about fast cars and comfort in Aden, and Derek had a horrific introduction into the violent world in which soldiers sometimes have to exist. He was driving Brigadier Kyte back to his Married Quarter late one afternoon and noticed an old civilian Land Rover in his rear view mirror. It was driving at full pelt and so he let the battered old vehicle overtake him. As the vehicle sped past he noticed at least two scruffy young Arab's in the front seats. The Land Rover accelerated away and as it drove over a hump in the road Derek and the Brigadier were now trailing about 30 metres behind them. It was at that point that the Land Rover exploded into a million pieces and one of its occupant's arms bounced off the bonnet of Derek's Staff Car. Derek's initial shock of the explosion didn't stop him from slamming on the anchors and pulling over to the side of the road. It was after the Brigadier had pulled a shocked Derek out of the Driver's seat that he noticed the windscreen, bonnet and roof of the car was covered in bits of human flesh and blood. Army and Police patrols soon swamped onto the site and Derek knew he should get his senior officer away from the danger area, there was little they could do to help anyway. Derek tried to reassure Brigadier Kyte that he was alright and that he could continue to drive him home, but the wartime officer wouldn't listen to any protestations. He ordered Derek into the back of the car and drove them both to his official Officers Married Quarter. Once inside Derek sat down on the settee whilst his senior officer poured him a tumbler of brandy, he handed it over to Derek with the instruction, "Here you go Lance Corporal Gale, drink this down and you'll be fine." After quickly drinking the five star brandy Derek was so pissed that the Brigadier had to drive him back to his Steamer Point accommodation, he also picked him up again the following morning.

Derek was given a brilliant confidential report before he left Aden which included a strong recommendation for his promotion to Full Corporal. He was also given a prestigious posting to 20 Squadron RCT at Regents Park Barracks in London (the RASC had been de-commissioned and by now it was called the Royal Corps of Transport). As a full Corporal Derek was put in charge of three large vans that were used for the Royal family and Very Very Important Persons (VVIP's) baggage details. The vans had to be kept in an immaculate condition and were generally polished several times a day. Every day Derek and the RCT Drivers who worked for him had to wear their best boots which had to be bulled up to a shine that would put a Guardsman to shame, they also had to wear their Number 2 Service Dress (SD) and Number 1 (No 1) hats, commonly referred to as 'Twat Hats' because any soldier wearing one looked like a right twat! They were on call 24 hours a day. The team of Drivers from 20 Squadron were always busy collecting and delivering all sorts of gear from Buckingham Palace, Sandringham House, and both Windsor and Balmoral Castles. The Squadron once had to load up a van with cinema equipment so that the Royal Family could watch films at Balmoral, (this was in the antediluvian days before all of the recent digital gizmos).

On one particular detail Derek and his team were given a police escort to Heathrow Airport where they had to collect all the baggage of a visiting VVVIP official from the Russian government and his support team. The visitors were staying at Buckingham Palace as guests of the British Royal family for seven days. Derek guided each van in turn as they reversed up to the aircraft for loading; the first two vans were loaded up to the gunnels with luggage and the last van was loaded with thirty unmarked and heavy boxes which collectively amounted to about four tons in weight. On arrival at Buckingham Palace everything was unloaded through a side entrance door where Derek asked one of the royal household flunkies, "What the hell is in all of those bloody boxes?" The flunky ripped open the top box and let Derek have a look inside, each box was full of bottles of vodka. The official told Derek, "This is for the VVVIP and his staff during their stay here at the Palace."

Late in 1965 Derek was posted to 62 Squadron RCT in West Berlin but he was only there for three months before being promoted to Sergeant and reposted to B Squadron at the Junior Leaders Regiment RCT in Taunton, Somerset. The Regiment received a royal visitor when a young Princess Anne came down to inspect the unit. Derek had previously bumped into Princess Anne when he was at 20 Squadron in London and so he was given the honour of driving the open topped Land Rover for her as she inspected the troops in Taunton. "She was a very nice girl" says Derek, "Very down to earth and without any airs or graces." During his time at Taunton Derek, who had played semi-pro football for Epsom FC and Hounslow FC, had the chance to play plenty of football and played alongside some Corps players like Alec Young, Chris Crowe, and Yonkter Yates, who'd actually played for Liverpool, Arsenal, and QPR.

After yet another great confidential report, Derek was promoted to Staff Sergeant and posted to 31 Port Regiment RCT in Hong Kong from 1972 to 1974 where he continued playing football at Corps level. Within the Regiment Derek was unfortunately made SQMS (Squadron Quarter Master Sergeant) and he was put in charge of all the maritime stores. "I was surrounded by anchors, ropes and all sorts of nautical equipment that was worth thousands of pounds, and yet I didn't know anything about bloody boats." His Regimental Sergeant Major (RSM) WO 1 PP D (Peter) Quinn MBE RCT and the subordinates within the Quartermaster stores were a great help to him though and he soon started to learn what bit of kit went where on each type of vessel. Derek also played a lot of Corps football in Hong Kong and he captained the RCT Far East side against the Royal Air Force and the Royal Marines. When not playing football or in the stores he spent the rest of his time on board ship.

From 1974 to 1980 Derek was the Troop Staff Sergeant in C Troop 17 Squadron which was part of the notorious 10 Regiment RCT in Bielefeld West Germany. During his tenure in 17 Squadron he did a six month tour in Northern

Ireland throughout which he was based at Moscow Camp in Belfast. The Squadron operated in support of 1st Battalion the Black Watch and 2nd Battalion Royal Anglian Regiment whilst deployed to the Province. Derek and his Troop Commander used to visit the Drivers of C Troop at their various locations which were spread all over West Belfast. After his experiences in Aden, Derek made sure he kept a fatherly eye on his baby Lieutenant.

Staff Sergeant Windy Gale behind the wheel of a 17 Squadron MkIII 'Millie' with some of his lads.

On promotion to Warrant Officer Class 2 (WO2), Derek was posted from C Troop 17 Squadron to the Regimental Training Wing in 10 Regiment RCT. This job involved him superintending every Driving, Promotion and Trade Training course. Even though it was mainly an administrative post, Derek was kept extremely busy and he loved the work. His dedication to the job led to him being promoted to WO1 Regimental Sergeant Major (RSM). He was given a choice of postings - he could go to the beautiful and sunny island of Cyprus as the Garrison Sergeant Major (GSM) of Dhekelia Garrison, or he could snatch a Territorial Army (TA) attachment as RSM of 151 Transport Regiment RCT, based in Croydon, South London. Unbelievably, Derek chose the latter option for reasons best known to himself. As his career was coming to a close Derek decided to apply for a commission within the army but he was subsequently turned down. The board in those days didn't have to give any reasons why they turned him down so Derek is none the wiser about where he went wrong. Authors note: (*Must have been that bloody West Country accent Derek*) and so he left the Royal Corps of Transport and British Army on 28th December 1982.

Derek moved to Southampton where he worked as a long distance lorry driver, which paid the bills but was quite a lonely existence. After working part-time behind the bar in a friends' pub Derek decided to enter the licencing game himself and he eventually took over a Free House in Woodchester Gloucestershire. Derek retired from being a landlord in 2007 and now works part time as a courier, he is a committed member of the Warrant Officers and Senior Non Commissioned Officers RASC/RCT Club and the RASC/RCT Association (Aldershot Branch) and is now their Vice Chairman.

He married his beautiful wife, June in 2005 and they now live in Basingstoke, Hampshire.

WO1 RSM Gale at his nephew's Royal Signals passing out parade at Abingdon. At the time Derek was serving at 151 Transport Regiment.

24115820 Sergeant Seamus O'Callaghan
RCT 1967 - 1991

At the age of nine years old Seamus Patrick O'Callaghan was caught brawling with his friend Sam Morris on the streets of Clipstone and his dad was furious at their disgraceful behaviour. Jimmy Patrick O'Callaghan was a miner at Clipstone Colliery in Nottinghamshire, he was a tough but disciplined man who'd fought many a fight, but always in the boxing ring. Jimmy and Sam's father decided that their sons should settle their differences by boxing under the Marquis of Queensbury rules, the locals from the community made a peoples ring and stood shoulder to shoulder to form a human square. Both fathers and sons agreed to a fight being held in the improvised boxing ring, but it had to be done fairly and under strict disciplinary rules. The young boys contest only lasted for three rounds after which they shook hands with each other and remain good friends to this day. Seamus had an epiphany that day because he'd secured a desire to get back into that boxing ring again. His dad was already a keen boxer and Seamus fell in love with the sport, a sport in which he would become synonymous within the British Army.

Whilst walking back home after the fight with Sam Morris, Jimmy told his son, "You've got to move your head more when you're boxing lad!" He then took Seamus into the family's backyard and made him stand on a handkerchief with the instruction of not to move his feet but to bob and weave away from his dad's punches. Seamus received plenty of clouts from his dad before they swapped places and reversed roles. Seamus couldn't land one punch on his dad as the 'old fella' ducked and dived without moving off the small white cloth, it was a great initial lesson for Seamus and one which he never forgot, it was to stand him in good stead for the future. Seamus joined the Forest Town Gymnasium and mixed with the likes of Mickey Oswald (Mickey became an England schoolboy's champion) and Jake Cheetham, both of these young lads became extremely good boxers with the 2nd Battalion Royal Green Jackets but they never boxed competitively against Seamus. After becoming hooked (pardon the pun) by the boxing bug, Seamus wholeheartedly threw himself into the sport and he eventually became good enough to box for the 'England Schoolboy's' team in 1966 in London.

Seamus once boxed for England against Wales and he was paired up against a young lad called Shearer and it was one of the worst fights of his entire career. In the first round both boxers just danced around each other and hardly landed any punches. When the bell sounded, Seamus went back to his corner where his trainer slapped him in the face and shouted, "What do you think you're doing?" He wouldn't let Seamus sit down on the stool and refused to give him any water because his performance was so poor. The trainer gave him some stern instructions which ended with, "Now get out there and bloody well fight him." In the second round, Seamus's work rate was much better and by the end of the third he'd won the bout on points. That lacklustre performance would never be repeated whilst he boxed in the British Army, but during one particular fight as a soldier he became a bit too cocky against a German civilian boxer, more on that later though.

Patrick Carol was Seamus's best friend throughout their time at St Philips Junior and St Bede's senior schools. After graduating they both decided to join the Armed Forces. At the time Seamus had two uncles who were serving in the army, his Uncle Martin was in a Battalion of the Royal Irish Rangers and his Uncle Jimmy was in the Royal Army Ordnance Corps (RAOC). Both were desperate for Seamus to join their units but a cousin had warned him that on joining the Royal Irish Rangers he'd been mercilessly picked on just because his uncle was a Warrant Officer within the Battalion. He warned Seamus, "Don't listen to either of them, go your own way." Seamus had already decided he wanted to see a bit of the world and get away from the local area so he approached the Royal Navy (RN) desk in Mansfield's Armed Forces Recruiting Office. He had aspirations of sailing all around the world. Fortunately for the Royal Corps of Transport the RN recruiter was away from his desk at that moment and so Seamus followed his mate Patrick to the army desk where they both ended up joining the Junior Leaders Regiment of the Royal Corps of Transport (RCT). Seamus didn't have a clue what RCT soldiers did for a living or that the Corps already had some of the best army boxers within their ranks.

The Junior Leaders Regiment RCT was based at Norton Manor Camp in Taunton, Somerset and on his arrival there, Seamus was placed into Dalton Troop, C Squadron. His Troop Sergeant was a man called Sergeant Roy 'Donkey' Owens who encouraged Seamus to get into the inter Squadron boxing competition. Seamus's first fight was against Junior Driver Bob Ford who was also a very good young boxer, but not good enough as it turned out, Seamus gave him a lesson in how to be an even better boxer. 24115820 Junior Driver O'Callaghan threw himself into most of the military training and describes all the usual spit and polish bullshit as "Awesome", which will be a surprise to most other ex-soldiers because that element of Basic Training is usually detested. Seamus loved every minute of a training schedule that was devoted to Drill, he preferred being marched up and down the main parade ground all day rather than taking part in any of the other training schedules. Even though he found weapon training boring (a key part of being a soldier which most enjoy) he rose to the giddy heights of Junior Corporal and was eventually moved out of the twelve man room and allocated his own bunk. It was there that he started a card school with other Junior Drivers who he supplied with some locally acquired scrumpy (locally brewed cider). Seamus just indulged in cups of tea during their card games and unsurprisingly won a lot of money off the other, pissed, Junior Leaders. Towards the end of his training Seamus progressed onto the Driver Training phase where he suffered from a couple of disabilities, his right boot was filled with rocks and the tendons in his right wrist were overenthusiastic. Both infirmities caused him to break the speed limit on several occasions whilst on Driver Training and he was appropriately warned about his 'need for speed'; he failed his 'very fast' motorbike test and 'Passed Out' of Taunton without a motorbike licence. Though that minor inconvenience never stopped him from being a Don R, (Dispatch Rider - motor-bike escort), throughout his military career.

Seamus's plan of seeing the world hit a bit of a setback when he received notification of his very first posting. RCT Manning and Records were sending him from the Junior Leaders Regiment in Taunton to 19 Tank Transporter Squadron RCT which was based at Retford, a mere twelve miles from his home town, "I didn't join the bleedin' army just to be posted a couple of miles from where me parents lived!" Seamus complained bitterly to his Troop Commander and was given one other choice of posting which was to 22 Air Despatch Squadron RCT based at Emsworth near Portsmouth. From 1969 – 1972 Seamus flew 108 missions with 22 AD Squadron, 47 AD Squadron and 55 AD Squadron. He flew operational tours in most of the current RAF aircraft at that time:

The **Lockheed C 130 Hercules** four engine turbo prop military transport aircraft.
The **Armstrong Whitworth AW660 Argosy** four engine cargo aircraft.
The **Hawker Siddley Andover C1** twin engine cargo aircraft.
The STOL (Short Take Off and Landing) single engine **de Havilland Canada Beaver AL Mk 1**.

Seamus even flew missions on the RAF's Wessex Helicopter for which he had to attend a Royal Navy underwater emergency evacuation course in Portsmouth. Eight candidates were allocated seats on a mock up helicopter that was immersed into a large tank of water and then turned upside down to simulate the scenario of crash landing in a body of water. The students had to calmly hold their breath and wait until the mock-up aircraft was fully submerged, had been rotated into the inverted position, then, and only then, could they remove their seat belts and swim out of the nearest exit with composure and strict military discipline.

The six weeks training to become an RCT Air Despatcher was extremely hard work. Sergeant Pete Smyth was one of Seamus's initial course instructors who'd originally thought he was going to 22 AD Squadron RCT as an Admin Sergeant, however, he eventually qualified as an Air Dispatcher and went on to became the units' Regimental Sergeant Major (RSM) at 42 AD Squadron. The candidates had to learn how to prepare all sorts of stores and vehicles for airdrops, each pallet's weight, strapping, and positioning on the aircraft was essential for a safe flight, safe despatch, and hopefully, successful landing. A load might look good as it was being loaded but if it disintegrates on landing then the whole process would have been a total waste of everyone's time and effort. The soldiers on the Drop Zone (DZ) who needed the resupply were also put under the extra pressure of having to soldier on without the necessary resupplied rations, water and necessary kit. Preparing palletised vehicles for a heavy drop wasn't the only part of the students training, they also had to learn about preparing SEAC (South East Asian Command) packs which were originally designed for despatching into Jungle environments', these were coffee table sized canvas bags that were thrown out of the side doors of a cargo plane that could penetrate a jungle canopy and reach SAS soldiers living in remote areas. On one particular mission Seamus had to pack and deliver a cage of live chickens to some Ghurkha's exercising in the desert. The Nepalese soldiers were so grateful for the delivery of fresh meat that they later rewarded the Air Despatchers with bottles of beer. All RCT Air Despatchers had to be trained on how to drive and operate the army's perplexing Eager Beaver Fork Lift Truck. These trucks were also dropped by air because the Air Despatchers sometimes had to work on the DZ moving the received stores - chickens or otherwise.

Once qualified as an Air Despatcher, Seamus had to have his kit constantly packed and be ready to deploy within an hour. During his three years with the

RCT AD Squadrons, Seamus deployed to Gibraltar, Malta, Salala, Sharjah, Bahrain and Cyprus. Each morning when he reported to the Squadron office he would have a conversation with his Troop Sergeant that went along these lines:

Troop Sergeant: "O'Callaghan!"

Seamus: "Yes Sergeant!"

Troop Sergeant: "In here now!"

Seamus: "Sergeant!"

Troop Sergeant: "Kit packed?"

Seamus: "Yes Sergeant!"

Troop Sergeant: "Inoculations up to date?"

Seamus: "Yes Sergeant!"

Troop Sergeant: "Got your passport handy?"

Seamus: "Yes Sergeant!"

Troop Sergeant: "Good, you're off to Bahrain for the next four months, Bye Bye."

Seamus: "When do I leave Sergeant?"

Troop Sergeant: "Don't worry, I'm sure you've got plenty of time to get ready. The pilots are warming up the engines now!"

Seamus: "Oh shit!"

Troop Sergeant: "Oh shit indeed! Now off you go lad, we don't want to keep them RAF types waiting, they're not real men like us Trogg's you know - they're sensitive!"

Seamus loved working on aircraft and found standing on the edge of an opened back ramp or side door of a flying C 130 very exhilarating, especially when he didn't know he was being shot at by someone on the ground. The RAF were doing a resupply drop during the Dhofar rebellion (1969–1970) and when flying over the DZ after despatching SEAC packs out of the side door, Seamus wrongly thought that some bees had somehow got inside the Hercules aircraft and were buzzing around his head. He was very surprised and somewhat alarmed when an RAF Flight Sergeant pointed to a few bullet holes in the aircraft's fuselage.

Deployments to Bahrain, Cyprus and Sharjah were the most popular with the RCT Air Despatchers because they were usually a 4 – 6 months detachment. After completing one four month tour, Seamus went home for a couple of weeks leave and was lucky enough to be sent straight out on another four month tour. Seamus recalled that, "Everything was so cheap out there, you could buy a really good quality hand stitched and made to measure suit, shirt and tie set for only a fiver and I once bought a beautiful pair of made to measure Chelsea boots that only cost me two quid. And when you weren't flying your time was usually taken up with swimming, sunbathing or sailing. It really was the worst time of my entire career. When we weren't enjoying our time in the sun we spent a lot of time doing some hard drinking, you could also buy a large bottle of Chivas Regal whiskey for only two shillings and six pence (12p in today's money)." To avoid the strain of living out in Bahrain the lads were frequently given some Rest and Recuperation (R&R) time in Cyprus. There were several flights a day running between Bahrain and Cyprus so it was just like hopping onto a bus to get down to your local pub. The RCT lads worked in pairs when they were on duty and despatching loads and they did the same when they went on R&R. Seamus flew to Cyprus with Driver Ronnie Hope for one particular weekend in RAF Akrotiri.

On arrival at the RAF Station, Seamus dumped his mate and spent the weekend in Nicosia with a Women's Royal Army Corps (WRAC) Warrant Officer that he was particularly friendly with, he also got the chance to visit his cousin Geraldine who was living nearby. Seamus had a great time and a bit too much booze which resulted in him getting back to RAF Akrotiri after his return flight had already departed the Island. He was met in the departure lounge by his mate Ronnie Hope, Seamus asked him, "Why the fuck are you still here?" Ronnie answered, "Couldn't go back without you my mate, I'd have got so much shit in the bar from the other lads in the Squadron." If a soldier doesn't have a valid excuse when he's overdue returning from leave, the offence is considered a crime within the British Army and these misdemeanours usually result in the offending soldier being placed on a military charge, using the infamous Army Form B 252 (Charge Sheet). If found guilty of the charge, the soldier's Squadron Commander would then relieve the offender of some of his hard earned wages or give him some extra duties. Seamus and Ronnie jumped on the next RAF flight to Bahrain, but not before buying the largest bottles of booze available from the duty free shop. On arrival at their Squadron office they were met by Sergeant 'Paddy' Cumming's who was on duty as the Orderly Sergeant. The three of them had the following conversation:

'Paddy': "YOU'RE LATE BACK! You two are in deep shit right up to your ears."

Ronnie: "We're really sorry Sergeant, we didn't realise the time was that late."

'Paddy': "That's not an excuse Driver Hope! I'm going to put you both on a charge for being Absent Without Leave. You'll be marched in front of the old man on Monday and I'm sure he'll fine the pair of you."

Ronnie: "Oh dear, I don't suppose the fact that we bought you back some presents will make any difference will it Sergeant?"

'Paddy': "Well that's very nice of you Driver Hope. What exactly have you bought back from Cyprus for me?"

Ronnie: "I've bought you a barrel of very expensive sherry sergeant."

'Paddy': "Hmmm, that's very kind of you Driver Hope. And what about you Driver O'Callaghan, did you bring me a nice present back from Cyprus?"

Seamus: "Yes Sergeant, I've bought you a very large bottle of 5 star brandy, do you like it Sergeant?"

'Paddy' "Yes Driver O'Callaghan, I like it very much indeed. Listen you two, I've had a rethink. The boss will probably be very busy on Monday so I'm putting you both on the late shift for a week instead. Now, leave the presents here and bugger off out of my sight."

A week on the late shift was a bit of a pain because it involved being on standby and working in the packing shed from 0800 hours until 1600 hours, during which time on duty they'd be prepping SEAC loads for future despatches and the tardy pair wouldn't get the chance to do any sailing, swimming or sunbathing. Still, it was better than being put on a military charge and losing money.

In 1972 Seamus was summoned into the Squadron office at Emsworth for a chat with 55 AD Squadron's Admin Officer, Captain Ford, who was a big boxing fan (the Squadron had recently been re-designated its new number). Captain Ford told Seamus that 10 Regiment RCT had been in touch and they had asked if he'd like a posting to 17 Squadron RCT based in Bielefeld West Germany. The Admin Officer also explained that the Regiment was putting a new boxing team together and that he'd already told Manning and Records about Seamus's prowess in the ring. Captain Ford had been very forthcoming with both RCT Manning and Records office and 10 Regiment RCT about Seamus and some of his recent fights. WO2 Gill O'Neil (the Army Boxing team trainer) had already recruited Seamus into the Army team and Seamus had recently only just lost on points to Private Benny Walmsley of 2 Para in the Senior Army Finals. 10 Regiment RCT definitely wanted him at Bielefeld. With the chance of getting involved in some regular boxing training and competitions, Seamus bit Captain Ford's hand off but after the interview Driver Burt Royal told Seamus a few alleged home truths about 10 Regiment RCT:

Seamus: "Hey Burt, 10 Regiment have been asking for me and I've accepted a posting to 17 Squadron in Germany."

Burt: "Why?"

Seamus: "Their putting a new boxing team together and I'm joining them."
Burt: "Fuck me Seamus, 10 Regiment is a punishment posting! All the toe-rags and knobber's get sent there, mate."

Seamus: "But it's a boxing regiment."

Burt: "Yeah but they'll all be thugs! You don't need any of that shit mate."

A worried Seamus went straight back to Captain Ford's office and asked if he could change his mind over the posting to Bielefeld. The answer was an emphatic, "No!" The posting went ahead and Seamus left 55 AD Squadron RCT in August 1972. At his leaving party the RCT lads made him drink an unmeasured alcoholic cocktail out of an old and sweaty flying boot.

Seamus got married to his girlfriend Susan just before he set off on his new posting to 10 Regiment and unfortunately it was when both sets of parents were away on holiday. The hastily arranged ceremony was held in the local registry office because of Seamus's rapid posting and Titch Haywood, a good school friend, was present as his Best Man. When Seamus's mum returned from her Skegness Caravan Park holiday and was informed of the happy occasion, she wasn't very happy at all. Mrs O'Callaghan (not the new Susan one) virtually frog-marched the newly married couple down to the local Catholic Church to make sure the wedding was blessed and that the Priest could confirm that Seamus and Susan were properly married. Susan had to continue living with her parents in Clipstone for the next three months before joining Seamus in Bielefeld. At that time there just weren't enough Married Quarters available for soldiers and Seamus struggled to find a decent Private Hiring. Seamus therefore had to live in the 17 Squadron 'singlies' accommodation block for those three months until the whole process of getting Susan over to Bielefeld was finalised. Within three weeks of joining 17 Squadron Seamus got himself into trouble by going on the piss with Burt Royal who was one of his best mates. They'd been down town and returned to camp absolutely bladdered out of their tiny skulls. The guard quite rightly arrested the pair of them because they were being raucous as they entered 10 Regiments' camp gates. The two of them were locked up in the cells for the rest of the night.

In the morning the Regimental Sergeant Major, WO 1 (RSM) G (Gordon) Pengelly RCT stormed into the corridor where the cells were located and confronted Seamus in his cell, Seamus picked up a chair:

Seamus: "I've heard about you sir, if you try to knock me about I'll mark you with this chair......Sir".

RSM: "And why would you do that Driver O'Callaghan?"

Seamus: "Well, if we're both marked and it comes to a Court Martial, I can prove that I were just defending myself sir."

RSM: "I'm not going to hit you O'Callaghan, now put that chair down!"

Seamus put the chair down and the RSM walked towards him and snarled while they stood face to face:

RSM: "You're supposed to be a 10 Regiment boxer, not a fucking drunk!"

Seamus: "Sir!"

RSM: "If I ever catch you in this jail again then I will break your fucking neck, do you understand me boy?"

Seamus: "Yes Sir! You'll not catch me in here again!"

RSM: "Good, now get out of my fucking sight before I lose my temper with you."

Seamus: "Thank you sir!"

Seamus wasn't charged with being drunk and he never booked into Pengelly's Prison ever again!

Seamus was involved in the 10 Regiment boxing teams tours of London, the home-counties and a few boxing clubs up North. At his old unit in Emsworth Seamus watched Driver Stevie Johnson, who'd won the RCT Hemming belt trophy a record five times, go up against a really good Army Boxing Association (ABA) boxer. Stevie lost the fight and Seamus fought the same boxer on the same night. Seamus lost his fight as well and he said to Stevie in the changing room afterwards, "We boxed the same bloke on the same night and neither of us did any good, how bloody crap are we mate?"

During his time as a Regimental, Corps, Army and International Schoolboy boxer, Seamus had participated in over 500 fights and won at least 450 of them. He'd boxed at Bantam, Feather, Light and Light-Welter weights. In 1975 Seamus was part of the 10 Regiment team that did an exhibition tour against the American Forces in Southern Germany. Seamus was put up against a black soldier who'd won an American 'Golden Gloves Champion Trophy.' His opponent was disliked by the US Troops because they deemed him to be a show off and too arrogant. During the fight the US soldier never laid a glove on Seamus, which goes to prove that all of his dad's training on the handkerchief

Seamus O'Callaghan's fight against the Paras in Berlin. He's the one without the mangled face.

The famous 10 Regt RCT Boxing Team.

really did pay off. Seamus battered the Yank all around the ring and he was ceremoniously applauded by both British and US supporters at the end of the fight. Seamus always said he would retire from boxing if he was ever knocked out by a plum. He was referring to any boxer who was slow, couldn't punch very hard and was heavy on his feet. In a locally organised exhibition match the lads in the 10 Regiment team were fighting a local German club from Bielefeld in which Seamus was paired against a real German plum. He explains exactly what happened during that fight:

"There wasn't a chance in hell of him beating me. I was boxing in front of the Commanding Officer of my Regiment and so a lot of pride was at stake. On the night I, unfortunately, decided to put on a bit of a show for the Colonel and our supporters. I did a sort of Mohammed Ali shuffle and danced around with my gloves down. The German boxer caught me with a reasonable punch and dumped me right on me arse. I received a standing count from the referee before continuing with the fight and the plum then proceeded to put me down a second time and knocked me out. I totally underestimated my opponent and got what I deserved. It was really embarrassing for me, especially as the Commanding Officer, and my Regiment, were there in force to support me, and so I decided to hang up my gloves."

Seamus was persuaded to stay on with the 10 Regiment Boxing team for one more year though and he went on to help them win the BAOR and Army Championships.

At 10 Regiment it wasn't all about boxing though, because from 1974 to 1978 Seamus completed four tours of duty in Northern Ireland. In fact he cut his 'Internal Security' teeth as a Lance Corporal whilst commanding an RCT Section at Blair's Yard in Belfast. His lads were operating in support of a Royal Artillery unit and Seamus always made sure he worked his fair share of patrols and riots with the Gunners. In 1982 Seamus received his second stripe when promoted to full Corporal and was posted to 42 Squadron RCT AMF (L) (Ace Mobile Force Land) based in Bulford, Wiltshire. The unit was a Quick Reaction Force (QRF) trained to deploy onto NATO's Northern Flank in Norway and Denmark, just in case the Russians cut up rough and started a Third World War. By this time Susan was living in their own home in Mansfield with their two sons Seth and Liam. Seamus was away on so many Military Exercises in either Norway or Denmark that there was no point in living in a Married Quarter in

Bulford. The army-enforced separation hit Seamus very hard because deep-down in his heart he was a family man. He missed Susan and the boys so much that it unfortunately resulted in him hitting the bottle very hard. On most days Seamus was drinking a full bottle of Vodka and at least 8 pints of beer a day, which if he carried on like that his career was going to end catastrophically. Seamus's Troop 'Staffie', Staff Sergeant Matt Matthews RCT came to the rescue because he always told it like it was. He took Seamus to one side and said, "Listen to me Seamus, if you carry on like this you'll be finished by the army, but if you cut out the shorts and half of the beers, I can guarantee you'll be promoted to Sergeant within six months." Back in his room Seamus poured half a bottle of vodka down the sink and never opened another bottle of spirit, and true to Matt's word he was promoted to Troop Sergeant in three months.

Whilst on one of his three trips to Norway, Seamus was acting as the Squadron Quartermaster Sergeant (SQMS) for his unit, responsible for paying all of the bills for the military damage done to the training area by his squadron. Everything in Norway was expensive, which not only included the bills for damages, for example a broken window could be as much as £500, it also included the average price of alcohol for the entire Norwegian nation. Seamus had learned an important lesson from previous deployments and had brought plenty of bottles of whiskey with him, not to drink himself, but to bribe the Norwegian Army's RQMS into putting some of the damage down to local wildlife rather than 42 Squadrons vehicles. Sergeant Seamus O'Callaghan saved the British Army a fortune in damage repairs. It was during his last Exercise in Norway that Seamus was informed his dad was dying and that he had, at best, only days to live. WO 1 (RSM) Pete Smyth sprang into action and organised civilian flights, cars and he even tried to get a military helicopter to fly Seamus from London Airport to his home town, but the fog was too severe. Nevertheless Seamus still made it home in time and was holding his dads hand when he died and it was all thanks to Pete Smyth about whom Seamus says, "I have the greatest respect for that man, he was absolutely fucking brilliant."

After postings to 20 Squadron RCT in London and 4 Squadron in Bunde, Seamus was posted back to 17 Squadron in Bielefeld as a Troop Sergeant. It was here that he and Staff Sergeant 'Tam' Forrester initiated and organised a boxing ring and Gymnasium in the Squadron's attic. Any new arrivals into the Squadron were given the opportunity to try out their boxing skills against Seamus and Corporal Lionel Braithwaite. One new arrival from Buller Barracks was a young lad called Driver Dave Walker who noticed that his new

Troop Sergeant had a slightly rotund figure and had a leg in plaster. Seamus's tibia and fibula had been fractured in the Sergeant's Mess when two Mess members were larking around and they fell onto his knee, their full weight breaking his leg, while Seamus was sitting on a chair and was resting his foot on a coffee table. Dave knew nothing about Seamus's career as a boxer and even though he'd gained a little weight because of his broken leg, Seamus was still fit and very quick with his fists. After giving Dave the grand tour of 17 Squadron's Headquarters, Seamus took the 'Nig' (New in Germany) up to the attic and showed him the Squadron's private gymnasium. Seamus asked Dave if he was any good at boxing, to which he jokingly replied, "I did karate lessons as a kid so I think I could definitely take you on Sarge." Seamus bit his tongue and told Dave that he could batter him around the boxing ring with one hand tied behind his back. Dave picked up the challenge and they both got gloved up. That morning Driver Dave Walker received a lesson in humility that he has never forgotten, "I was clinically taken to pieces by an old, overweight sergeant who not only had one hand tucked into his shorts, but he also had a fucking broken leg."

Seamus finished his RCT career as the SQMS at 42 Squadron RCT in Bulford and on discharge from the British Army he worked at Centre Parcs for six years as the Assistant Manager. He also worked in the pub and catering trade before becoming a security guard. In 2011 Seamus came home from a work out at his local Fitness Centre and whilst enjoying a cup of coffee on the sofa with Susan he suddenly developed quite severe chest pains. Putting the pain down to indigestion he took some Gaviscon indigestion tablets and went upstairs for a lie down on the bed. The pain didn't go away though and so Susan asked her brother-in-Law Duncan and their son Liam to come and see what they thought, Liam immediately took Seamus to hospital in his car. The local hospital gave Seamus an ECG test and told him that he'd had a heart attack and within ten days a surgeon had inserted three stents on the right side of his heart, and a week later they put one on the left side. After everything Seamus had given during his time served in the Royal Corps of Transport and British Army (he'd competed at Rugby, Football and Boxing at Corps and Army levels) it was no wonder that he suffered with Type II diabetes and has severe arthritis.

Seamus is now fully retired and spends a lot of his time walking, fishing and annoying his wonderful wife Susan. Both of their sons enlisted into the British Army and have served in the Royal Electrical and Mechanical Engineers

(REME) and Royal Signals, where, unsurprisingly they have both represented their individual Corps in the boxing ring.

533840 Lieutenant Colonel Peter Joseph Shields
MBE, QGM, F Inst LM
RCT and RLC 1968 – 2005

Driver Peter Shields RCT on his first tour of duty in Northern Ireland in 1972, at the time he was serving in Belfast with 3 Tank Transporter Squadron RCT.

Because Peter Shields comes from a Glasgow background it will automatically be assumed that he's be a bit of a hard-case, and growing up there during the 1950's and 1960's will only add weight to this impression. Well, he's probably better described as tough rather than a hard-case. In truth Peter is not a man to be trifled with because he doesn't suffer fools gladly, mainly because he's a very determined man who won't let anyone stand in his way. Having said that, he is also an idealistic man who will move heaven and earth to do the right thing for anyone who needs his help.

Peter's dad had served in the Highland Light Infantry (HLI) and the Seaforth Highlanders and his uncle in the Queen's Own Cameron Highlanders during the Second World War, and so in 1968 when he told his dad he was joining the British Army, his dad automatically asked,

Mr Shields: "So, what colour's your tartan?"

Peter: "I don't have a tartan."

Mr Shields: "What kind of army are you in that doesn't have a tartan?"

Peter: "I'm joining the Royal Corps of Transport."

Mr Shields: "Never bloody heard of it."

Peter: "It might have been called the Royal Army Service Corps in your days."

Mr Shields: "Christ! You're a bloody chef!"

Peter: "I'm not a chef, I'm going to be a truck driver."

From the age of 8, Peter had worked for just about every dairy in Glasgow but primarily with Sloane's Dairy. He'd always wanted to drive and so some of the Milkmen he worked with occasionally allowed him to drive the electric float to the end of the street. During the early 1960's the streets of Glasgow saw very little traffic at 4 o'clock in the morning and so the chances of hitting another vehicle was minimal to say the least. As time went on the Dairy progressed onto petrol driven vehicles and Peter's driving skills developed accordingly. By the time he was fourteen years old Peter was a competent, albeit illegal and unqualified driver on the roads of Glasgow. Peter was married at sixteen and a father of two babies by the time he was eighteen. With his new responsibilities as a husband and father he had to start earning enough money to support his young family. As if one job wasn't tiring enough, Peter took on any other available work that would earn him some extra cash, after finishing his milk round he worked long hours Hod carrying for a firm called Lawrence builders. For any younger readers who need some clarification, a Hod is a long handled metal box that was used on a building site to carry heavy bricks on the shoulder whilst climbing a ladder. Be under no illusion kids, this was back breaking work. When not required as a Hod carrier Peter worked for a precast concrete company making bricks, and when not doing that he worked for his self-employed uncle laying kerb stones and concrete slabs in the streets of East Kilbride. The last job he took on before joining the Territorial Army (TA) was as a Bus Conductor. Some people might consider this a relatively easy job, except that Peter had to get up at 5 o'clock in the morning and cycle twelve miles to the bus depot before starting his shift. Peter has always had a phenomenal work ethic which won't allow him to laze about on a beach during his holidays.

Peter was encouraged to join 154 Lowland Regiment RCT in 1968 by his bus conductor mate Andy West. Andy and Peter not only worked at the same bus depot but they also lived in the same street; their TA wages helped both of them supplement their weekday wages. With his first end of year TA bounty Peter bought a split screened Morris 1000 car from a car market in Glasgow. The car only lasted for about a fortnight because in those days most engines had core plugs which popped out when the wrong type of coolant was used. If the coolant wasn't changed before replacing the core plugs then the working parts of the engine could be seriously damaged due to overheating. Because his core plugs kept popping out Peter simply hammered and glued them back into place without replacing the coolant in the engine and within two weeks the engine stopped working. In the end he sold the car for scrap, recouping a miserly six quid for his trouble. Peter's next motor was a 1963 four door Vauxhall Cresta PB family car which cost him £35 from the same second hand market. He used it to take his friends to parties and once when they arrived at a party in Drumchapel one night they found that the doors wouldn't open and everyone was trapped inside the car. The welding on a chassis seam had rusted through allowing the car to bend in the middle which jammed the doors in the closed position. Using Scottish ingenuity the revellers simply climbed out of the car windows so that they could get to the party.

After two years in the TA Peter went along to 581 Sauchiehall Street to see if he could enlist into the Regular British Army. As a fully trained Territorial soldier with an HGV III Licence it made sense for him to try and make a long term career in the professional army. The recruiter talked Peter out of joining the Infantry because he deemed it would be a waste of his driving licences and training in the RCT to enlist into any other branch of the army. The medical took place upstairs from the recruiting office and was carried out by a five foot three inch rotund man who told Peter to stand in the corner of the room facing the wall. The 'Witch Doctor' then jingled the loose change in his pocket and whispered the words, "Daily Record." When asked what he'd just said Peter correctly repeated "Daily Record" and the 'Quack' told him, "Yeah, your hearing's fine."

In 1971 Peter headed off to Aldershot and joined Intake 263 at the RCT Depot in Buller Barracks where he was issued his Regular Army service number 24157149. Basic Training was very easy for Peter because he already knew how to march, iron his kit, bull his boots, fire and maintain service weapons as well as being a qualified army Driver. Peter was a bit of a shining star at Buller, particularly with his fellow recruits who turned to him for help if they were struggling with any of the training syllabus. After finishing Basic Training, Peter opted to become a BIII Radio Operator because, "With my own myopic vision of army life, I had dreams of driving all over the world in my own Land Rover with a radio in the back, the idea of this delusion suited me down to the ground." The now trained soldiers of Intake 263 all went home on leave for a week before proceeding onto their first postings. An incident whilst on leave would result in a change of posting for Peter that would shape the rest of his military career.

One night in Glasgow City centre Peter was attacked by seven or eight long haired drunken yobbos. The cowardly and unprovoked attack was caused simply by the fact that Peter had a short haircut and looked just what he was, a soldier. The beating was severe enough to keep Peter in hospital for a few days and by the time he got back to Aldershot his posting as a BIII Radio Operator had been taken by someone else. Within seven days he was called into the main office and given a Posting Order sending him to 23 Tank Transporter Squadron RCT, based in Sennelager. Peter handed in his bedding before leaving Buller Barracks and the Scottish bedding storeman (an ex RCT Tank Transporter Driver) told him, "You're going to the best RCT Squadron in the British Army." The journey out to Sennelager had to be done whilst wearing Number 2 Service Dress Uniform complete with a tie and peaked Twat Hat (so called because a soldier felt a right twat whilst wearing one on his head). Everything a soldier possessed in the world had to be carried in either his army suitcase or sausage shaped kit bag, if it didn't fit in either of these, then it didn't go at all.

After alighting from the Deutsche Bahn train at Sennelager railway station, Peter was met by Driver 'Ginge' Smith who was also wearing a Number 2 Service Dress Uniform and a Side Hat (known as a chip bag). He'd arrived in an immaculate and very shiny army Half Ton Land Rover, sporting large RCT emblems on each door. 'Ginge' drove to the camp and dropped Peter outside the Squadron Office which was like a ghost-town, unbeknown to him it was completely deserted because everyone was busy drinking down in the Squadron bar. The Squadron Bar was, (and still is today), a precarious world in any army unit and if a soldier looked around a bar without recognising any one of the forty soldiers present then he knew he was the one that was going to upset the applecart just by breathing.

There was a pecking order within a Tank Transporter Squadron because every Thorneycroft Antar Tank Transporter crew was made up of just two operator's. The Number 1 was the most experienced and he alone drove the tractor unit, the Number 2 being responsible for the massive trailer, although he occasionally got to drive the tractor unit. Anyone who wasn't a Number 1 or Number 2 operator in a Tank Transporter Squadron was quite simply dog shit on an army boot, and didn't get to drive the tractor unit. Only Number 1's and Number 2's could order drinks from the Squadron bar and everyone else had to make a point of buying the crew members a drink just so they could order themselves a drink at the same time. The system was more theatre than anything else and if you played the game properly then you got along fine within the Squadron.

On arrival at 23 Squadron, each RCT soldier had to initially spend three months on the Regimental Police (RP) staff in the guardroom, a mind numbing job for soldiers that was commonly advertised as, "If a soldier can't do anything useful, then put him on the RP Staff so at least he can open the camp gates for someone." The Regimental Sergeant Major (RSM) arrived at the Guardroom every morning and insisted that the incoming and outgoing RP's were mixed up before he inspected them. Any unfortunate whose uniform and boots looked like they had just spent twelve hours on duty would suffer his wrath. Without exception, everyone going off duty had to look as if they'd just arrived on guard, (this bearing in mind that throughout the night the RP Staff constantly had to dispense fuel from the POL point to any Garrison duty vehicles).

After serving his time on the RP Staff, Peter was moved into C Troop where he worked in the MT Section. His Troop Commander then sent him on his Junior Military Qualifications Course (JMQC) and on the last day Peter was presented with the top student award. As a result of this achievement he was immediately promoted to Lance Corporal, and within twelve months was sent to 10 Regiment RCT in Bielefeld to complete his Senior Military Qualifications Certificate (SMQC) which would qualify him up to the rank of Sergeant and beyond. Three RCT soldiers from 23 Squadron RCT were allocated places on the course and when it ended Peter was once again nominated as top student, his mate Dave 'Trigger' Johnson coming second. Peter eventually moved across into A Troop and started work on becoming a fully-fledged Number 2 on a Tank Transporter. His Troop Commander, Lieutenant Gibson, and Staff Sergeant Dave Jurgens allocated him a space on one of the tractors. Peter was merely used as a grease monkey within the crew because essentially he was considered just a spare part every time the vehicle was taken out on a drag. The Number 1 drove, the Number 2 looked after the trailer and the spare bod watched and learned whilst doing all the trivial jobs for the other two. Lieutenant Gibson and Staff Sergeant Jurgens received glowing reports from Peter's Crew Commander and were so impressed with his enthusiasm and quick learning that they offered him the place as a Number 2, so one Monday morning he was told to go and sign for his own trailer. There were two types of trailer in use, the 50 ton Tasker which had manual ramps and the 60 ton Sankey that had two massive hydraulic ramps measuring eight foot high by two foot wide. The 60 Ton Sankey had been used mainly for the sixty ton Conqueror tank that went out of service in 1966. At the same time, the Number 2 had to learn his A Trade Training which incorporated knowledge about the trailer, how to recover vehicles, where different oils and lubrications were used, how to tie down different loads and a plethora of other MT duties. Tank Transporter Drivers were considered to be on a higher level than the usual run-of-the-mill RCT Drivers because of the complexity of the job and the value of the equipment they had to look after. That is why they were an A Trade and paid significantly higher trade pay.

The process through which Tank Transporter Drivers progressed meant they had to pass their HGV I driving test even before they became a Number 2 and signed for their first trailer. The Antar tractor had a huge five speed gear box with overdrive and the gate alone was 400 centimetres wide, which occasionally caused Peter to crunch the odd gear or two. Whenever he did this he was rapped on the knuckles with a wooden traffic lollipop by his Mixed Services Organisation (MSO) Driving Instructor. 23 Tank Transporter Squadron RCT Drivers also went down to the neighbouring armoured unit in Athlone Barracks and learned how to drive a tracked vehicle in a 432 Armoured Personnel Carrier

(APC) because only Tank Crews and the RCT Drivers were allowed to drive a tank onto the back of an Antar Trailer. The Number 1 would line the tank up with the trailer ramps, bearing in mind that there was only a two inch margin for error on either side, the Number 2 would then stand on the swan neck - the highest point on the trailer, and then wave the tank forward. As the tank started to climb onto the trailer the driver had to put his arms outside the driving cupola to prove he didn't have his hands on the tanks steering tillers. Essentially the tank driver was now just looking up at the sky, which could have an unnerving effect that might make him suddenly grab the tillers, causing his tank to fall off the trailer. There comes a critical point on loading when the tank reaches the top of the ramps and it is at this stage that the driver must briefly halt before continuing onto the trailer. If he doesn't, the tank can damage the trailer and or topple off the side.

On 28th February 1972, Peter deployed with the now named 3 Tank Transporter Squadron RCT on his first of four tours of Northern Ireland. From this date the RCT became responsible for driving and maintaining the roulement Infantry Battalions APC's. Up to that point the Infantry Battalions had used drivers from their own MT Section which had proved unsatisfactory for two reasons. The main problem being that Infantry drivers were not maintaining their vehicles properly, leading to an unacceptable amount of mechanical breakdowns. Secondly, using a soldier from the Battalion as a driver depleted the amount of Infantry men available for use on foot patrols and guard duties. "The first of my four tours was by far the worst" says Peter. "Seven members of the Squadron were shot and Lance Corporal Mickey Bruce was killed. Mickey was a cracking bloke who was always playing football with the kids. He was everybody's pal, if ever there was a guy who should never have been shot it was Mickey." The famous RCT base in Moscow Camp didn't exist in these early days of 'The Troubles' and so home for Peter and his fellow Troggs was on HMS Maidstone in Belfast Docks. Incidentally, the ship was actually moored in the docks next to where Moscow Camp's Servicing Bay would eventually be built.   The RCT Drivers shared their very cramped accommodation with soldiers of the Welsh Guards and Peter slept on the top of three very poky naval bunk-beds.

A Ministry of Defence ruling at the time decreed that soldiers had to adopt a non-aggressive posture whilst on the streets of Belfast which meant that RCT Drivers had to patrol with both back doors of their 'Pigs' left wide open. The reason why so many RCT Drivers were injured is because IRA gunmen waited for a 'Pig' to pass a side street before jumping out and emptying their magazine of ammunition into the centre spot of the rear of the vehicle. Infantry soldiers travelling in the back sat on benches over the rear wheel arches at the sides of the 'Pig' and so the bulk of the incoming rounds hit either the patrol Commander or the Driver because they were positioned in the middle at the front. Drivers Bob Hadley and Neil Clarke were both wounded when shot in the shoulder and Driver Ray Veasey was shot across the back of his neck and shoulders. Driver 'Black Mac' MacDonald BEM was also shot, unfortunately he got hit in the backside.

Lance Corporal Mickey Bruce RCT. Killed by a sniper in Andersontown Belfast on 31st May 1972.

Saturday afternoon the 4th of March 1972 is permanently etched into Peter's brain. On that day a 5lb gelignite bomb exploded in the very crowded Abercorn Restaurant killing two young women and causing a multitude of gruesome injuries to more than 130 innocent shoppers. Many of the injuries included traumatic amputations and blindness caused by flying glass and other shrapnel that had been packed around the explosive charge. Folklore has it that two young girls aged between sixteen and eighteen years old were coerced into leaving the bomb in the restaurant where it was remotely detonated after they'd left the building. No-one claimed responsibility for the bombing but it is widely believed that the IRA were responsible. The young girls were never traced.

Peter initially turned up at the incident thinking he was going to form part of a cordon around the shopping mall, but on arrival at the scene he and several other soldiers were given black plastic bin liners and sent into the bombed building. They were ordered to, "Collect any bits of flesh that looks like it belongs in a butchers shop window." After reminiscing about this awful incident Peter poignantly said, "People sometimes forget about Northern Ireland and what we British soldiers went through. In the 1970's Ireland was not a nice place to be. I kept a scrap book back in those days, in fact I've still got it at home."

Peter enjoyed his first tour of Northern Ireland. "It seems kind of a stupid thing to say after what I've just mentioned but I think it was because we were young soldiers and the tour was something completely different from anything we'd done before. The Infantry we worked with were great. After the Welsh Guards left, the Glosters took over and they were absolutely fantastic." By the time the Glosters had taken over control of Belfast, Peter had moved accommodation from HMS Maidstone into the Albert Street mill. On the second half of his tour, Peter spent more of his on-duty time taking part in Foot Patrols around the infamous Divis Flats area. The Infantry always made him carry the first aid bag in the belief that the Red Cross emblem would in some way give him added protection from IRA snipers! By this time Peter and his wife were now divorced, so he spent all four days of his Rest and Recuperation (R&R) leave completing personal admin in Albert Street Mill and catching up on some desperately needed sleep. Peter's subsequent tours of Northern Ireland were all in Belfast where he was accommodated in Albert Street Mill and Palace Barracks. His last tour of duty in the Province was in 1976, but none of those other tours compared to the sheer horror of his first one.

After returning to Sennelager, Peter was promoted to full Corporal and he became a Number 1 on his own gigantic Antar Tank Transporter. Because of his drive and enthusiasm it didn't take him long to be recommended for promotion to Sergeant and in 1979 he was posted to the Junior Leaders Regiment RCT at Colerne near Bath as a Troop Sergeant/Drill Instructor. The role of Troop Sergeant in Masters Troop suited him very well because he loved to encourage and nurture the 16 year old Junior Leaders. Major B (Bruce) J Burgess RCT was his Officer Commanding and WO2 D (Dave) S Turner-Swift RCT was his Squadron Sergeant Major. Dave was a pencil moustached archetypal Sergeant Major character who could have come straight out of a children's comic book. These two were obviously impressed by Peter's attitude and teaching skills because after just one and a half terms they recommended him for promotion to Staff Sergeant. Peter had already made a name for himself in the RCT Tank Transporter world and so a posting to 414 Tank Transporter Troop in Bulford on Salisbury Plain duly followed. As a Staff Sergeant Peter, wouldn't be going back to simply driving an Antar up and down the roads at 18 mph. The novelty of doing that had worn off a few years previously. As a Senior NCO, Peter now worked in the unit Operations Room on a new fuel accounting system called Traffic Management Accounting (TMA). During his tenure at 16 Tank Transporter Regiment he also did a stint as a Troop Staff Sergeant and also became the Unit Fitness Officer.

Peter was selected for promotion to WO2 at the very young age of just 33, (most soldiers aim to reach the rank of Sergeant by the time they're 30) and he was posted back to Sennelager to 7 Tank Transporter Regiment RCT as their Training Warrant Officer. Peter was responsible for putting together and teaching Tank Transporter trade training courses to all RCT units in BAOR. After only 18 months in the job he was cherry picked to become the first British Sergeant Major of a predominantly Polish Mixed Service Organisation (MSO) Tank Transporter Unit. 617 Tank Transporter Squadron RCT was based in Cromwell Barracks, Hamm and Peter describes the civilian drivers as second to none. "They were the best Tank Transporting unit I've ever worked with. Guy's aged 55 to 60 years old were still lifting ¼ ton spare wheels and they could drink most seasoned soldiers under the table without batting an eyelid. They were absolutely brilliant." 617 Squadron's OC, Major R (Robbie) G C Campbell RCT, and Peter were invited to a 'Burial Party' within the unit and when Peter asked who had died he was told, "No-one. The Squadron is going to bury one thousand Deutsche Marks of beer at a party." Peter sat next to the OC at the opening ceremony which was called the 'Talking Party' and they were served many ½ litre bottles of beer which everyone drank whilst talking to each other. The congregation was then served 'Besucher Teller' (visitors plate) a platter of open sandwiches, whilst they all watched old cine films showing movies about Tank Transporters. This was followed by an 'Eating Party' where they were served a huge boiled knuckle end of pork…one each, which was scoffed with a very hot radish sauce. The last part of the festivities was called the 'Drinking Party' where bottles of Whiskey and Vodka were opened and placed on each table and whenever someone shouted "Na zdrowie" (cheers/bless you), everyone had to drink a shot of spirit. Luckily these burial parties were only held every three to four months.

The Civilian Figurehead within 617 Squadron was a man called Staff Superintendent Wladislaw Paterek MBE, a Pole who had served as a Lieutenant in the Polish Infantry and actually fought against the invading German Army in 1939. Although Paterek and his comrades were eventually surrounded he escaped capture by crawling through the sewers of Warsaw and went on to fight during the Italian campaign. Wladislaw was a tough, intelligent man who could speak several European languages. He once received a letter from Lieutenant Colonel Derek Braggins RCT, the Commanding Office of 7 Tank Transporter Regiment RCT. The routine letter opened with the usual niceties calling him 'Dear Wladislaw' and although he could speak several languages the written word was a totally different ball game. Before replying to the letter, Wladisaw checked in an Oxford English Dictionary to find out exactly why the Colonel had called him 'Dear'. The Oxford English Dictionary defined the word as, *'expensive, at great cost, exorbitant, highly priced, and treasured'* and so *Wladislaw* replied to the CO's letter with the opening nicer nicety, **'To my very expensive friend.'**

Having been promoted every two years and staying mainly within the Tank Transporter fraternity, RCT Manning and Records decided that Peter should step outside of his comfort zone and accordingly posted him to 42 Squadron RCT AMF (L) (Ace Mobile Forces Land) in Bulford as their Squadron Sergeant Major. Over the next fifteen months Peter guarded the Northern and Southern flanks of NATO in Turkey, Norway, and Italy before being promoted to WO1. The AMF tried to lure Peter into becoming the Logistic Support Regiments RSM but 7 Tank Transporter Regiment RCT had got in there first, they'd already cordially invited him to be their RSM and Peter grabbed the position with both hands. To go back to his old unit was going to be great fun because he still knew the majority of the men who remained there. On the other side of the coin was the fact that Peter was now the main 'Stick-man' in the Regiment and so had to maintain discipline and remain aloof, not only to the Drivers, but also with his old friends who were by now mainly Senior NCO's. One of Peter's many duties as RSM was being President of the Regiments' Warrant Officers and Sergeants Mess. On his first Mess Meeting he announced, "Gentlemen! I have to make a sad announcement this evening, Peter Shields is dead and I'm his replacement! You may all call me Sir!" He went on, "On the odd occasion when I call you by your Christian name please do not feel obliged to return the compliment." After closing the Mess Meeting Peter went up to the bar to buy a drink and a Sergeant patted him on the back and said,

Sergeant: "Nice one Pete, great speech."

Peter had to set his discipline stall out and so he gritted his teeth as he spoke to the Sergeant.

Peter: "I don't know why you think it was such a great speech because you obviously weren't listening."

Sergeant: "Oh for fucks sake Pete…"

Peter: "That's twice now, see you at my office 0730 hours tomorrow morning."

Sergeant: "I can't Pe…Sir, I'm travelling back to my Fallingbostel Married Quarter tonight and I'm catching a ferry tomorrow because I'm on leave after this Mess Meeting."

Peter: "Let me repeat myself just one more time! **Be in my office tomorrow morning at 0730 hours!**"

Sergeant: "Yes Sir!"

At 0730 hours the next morning the Sergeant marched into his Regimental Sergeant Majors' office and smartly halted in front of his desk. Without so much as an upwards glance Peter said:

Peter: "Take seven extra duties and fuck off!"

Peter had been applying for a Commission in the British Army since he was the Training WO2 at 7 Tank Transporter Regiment, but each application had been rejected because interviews weren't even considered until the applicant was at least a Warrant Officer Class 1 and with at least one operational tour under their belt. After serving three years as a Regimental Sergeant Major, Peter again applied for a commission. As per the rules he applied to his own Corps first, followed by the Army Air Corps (AAC) and the Royal Army Medical Corps (RAMC). Peter received a phone call from AAC Headquarters inviting him for a commissioning interview in Bielefeld with the Director of Aviation. The interview was conducted whilst wearing full leather and medals and went along these lines:

AAC Brigadier: "Good Morning RSM."

Peter: "Good Morning Sir."

AAC Brigadier: "I hope you are well today, please take a seat and we'll get started immediately."

Peter: "Thank you sir."

AAC Brigadier: "OK RSM, tell me what you know about aviation?"

In his usual forthright manner Peter put his hands up and said,

Peter: "Brigadier, I sorry but I think we'd better stop right there, because if my success or failure is relying on my knowledge of aviation then I fear I'm wasting your time and mine."

The Brigadier changed tack and they chatted about different jobs and people they both knew within the AAC. Peter obviously shone in the interview because the Brigadier immediately offered him a commission in the AAC. The commissioning rules stated that each applicant's own Corps were to be given first refusal of all applications and Peter hadn't even done the RCT interview yet. Incidentally, the RAMC Commissioning Board offered Peter a commission without even bothering to interviewing him. For the RCT Board Peter was eventually interviewed by Brigadier John MacDonald late RCT. Peter's letter of introduction said "You are invited to speak in front of a panel of three senior RCT officers blah blah blah. Be prepared to talk on the following three subjects.

1. Critical factors for the continuation of peace in Europe.
2. If you don't like being yourself who would you rather be?
3. Was the collapse of the Berlin Wall inevitable?

Be prepared to talk for not more, or less, than three minutes on each subject, and all briefing notes will be handed in at the end of the interview!

Peter's Commanding Officer, Lieutenant Colonel John French, offered him a bit of advice, "Better start reading the Times then RSM!" Peter thought, 'Nah, I'm gonna wing it." And that's exactly what he did.

Brigadier John MacDonald: "Good morning RSM, please take a seat and we'll get started."

Peter: "Yes Sir!"

Brigadier John MacDonald: "You know the brief RSM. In which order would you like to answer the questions?"

Peter: "Critical factors for the continuation of peace in Europe are the most important so I'll answer that first, and with me being the least important I'll answer about who I'd rather be, last."

After Peter had been speaking for a while the Brigadier suddenly interrupted him.

Brigadier John MacDonald: "RSM? You do realise that you've been speaking for more than three minutes don't you?"

Peter: "Of course I have Brigadier but I can hardly be expected to talk about, and cover the continuation of peace in Europe, in under three minutes…sir."

Brigadier John MacDonald: "Ok, well we've got your salient points on the subject matter so could you now tell us about your thoughts on the Berlin Wall coming down?"

Peter: "It was inevitable Sir."

Brigadier John MacDonald: "Really?"

It was at this point that Peter heard a metaphorical JCB digging behind him and with his usual aplomb he winged it like a true professional.

Peter: "Well the way I see it sir….blah blah blah."

Brigadier John MacDonald: "Right, last question then RSM. If you didn't like being yourself, who would you rather be?"

Peter: "In all honesty Brigadier, I'm perfectly happy just being myself."

And with that last perfect answer the Brigadier asked Peter to hand his notes into the clerk on his way out. Peter apologised and told the board he didn't have any briefing notes because he didn't feel he needed any (cocky sod). A commission in the RCT was immediately offered by the Board and accepted by 533840 Lieutenant Peter Shields RCT.

Within days Peter reported for duty at 4 Squadron in 1 ADTR RCT (Armoured Division Transport Regiment) based in Bunde. Lieutenant Colonel G (Gavin) J Haigh RCT was the Commanding Officer of 1 ADTR and when his unit was called up for deployment on the First Gulf War, he ordered Peter to remain behind in BAOR as the unit Admin Officer. As it turned out, Peter eventually deployed out to Kuwait as a Battle Casualty Replacement (BCR). Peter's official job was as Officer Commanding Forces Kuwait and he was made the Camp Commandant of St Georges Lines in Doha. The encampment was home to both British and US Service personnel and their war stocks, the garrison also included 1 ADTR which was operating in support of the Royal Anglian Battle Group. It was at this time that Captain Peter Shields RCT displayed such courage and leadership that he was awarded a Queen's Gallantry Medal (QGM). This is how the official citation recorded the events:

London Gazette 23rd December 1991

533840 Captain Peter Shields QGM
'On Thursday 11th July Captain Shields was the Administrative Officer in the Garrison Headquarters, British Forces Kuwait, located in St Georges Lines, Doha. At 1030 hours a United States Army Artillery ammunition carrier, parked amongst scores of other combat vehicles all fully loaded with war stocks of combat supplies including ammunition, caught fire 100 meters away from the Headquarters. By 1100 hours the fire was out of control and the Americans warned everyone to leave the area as soon as possible. Shortly afterwards the ammunition carrier exploded with a massive blast while Captain Shields was still in the headquarters building checking everyone had left. Those inside immediately rushed outside to seek cover; Captain Shields marshalled them to the nearest vehicle and pointed out the safest escape route. The explosion had ignited other ammunition vehicles and a chain reaction of enormous explosions started at random intervals. There was no means of forecasting when the next blast would occur and it was extremely dangerous to move anywhere in the camp. Undaunted, Captain Shields proceeded on foot towards the corner of the

warehouse where other soldiers were gathering. He led the men to the perimeter wall of the camp and assisted them to scale its 3-meter height before climbing it himself and dropping to the relative safety on the other side. There were a few injured British and American soldiers whom he ensured received medical treatment from an ambulance nearby. He ran around the outside of the wall in a midday temperature of 50 degrees centigrade to report to the commander at the front entrance of the camp to see if he could assist anyone else, before returning to the ambulance. Captain Shields was concerned that there might be men trapped inside the camp, especially close to the continuing explosions. He asked for a volunteer to accompany him and check the area. With the willing assistance of Corporal Plant he took a stretcher and first aid kit and ran back inside St Georges Lines. Massive explosions continued and lethal debris fell around him; there was no safe cover. Quite apart from the shrapnel, unexploded shells, bomblets and mines, the hangar doors to the warehouse accommodation were being blown out of their frames, large pieces of vehicles were being propelled at great speed through the air and skylights in the hangars were showering glass everywhere. The force of the blasts was terrifying. With total disregard for his own safety and at very considerable risk to his life, Captain Shields systematically checked all the buildings and areas where soldiers might be lying injured or trapped. He confirmed that no men remained in the camp before returning over the perimeter wall and reporting the area was clear. Captain Shields' selfless action cannot be praised enough; in great danger he risked his life to ensure that other soldiers were safe. He displayed outstanding leadership and courage in the highest traditions of the service and his action merits public recognition. It is strongly recommended that Captain Shields be awarded the Queen's Gallantry Medal.'

The full story of why Peter was awarded the QGM is as follows and it fills in the gaps of the usually bland and inadequate military citation:

St Georges Lines and Hard Rock Camps were adjacent British and US military camps. Hard Rock was crammed with American M109 Self Propelled Artillery pieces and stockpiles of ammunition for the guns, and it was whilst Peter was looking out of his office window that he noticed smoke coming from one of the US guns. There had apparently been an electrical problem with the SP Gun which was why the fire had started and this particular artillery piece was attached to a limber that was fully loaded with live plutonium ammunition. Peter explains, "The US Forces mix their natures when storing supplies and so the compound was crammed full of Land Mines, Depleted Uranium shells,

Phosphorous ammunition, M1 Abrams Tanks, M109 Howitzers, fuel tankers, and they were all just dumped next to each other. The British operate on a Geographical Dispersal System where different volatile supplies were stored in their own relevant and suitable storage areas. I was about to depart St Georges Lines to go and pick up the entertainer Bobby Davro from the airport just as the fire started. The comedian was on a Combined Services Entertainment (CSE) tour to entertain our troops in Kuwait and I was given the job of picking him up and ushering him around." On seeing the smoke Peter went outside and spoke to an American Serviceman who was dealing with the problem, "You've got a vehicle cooking off over there." The Yank snapped, "Yes we're getting it sorted out now sir." Peter tried to encourage the obviously under pressure US soldier, "Well get it sorted out quickly man!" Peter went back a short while later and re-encouraged the Yank who was trying to extinguish the fire with a one inch garden hose, "Well that's not bloody working is it? Stick an M109 on the front and drag it out of the compound using a straight bar!" Within seconds the charge bags inside the M109 started to explode, the top cupola flew open and a pillar of solid red flame shot up into the sky. The on board fire extinguishers came into play and the air was suddenly filled with a dense black smoke. The two US Servicemen dealing with the fire suddenly burst into life and even Usain Bolt couldn't have caught them before they reached the camp gates.

When they came back to the burning vehicle, Peter gave specific orders to the obviously shaken up Yanks, "For Christ's sake get another M109 and straight bar, attach it to this burning vehicle and then tow the damned thing straight through these prefabricated camp walls. We need to get it away from the rest of these vehicles and stores." One of the Americans confirmed that he wasn't authorised to drive a vehicle and that his Master Sergeant, who had all of the keys, wasn't on the camp. It was at this time that the small arms ammunition in the burning M109 started to explode. Peter realised this problem was going to escalate and so he reported directly to a British ex-Special Forces Colonel who was also on the camp. Peter recommended that the whole camp be evacuated before someone was killed. The Colonel hit the fire alarm and the British Forces naturally behaved in an exemplary manner, whilst the troops calmly filed outside Peter noticed some of them were only wearing their Calvin Klein underwear and combat boots, but at least they all had their webbing, helmets and were carrying weapons. Peter explains, "If there is one thing we Brits are really good at, its drills. Our lads paraded, the nominal roll was called, after which the Squadron Sergeant Major called them to attention and quickly marched them out of the danger area and into the desert. Job done!" Peter went back inside and started videoing the fire and damage to provide evidence for a board of enquiry. Whilst in the Headquarters, Peter was just walking down the stairs when an almighty explosion completely destroyed his Headquarters building. Windows, desks, chairs and walls were thrown all over the place. The massive shock wave from the explosion propelled him down the rest of the stairs and slid him along the entire length of the corridor on his arse, he was thrown out of the fire doors at the end and dumped outside on the vehicle park. He continued to video the carnage around him and witnessed an M1 Abrams Tank disintegrate in front of his camera lens. That explosion threw him backwards and he landed between two ISO containers, he continued videoing the sky for a few minutes. Whilst lying on the ground Peter could hear large pieces of shrapnel landing all around him and bouncing off the ISO containers. He got up and reported back to the Colonel.

Colonel: "Hello Peter, are you ok?"

Peter: "Yes I'm fine sir, but it looks like the camp's had it."

Colonel: "Is everybody out Peter?"

Peter: "I don't know sir. The camp is over five kilometres in diameter."

Colonel: "Well I need to know if they're all out."

Peter: "Well the only way to do that is to go round and check every single room in every single building sir."

Colonel: "Well, off you go then Peter."

Peter: "Yes Sir!"

Corporal Paul Plant volunteered to assist in searching the camp and Peter selflessly gave him his helmet to wear because he didn't have one. They both collected a stretcher and first aid bag and started a systematic exploration of the camp to find any trapped or injured personnel. The only soldiers they had to rescue were US Servicemen because the Brits had already sensibly evacuated the area. The two rescuers did find some injured American Servicemen and they evacuated them to a nearby ambulance where they received dedicated medical attention. During the search for casualties both Peter and Paul Plant were constantly flinching away from exploding ordnance and flying debris. Peter spoke to the 11th Cavalry Regiment Brigadier General, "Compliments of Commandant British Forces sir, this is what's happening. We're evacuating the camp because of a fire and exploding munitions." The condescending American Senior Officer simply replied, "Listen here little feller, the British might run away but we Americans don't." Peter told him, "Suit yourself but just remember you heard it here first." It is believed the Brigadier General was later Court Martialled for the ensuing colossal damage and loss of stores and equipment. In the end the entire compound was completely obliterated. The widespread damage and contamination was so bad that the MOD sent a Royal Engineers Lieutenant Colonel Bomb Disposal expert, and his WO1 sidekick, out to assess the damage. The RE Lieutenant Colonel had already won a George Medal and an MBE so he wasn't exactly a scaredy-cat, but even he refused to do anything with it and declared it a dirty area, he crossed the area off the British military maps. The Americans, however, insisted on moving back into Hard Rock Camp immediately and so the RE Lieutenant Colonel made them sign and take over responsibility for both of the contaminated camps.

Later on that afternoon Peter suddenly remembered he had to pick up Bobby Davro from the airport and so he jumped into his staff car and headed off to Kuwait Airport. As he walked through the arrivals lounge he noticed everyone was staring at him because his T shirt was torn to shreds and his face and arms were covered in black grime. He instantly recognised Bobby Davro and went up to introduce himself. The comedian took one look at Peter face and said, "Fuck me! What happened to the other bloke?" Peter apologised and told him he'd had a wasted journey because there wasn't a camp to hold the show in, the enduring Bobby Davro said, "Bollocks! If you can shine a torch on me I'll do a show for the boys, let's go!" By the time Peter and Bobby had returned to the temporary camp area in Kuwait docks the Royal Engineers had constructed a stage using a huge trailer, some black hessian material, and a few spotlights. Half way through the show Peter saw a cavalcade of blue flashing lights approaching the show. It was some US Military Policemen who were investigating the hullabaloo and bright lights. Peter explained about the CSE show and a bemused Yank said, "You guys were bombed out of your camp today and you're holding a comedy show?" Peter smiled and told him, "Well the show must go on old boy!"

The next day Peter found a camp that the Brits could move into. Camp Bibby was an ex-Pats site from where the DJ Simon Bates was going to do a radio broadcast, but the American Forces objected to the transmission because they didn't want anyone knowing about the previous day's debacle. After finding the new camp, Peter set about replacing every destroyed piece of personal equipment needed so that the Brits, including 1 ADTR, could continue with their missions. The American material losses alone included three M1 Abrams tanks which at $4.3m a pop came to $12.9m, nine M109's at $2.68m a pop came to $24.12m and this total doesn't include the limbers. Throw in numerous fuel tankers and multiple thousands of tons of ammunition and you've got yourself one hell of a tax payer's bill to pay, my friend. When everything had quietened down Peter was taken to the British Embassy in Kuwait and he personally spoke on the telephone to the Defence Secretary Tom King, the Head of the Ministry of Defence asked Peter what had happened and who he thought was at fault. Peter was completely honest and said, "Sir, I don't think I'm qualified to answer those kind of questions but suffice it to say, we Brits would never store ammunition in such a manner." He also informed the Defence Secretary that he'd videoed much of the incident.

The following day a US car pulled up next to Peter and two 'Black Suits' climbed out. The Secret Service 'Gentlemen' wore dark sunglasses and had white curly earpieces in their ears. Peter felt as if he was taking part in a scene being filmed for the next 'Men in Black' movie. The Spooks were accompanied by a Captain from the British Intelligence Services who said, "Peter, these two guys want to speak to you." One of the American Moles told Peter that he knew about the video tape and asked if could borrow it so that the Americans could make a copy. The Agents would of course return it to Peter within the hour. Peter said, "No! That tape is the property of the Ministry of Defence and I would need permission from a higher authority before handing it over." That bit of bollocks was a little white lie because the camera and tape were Peter's private property and his boss told him that he shouldn't feel pressurised into handing over any private property. The next day Peter was put under more pressure when he was whisked away to the US Embassy where a large Texan diplomat apologised for dragging him away from his duties, but he definitely needed that video tape. The Texan offered to take it from him there and then and they wouldn't need to bother him anymore, and of course they would make sure the tape was returned to him as soon as they'd made a copy. Thinking on his feet Peter said, "I'm sorry but I don't have the tape with me, your guys unceremoniously dragged me away from a convoy that I was leading down South and all of my kit, including the video, is still on that truck. There is nothing I can do about it at the moment but I'll catch up with you later after I've made a copy of the film for you." A week later Peter did give Agents J and K a copy of the film but before handing it over, he made them sign a disclaimer that the US Government did not have permission to copy, or use it for any purposes, without the express permission of Captain Peter Shields, Royal Corps of Transport.

After the war had ceased Peter returned to Bunde and as time moved towards winter he was given a posting to 62 Transport and Movement Squadron RCT in Berlin. Whilst packing up his Married Quarter on Christmas Eve he heard the front door bell ring and on opening the door he saw his Commanding Officer, Lieutenant Colonel Gavin Haigh, standing outside.

Peter: "Good evening Colonel. What a pleasant surprise."

Gavin: "Good evening Peter, I thought I'd pop across with a present for you."

Peter: "Well that's very kind of you Colonel, come on in but you'll have to take us as you find us I'm afraid. Pull up an MFO box and sit yourself down."

Gavin: "Not a problem Peter, I've just bought you a bottle of Whiskey."

Peter assumed that the whiskey was a leaving present from the Officers Mess.

Peter: "Thank you Colonel."

Gavin: "There's a card for you as well."

Peter opened the card and read, 'Congratulations on being awarded the Queen's Gallantry Medal'. Gavin Haigh.

Peter was gobsmacked, there isn't a process where someone calls you into an office and says' "Listen Peter, I'm going to write you up for an award blah blah blah." The QGM was a bolt out of the blue for Peter because he hadn't been given any indication that he'd even been recommended for any sort of award. On the day that the Queen presented him with his medal Peter took his wife and two children with him to Buckingham Palace. At one stage those accepting awards are whisked away into a corridor to await being called forward and the family members are taken into the main auditorium to watch the presentation. It is a well-oiled machine at Buckingham Palace because wherever you go someone is available to point you in the right direction and tell you what you need to do. In a large room a Brigadier instructed that morning's 120 recipients on what was going to happen next. Knights always took precedence, then the awards and decorations are awarded last and in order of seniority. Peter was to be the last decoration that morning.

Captain Peter Shields QGM at Buckingham Palace.

The SSAFA Sisters, Ladies from the Women's Institute and Foreign Commonwealth Dignitary's all went through before Peter and when he was eventually called forward he walked along the red carpet, turned left and faced the Queen, nodded, and she then pinned his medal onto an already fitted clasp on his uniform. HM then briefly shook his hand and motioned him to leave by pushing his hand away on the second shake. Peter then found himself in another corridor where the medal was whipped off his uniform, put into a presentation box and then given back to him with a certificate. At this point he was ushered into a different corridor by another 'Jock in a Frock' (Peter Shields words, not the authors), with Dame Billie Whitelaw and Richard Stilgoe who had just been awarded an OBE. Peter says, "It was an absolutely fabulous day and I was elated with the award."

On arrival in Berlin Peter was initially employed as B Troop Commander of 62 Transport and Movement Squadron. However he was soon moved to become Admin Officer and QM and subsequently Theatre Drawdown Officer. Once again fate intervened and Peter was appointed OC of the Squadron by Brigadier David Bromhead on departure of Major Paul Brook. This senior officer was the Great Nephew of Lieutenant Gonville Bromhead VC who assisted Commissary Dalton (an RCT predecessor) in saving the Mission Station and military outpost at Rorkes Drift. The Brigadier effectively threw some Major's rank slides over the desk to Peter and said, "You're now the OC 62 Squadron, crack on Peter." A few feathers were ruffled within the Corps because Peter was a junior Captain and now an Acting Major, but with the backing of the Brigade Commander no-one dared argue the case. Peter was the last OC of 62 Squadron RCT because he eventually closed the Berlin unit down after the collapse of the East German Government and the Berlin Wall. When Peter was posted to the Scottish Transport Regiment (STR) in 1998 as the unit Quartermaster he was surprised to find his old mate Andy West was still serving in the unit as the Squadron Sergeant Major. Over a four and a half year posting with the STR, Peter did a phenomenal amount of work re-writing the Territorial Army's unit equipment tables. He also became a member of the Children's Panel, where he worked with troubled youngsters for two nights and every Saturday morning over a two and a half year period.

Peter's next posting was to 4 General Service (GS) Regiment RLC in Abingdon and during his tenure as Regimental Quartermaster he did Operational Tours of Bosnia and Kosovo. Because of his selfless dedication and hard work at the Scottish Transport Regiment, Peter was made aware that he was going to be awarded an MBE (Member of the British Empire). Again he knew nothing about this and was astonished when told of the award. A brief twelve month posting as the Chief Instructor at the RLC (Royal Logistics Corps) All Arms Wing in Deepcut was followed by a posting to the Defence School of Transport as the Quartermaster, DST Leconfield had an annual budget of £35 million a year and so there was plenty of work to be done over the next two years. Since leaving the Corps Peter has worked for Humberside Army Cadet Force and for the last ten years has thrown all of his boundless energy into working for BLESMA The Limbless Veterans which was formerly known as the British Limbless Ex Servicemen's Association.

Peter continues to work for BLESMA and lives in Barrow upon Humber with his beautiful wife Julie.

Major Peter Shields MBE at Buckingham Palace yet again.

24212479 Sergeant Roy Malkin
RCT 1969 - 1989

Harry Malkin had served in the British Army during the Second World War, in fact both he and his motorbike were drafted into the Royal Signals and Harry only just escaped being captured by the Wehrmacht at Dunkirk. Unfortunately, Harry's motorbike had to be destroyed by a Military Police Sergeants' pistol in France because, "There ain't no room on the boats to take 'er 'ome son, and we ain't leaving 'er 'ere for Jerry to use." The rescue mission to bring an overwhelmed British Army back to England in June 1940 was called **'OPERATION DYNMAO'** and the Manoeuvre saw Harry transported back to Dover on the PS (Paddle Steamer) Brighton Belle. He, along with 800 other servicemen, were lucky to be on the Belle's first rescue mission because on her second run she hit a recently mined underwater obstacle and sank. The men on-board, including the Captain's dog, were saved by PS Medway after she cross-loaded the stricken soldiers onto her own, already crowded decks, everyone safely returned to Dover and then the PS Medway returned to Dunkirk on five further rescue missions.

On arrival at Dover the defeated British soldiers were interned at what can only be described as a refugee camp. Conditions were so bad there that the disheartened soldiers virtually mutinied, throwing stones at the Officers' tents and chanting, "We want some money! We want some leave!" To solve the borderline riotous problem the rebels were herded onto a train by the Corps of Military Police en mass. They were then taken up to the middle of the Scottish Highlands where they could be dealt with once the Dunkirk crisis was over. Eventually they were re-equipped, retrained and rearmed before being shipped out to Egypt where they fought against the German Afrika Korps. Harry was wounded in the desert after being shot up by a Luftwaffe aircraft and as a result he was medically downgraded. No longer able to ride a Royal Signals motorbike, Harry was reassigned to the Royal Army Ordnance Corps RAOC) as a Storeman and eventually promoted to Lance Corporal. He was later busted to Private by the Commanding Officer for allowing some of the Italian prisoner workforce to smoke in the store area. After the war Private Harry Malkin RAOC returned to England and settled in the village of Meanwood in Leeds where he married and had two sons who were christened Lawrence and Roy.

Roy was an average student at school, he was more interested in playing rugby than reading books and eventually went on to play for Leeds City Boys. Before the war Harry had played football for Harrogate Town Football Club and he wanted his son to follow in his footsteps, so he was somewhat disappointed when Roy announced that he'd rather play rugby than football. Harry's wartime experiences had no bearing on Roy wanting to become a soldier because that was something he'd wanted to do for as long as he could remember.

When he went to the Army Recruiting Office, Roy remembers seeing a poster on the wall showing a Royal Corps of Transport (RCT) Air Despatcher (AD) pushing a load of cargo out the back of an RAF C 130 Hercules aircraft. The Recruiting Sergeant tried to steer Roy towards a career in the Royal Engineers (RE) or Infantry but Roy was having none of it. He pointed at the poster and said, "I want to do that." The Recruiter obviously had certain quotas to fill and so he tried to dissuade Roy, "Oh no, you don't want to join that lot, they're the Royal Corps of Transport, and anyway I think they are full up at the moment. We can get you into something much better than the RCT." Roy wouldn't be moved on the subject though because he wanted to stand on the tailgate of an RAF C 130 and watch a load of cargo gently float onto a Drop Zone (DZ). He told the Sergeant, "Well if I can't join that lot then I'll go next door and join the bloody Royal Air Force." Unsurprisingly, as Roy made for the door the Sergeant called him back, "Now hang on a second lad….give me a second and I'll see what I can do for you." Miraculously, he suddenly found out that the RCT did in fact have just one more space available, and in early December of 1969 Roy headed off to do his Basic Training in an under-heated RCT Depot at Buller Barracks in Aldershot.

Roy's Basic Training Troop Sergeant was a man called Baxter who Roy describes as being a drunken Scotsman with a handlebar moustache, "He was funny, firm and very fair." The Scottish Sergeant wasn't like one of the other Sergeant instructors who was positively racist against a black recruit. "I witnessed it on a couple of occasions whilst at Buller, I didn't like it but there was nothing I could do about it." The physical training at Buller Barracks was relatively easy for Roy because he was already a fit young rugby player before arriving at the Depot. After passing his HGV III and Land Rover driving tests, Roy was sent to Thorney Island to complete his trade training as an Air Despatcher. After alighting at Havant Railway Station he got onto a 1950's style single decker civilian bus that was commonly referred to as the Thorney Flyer, which took him to the RAF Camp where he was dropped off outside the main gates. The whole camp seemed to have been caught in a time warp and it appeared to Roy that nothing had changed since the 1940's. Some of the original photos taken during the Second World War were displayed on the walls in the corridor of 47 (AD) Squadron RCT and they were testament to a lack of change in the landscape of Thorney Island, the smell of floor polish probably hadn't changed much either.

It took about eight weeks to train an RCT Air Despatcher and on the trainees first day they were equipped with flying coveralls and a riggers knife which was invaluable when they were making up packed loads ready for despatch. Flying helmets weren't issued until they'd progressed onto the final phase of their training and curiously, all helmets and flying coveralls had to be handed back into the stores on completion of the course. It might have been a better Idea to do a one-time issue of flying kit during their training phase and add the items onto their Army Form B 1157 Clothing and Equipment Record, but instead the Despatchers had to sign out a different set of flying kit and helmet every time they were posted to another AD unit, still, the army probably knew better. Initially the trainees did lots of classroom work and written exams before moving onto the mock up aircraft fuselages in one of the hangars. It was in these hangars they learned the practical side of Air Despatching, like making up Medium Stress Platforms (MSP) which cradled larger loads like vehicles and the smaller South East Asian Command (SEAC) packs. Trainees practiced their despatching drills in the mock-up fuselages over and over again because they had to get everything right before doing the real deal over the DZ, Roy and his fellow candidates also had to learn how to drive and operate an Eager Beaver Fork Lift truck, how and where to hook up their safety harnesses and wires in all of the RAF's cargo aircraft like the Lockheed C130 Hercules, the twin propped Hawker Siddley Andover C1 and they even got to work with the smaller de Havilland DHC-2 Beaver aircraft. Roy's first practice despatch was from an Andover C1 over the Tangmere DZ and he was elated that he and the other trainees got everything right and their stores landed, undamaged, smack on the target area.

After completing his Air Despatch Training, Roy was posted to 47 (AD) Squadron RCT where he spent the next six years with the RAF Lyneham based unit. During that time he flew famine relief missions to both Nepal and Africa. He also went to the United States of America two or three times a year on demonstration Exercises and deployed out to Cyprus and the Middle East on numerous occasions. The RAF and RCT Air Despatching records showed that they were accurately hitting their DZ targets with only 10% of the load being written off after landing. In the 1970's, Air Despatching units thought that a 20% to 30% stores write-off on landing was an acceptable loss due to MSP failure and poor landings. The Brits had the best and safest international record at Air Despatching and were so good that they often taught their techniques to the Americans, Italians, French and Dutch. RCT Air Despatching (with a little bit of help from the Royal Air Force) was the envy of the military world. On each flight the RCT AD team consisted of one Corporal, one Lance Corporal, and two Drivers. They worked under the direction of an RAF Flight Sergeant Air Load Master (who was always called 'Loadie'), the Loadie and RCT Corporal both had direct helmet communications with the pilot during each mission. In the early 1970's Nepal suffered from a rice famine and because a lot of the Nepalese people lived in remote and inaccessible villages, 47 (AD) Squadron RCT was tasked with providing famine relief by distributing food and other essential supplies by air. The RAF C130's were based in Kathmandu for two months where all the servicemen lived in tents when they weren't on flying duties. Some helicopters were also sent out to assist in distributing the supplies but in the main Hercules aircraft were used because they could carry larger loads, had better navigational equipment on board and could fly further because of their fuel capacity. Roy states, "We constantly flew through 'Eddies' which were a drop in air pressure, resulting in the crews being buffeted around in the back of the aircraft. The RAF pilots were brilliant at low level flying because they'd practiced it time and again through the hills and mountains in Scotland." The scenery in Nepal was outstanding and Roy was living the dream as he stood on the ramp at the back of the aircraft. As he looked down at the luscious Nepalese jungle, which was surrounded by beautiful mountains, he was euphoric, "I felt like I was on the top of the world." There were times though when even the RAF couldn't fly through some of the atrocious monsoon weather. The long working hours were pretty much the same when they took part in the North African famine relief work, one big difference was the fact that the crews were based in Cyprus and they lived in decent RAF accommodation with plenty of fresh rations.

In 1972/1973 Roy was a member of C (Dakota) Troop in 47 AD Squadron RCT when the whole Troop was temporarily attached to 7 Tank Transporter Regiment RCT for their Roulement tour of Northern Ireland, the Troop was based in Palace Barracks where the Drivers mainly drove Bedford RL's and Patrol Land Rover's for the resident Infantry Battalion. In these early years of the Northern Ireland 'Troubles', Roy and every other RCT Driver were regularly stoned and shot at by small arms and RPG (Rocket Propelled

Grenade) weapons when they drove up and down the Crumlin Road. On the plus side of life, the local Belfast girls were allowed into Palace Barracks on disco nights and Roy met Patsy who he married after the tour ended, they lived in Married Quarters in Lyneham and BAOR and had two lovely daughters called Catherine (born. 1974) and Nichola (born. 1976). But unfortunately, like many army marriages of the time, Roy and Patsy drifted apart because of the time Roy spent on Exercises and overseas Detachments, they eventually divorced and Patsy returned to her home town of Belfast.

SEAC (South East Asian Command) packs on an RAF Hastings Aircraft.

On a later trip to Fort Bragg in North Carolina, things got even better for the crews because they were billeted in Motels and received Local Overseas

Allowance (LOA) to the amount of 22 US Dollars a day, which in the 1970's was a considerable increase to any British serviceman's monthly pay. Married soldiers usually saved the money and took it home to their wives but being young free and single, Roy blew the lot on wine, women, and song and wasted the rest. Roy went on the piss with his mate Driver John Clarke RCT in the town of Fayetteville just outside Fort Bragg. They noticed that the majority of the local population were black and they all seemed to be glaring at them whilst quietly muttering under their breath. The lads enjoyed a slightly uncomfortable couple of beers before walking up the street and buying hamburgers and fries from a fast-food joint. They then sat on some sort of monument with railings and scoffed their takeaway. Before they'd finished eating a Police Car pulled up next to them and a local Sheriff spoke to Roy and his mate John:

Roy: "Good evening Constable."

Sheriff: "What the hell do you two think you're doing?"

Roy: "We're just enjoying our burger and chips Constable, is there a problem?"

Sheriff: "Do you two have any idea where the hell you are?"

Roy: "I believe we're in the land of the free and the home of the brave."

Sheriff: "Get in the car smart ass!"

Roy: "Why?"

Sheriff: "For Christ's sake, just get in the goddam car... NOW!"

Somewhat bemused and slightly alarmed the two lads climbed into the back of the police car where the local cop explained that the bars they'd recently been drinking in were no go areas for white people. He went on to explain that they had just been eating their hamburgers on a local monument that marked the spot where an American slave market was situated in the 1800's, the railings they were sitting on where actually part of the original slave pens.

Sheriff: "You guys were lucky to get out of there alive, most white people are unwelcome in this part of town."

Roy: "It could be that we British have a lot in common with the black Americans."

Sheriff: "I don't understand, what do you mean?"

Roy: "Well, we've both had the shit kicked out of us by your lot."

Roy felt that the average RCT Air Despatcher was nothing more than a spoilt brat who would have struggled when put up against a General Transport (GT) Driver. "They were more disciplined and harder workers than we ever were and they didn't whinge and whine like a lot of the Air Despatchers did. In a Mechanical Transport (MT) role Drivers were commanded by Senior and Junior NCO's who wouldn't take any shit from an insolent Driver with a chip on his shoulder, we in the Air Despatch Role had an easy time of it really". A Scottish RCT Corporal was reposted back into 47 (AD) Squadron RCT from an MT role in BAOR and Roy started to get a taste of what it would be like in a normal RCT unit. The Corporal shouted, screamed, and threatened if things weren't done properly and to his satisfaction. It wasn't the sort of management system that AD crews were used to and Roy believes that Corporal must have gone on to become a Warrant Officer. In 1975 the Ministry of Defence (MOD) introduced changes into the Armed Forces establishment and the Air Despatching role was cut by fifty per cent. Roy had by now been promoted to Lance Corporal and was one of the reluctant Air Despatchers sent into that dreaded MT Role in BAOR.

The soldiers leaving 47 (AD) Squadron RCT weren't given a preference of posting and Roy ended up at 1 Armoured Division Headquarters and Signal Regiment, based in Caithness Barracks in Verden, West Germany. It was never going to be his dream posting because he'd already imagined it was going to be a shit job, as it turned out though he quite liked working with the Royal Signal soldiers. After being put into the RCT transport pool he drove the service children's school buses and the camp rubbish truck before being moved into one of the Troops in a Signal Squadron. Corporal 'Crinkle' had just been kicked out of Bravo Troop for Drinking and Driving and a Royal Signals Captain requested that Roy replace him to look after the Squadrons Land Rovers, trucks and water trailers. Roy had previously been tasked to drive for this Captain and had obviously made a good impression. The outgoing Corporal was cruelly christened with the nickname 'Crinkle' by the other RCT Drivers because his face had been burned in a servicing bay fire. The fire had erupted because Corporal 'Crinkle' was smoking in the Servicing Bay pit and his cigarette had ignited some fuel vapours. Even though Roy wasn't promoted to full Corporal when he took over from 'Crinkle'' he still took charge of the Troops box bodied trucks that held the 'Bleeps' signal equipment and their Command Post vehicles. Roy's job was usually done by a Sergeant or Corporal and when he eventually applied for Pay of Higher Rank, which meant he would be paid as a Corporal but not given the extra stripe on his arm, the Royal Signals simply posted in a 'Bleep' Sergeant who knew nothing about vehicles. Whilst at Verden Roy became interested in yachting and the sport eventually took up most of his leisure time which was a good thing because his drinking had spiralled out of control. He found that the alcohol distracted him from the tedium of soldiering with the Royal Signals unit. Each Field Exercise was pretty much the same as the last one and in 1980 Roy became so bored with the job that he was pleased when RCT Manning and Records posted him to 26 Squadron RCT in Northern Ireland.

After completing his Northern Ireland Relief Training (NIRT) Course at Ballykinler, the OC of 26 Squadron decided to send Roy up to D Troop which was located in Ballykelly, a mere twelve miles from the City of Londonderry. D Troop was located in a massive old RAF hangar that had previously been used to house RAF Shackleton aircraft. The place was big enough to hold all of the Troops civilian style cars, busses and ambulances, used to support the Londonderry Brigade and their families. One of Roy's peculiar duties as an RCT Lance Corporal at Ballykelly was to drive the army's civilian style Armoured Mobile Library. The vehicle had Makrolon Polycarbonate sheet armour attached to its bodywork for bomb blast protection and Roy drove to the isolated army locations in Londonderry to supply reading material (not the sort that squaddies usually peruse) for those soldiers on rest periods.

On 6th December 1982 during Roy's posting the Irish National Liberation Army (INLA) exploded a bomb at the Droppin Well pub discotheque in Ballykelly. The terrorists had reconnoitred the place and realised that it was often used by off duty British Army personnel. Eleven soldiers and six civilians were killed in the blast and thirty other civilians and service personnel were severely injured. Roy heard the explosion even though he was miles away playing darts in another pub. Everyone in the local area knew it was a bomb and the off duty army personnel immediately returned to barracks. Driver 'Chalky' White RCT and Roy Malkin drove the army ambulances that attended the incident and they were mentioned in a General Officer Commanding (GOC) commendation for their valuable work. A memorial stone was laid in Ballykelly to commemorate that terrible atrocity in 1982, the fallen soldiers and civilians were:

Corporal David Salthouse - Light Infantry
Lance Corporal Steven Bagshaw – Cheshire Regiment
Lance Corporal Clinton Collins – Cheshire Regiment
Lance Corporal David Stitt – Cheshire Regiment
Lance Corporal Philip McDonough – Cheshire Regiment
Private David Murray – Cheshire Regiment
Private Steven Smith – Cheshire Regiment
Private Neil Williams – Cheshire Regiment
Private Shaw Williamson – Cheshire Regiment
Private Terrance Adam – Army Catering Corps
Private Paul Delaney – Army Catering Corps

Alan Callaghan, Patricia Cooke, Ruth Dixon, Angela Hoole, Valerie McIntyre, and Carol Watts. *Belle! Horrida bella* - (War! Horrid War!) Virgil Aenied VI 86.

14 Intelligence and Security Company also had a compound in the corner of the Ballykelly camp which was cordoned off from everyone else. The detachment fort was made up of a twenty foot high corrugated stockade which no other soldiers from the camp were allowed to enter and they usually used their own raggedy arsed civilian cars. The Sneaky Beaky's operating from this fortress kept very much to themselves and they were very rarely seen entering or leaving the camp. D Troop were occasionally tasked with picking up some of these shifty soldiers who wore civilian clothing and had bulging jackets. Roy sporadically had to drive them out into the countryside and was told to simply follow their instructions. He'd drop them off at a hedgerow of their own choosing and they'd disappear into the darkness carrying a suspicious looking canvas holdall. The RCT Drivers designated to carry out these clandestine duties wore civilian clothing and were always tooled up with a hidden 9mm Browning pistol, they were also under strict instructions not to engage the operatives in conversation and they had orders not to return to camp using the same route. Towards the end of his tour with 26 Squadron Roy's drinking had escalated to an even higher level and it was fortuitous that he was promoted to full Corporal on posting to 1 Armoured Division Headquarters in Bielefeld, West Germany.

Lance Corporal Roy Malkin RCT (front rank far left) Note his AD badge on lower left sleeve.

Roy's new unit in Ripon Barracks had a very similar Role to the one played by his previous Royal Signals unit in Verden, except that in Bielefeld it was more of a Brigade unit than the previous larger Divisional organisation, which had more Officers and clerical staff but less vehicles. Roy extended his interest in Yachting and attended more Yachting Courses at the British Yacht Club at Dummersee where he qualified as a Class II Seaman and RYA (Royal Yachting Association) Sailing Instructor. He became Captain of his units' Yachting team and led them to a third place in the RCT Championships, this was quite an achievement bearing in mind that his team was made up from a Squadron sized unit and they were competing against Regimental sized units. Corporal Roy Malkin's crew bizarrely consisted of his boss Major Mike Hodson RCT and WO2 Ron Hughes RCT who were both his new OC and Squadron Sergeant Major respectively. In another competition Roy's yacht was involved in a collision with Warrant Officer David Flynn's yacht which unintentionally broke the other teams' mast. David Flynn was a large tough man who was a big name in the RCT sailing world because he'd previously won several major sailing trophies. He was also the main coach on the famous 10 Regiment RCT boxing team and between 1971 and 1976, he'd boxed twelve times for the Regiment, losing only four of those bouts and always on a points decision. Roy was privy to all this information and on seeing the look on David's face after the collision, and hearing the profanities coming from his bellowing voice, he did the sensible thing and 'Battened down the Hatches' before 'Cutting and Running.' Note: The author phoned David Flynn to get his side of the story and asked him if he was still angry. He jokingly replied, "Do you know where that bastard lives?"

In 1990 Roy was selected for promotion to Sergeant and at the same time was posted to Belize to take charge of the armoury in Airport Camp. The job was easy and therefore boring to say the least and so Roy started going out on patrol with members of the Royal Military Police. Whilst chatting with some of the local Civilian Police Officers in Belize City, Roy noticed that they were armed with World War Two .38 Cal Mark VI Webley revolvers which they carried on their webbed belts. He asked one of the 'coppers' if he could have a quick look at one of the guns. On opening the cylinder he found that the ammunition in the weapon was as old as the weapon itself. If they'd ever had to use the gun at any time the ammunition probably wouldn't fire and if it did, it would be more likely to injure the policeman rather than his target or any possible villain. When they got back to Airport Camp Roy happened to mention the state of the local coppers ammunition to the Quartermaster who told him to put up a letter to the Camp Commandant. As a result of his brief interest in the old style pistol, the British Army replaced the Civilian Police Forces' entire stock of .38 Calibre ammunition and the Commandant sent Roy out to check and service all of their revolvers. This involved travelling around Belize and staying with the local police force, Roy got to see examples of the seedier side of life in Belize.

Belize wasn't a good place to send Roy because he was a borderline alcoholic and when his six month tour was extended to a year his addiction to alcohol became worse. On his Rest and Recuperation Leave (R&R), Roy flew to Florida and stayed in a US Navy Submarine Training Base in Orlando where he went on the lash for three days and nights solid. On the third morning he was awakened in the base laundrette by a very attractive oriental woman who was the US Navy's laundry contract manageress. She apparently owned several other laundrette's in Florida and as she drove a Jaguar car Roy knew she was quite wealthy. After sobering up, Roy went out and bought the lady some flowers because she had been kind to him. It would ultimately be the start of a turbulent relationship after he left the army.
Roy flew back to Belize and was posted to Ripon in Yorkshire before being discharged from the British Army in 1990. With a £6,000 gratuity in his back pocket, Roy flew out to the Caribbean where he worked as a barman in Jamaica.

Every day he squandered his money on alcohol and some of that special Caribbean tobacco. Life was really cool for about a year until he started to run out of money and it was then that he headed back to his Oriental beauty in Orlando. Over the next five years or so the two of them built up a Laundry Empire in which they worked from 0700 hours to 2200 hours every day of the week, at the same time Roy's Oriental beauty had turned into a control freak. They had a large house and fast modern cars and by this time Roy was a millionaire, at least on paper. He was also an alcoholic and coupled with his partners eternal nagging, life was shit. Things were about to get even worse. Roy's partner had told him to dump the dripping condensation from under the Dry Cleaning machines outside the back door of their shop. He'd been doing this for a number of years and unbeknownst to him the condensation was full of Tetrachloroethylene, a chemical used in a dry cleaning process. It is now known to cause severe brain, liver, and kidney damage and can also affect the central nervous system and can cause cancer.

Roy's partner had decided to sell this particular shop and the new buyer insisted on having a full survey done on the building and its surrounding area. An Environmental Officer came to see Roy with the results of some soil tests and gave him a bit of bad news. The contaminated water he'd been dumping out the back had filtered through to the local drinking water table which was only eighteen feet below the ground. Roy was going to be prosecuted for the attempted manslaughter of a quarter of a million people. The Environmental Officer told Roy his future in no uncertain terms, "You're going to jail man because this carry's a minimum three year sentence and you'll also have to pay for the clean-up which is going to set you back at least half a million Dollars." That very afternoon Roy packed a suitcase full of money and flew back to the UK before re-uniting and living with his daughter Catherine in Belfast for a while. However, his alcoholism ultimately resulted in several failed business ventures and he was eventually declared bankrupt. After losing his home, Roy had to live on the streets of Belfast where he stole the collection money from several churches. He at least had the decency to listen to their sermons before running off with the cash.

One morning Roy woke up in a Belfast gutter after pissing his trousers and vomiting down the front of his jumper yet again. His thumping headache didn't deter him from going to the nearest church to steal some more collection money, he desperately needed the money to buy a bottle of anything alcoholic. His body and mind were crying out for the stuff and only those who have suffered from this kind of addiction can possibly understand what Roy was going through. He was at the lowest ebb of his life and couldn't sink any further. Looking for another opportunity to steal money from a collection plate, Roy sat in a pew at the back of the church. When the plate was passed to him he noticed it had a letter with his name on it. He opened the envelope and found a bundle of money that had been donated to him by the local parishioners, it sounds a cliché but from that moment onwards Roy turned to 'his Saviour' and prayed for help and guidance. Whether you believe in divine providence or not makes no difference, but Roy's life started to change for the better after the church-going people of Belfast showed him inordinate kindness. Over the years Roy ultimately beat his addiction to alcohol and also attained a Degree in Theology and a Diploma in Pastoral Studies.

Ray now lives in Wakefield with his amazing wife Maggie. He works tirelessly as a preacher helping alcoholics, those with drug problems, and women exploited by prostitution.

24242832 Driver Vince Rollock
RCT 1971 – 1976

Private Vince Rollock during his Basic Training at the Junior Tradesmen Regiment Rhyl in 1972. (Note the Light Infantry cap badge in his Beret.)

Vince Rollock was only eleven years old when he left Barbados. He arrived in a very cold, dirty, and depressing Huddersfield Town in 1967, his mum and dad having left the Island five years earlier in the hope of getting jobs in the UK where they could start a better life for their family. His dad, Ernest had previously reached the North of England in 1962 where he provided a cheap source of labour for the UK industry; he quite simply did all the jobs that other folks didn't want to do. By 1967 Ernest had earned enough money to send for the rest of his family who had remained living in Barbados.

By 1971 Vince had grown to be a tall and strong young man and even though he still wasn't as strong or tough as his dad, things were becoming fractious within the family household. Ernest outspokenly told his son, "This house isn't big enough for both of us!" At the age of 15, Vince left school without any qualifications because he'd had no interest in academic subjects, he also got into lots of fights at school and in all honesty admits to being a bit of a nuisance both at home and at school. He did however manage to get a job working as an apprentice book binder with a firm called Ben Riley's in Huddersfield. Even though Vince was now working, he still felt his mum and dad were treating him like a kid and the only way to resolve the household tension was for him to leave home, especially before things really boiled over. Vince hopped onto the number 70A bus and headed off into town, making his way towards the Army Careers Information Office. The recruiting Sergeant coerced Vince into joining the 2nd Battalion Light Infantry Regiment which in 1967 had absorbed the KOYLI (Kings Own Yorkshire Light Infantry) into its ranks. Vince was still only 15½ years old at the time and so he had to enlist into the Junior Tradesman Regiment at Rhyl in North Wales. This training unit supervised the Basic Training of soldiers from the Infantry and various Corps and Regiments, these included the RTR (Royal Tank Regiment), RMP (Royal Military Police), R Sigs (Royal Signals), and of course, the RCT (Royal Corps of Transport).

On arrival at Rhyl on 11th May 1971 Vince met another Junior Tradesman called Brian Yemm, they'd joined up at the same time and were both put into the same billet and room in 1 Platoon of Cambrian Company, however, 'Yemmie' had enlisted into the Royal Corps of Transport as a Junior Driver and not the Infantry. 'Yemmie' came from Kirkby-in-Ashfield which was a mere sixty miles away from Huddersfield and so he and Vince had an instant geographical rapport. Having said that, it must be pointed out that Vince was 6 foot 3 inches in height and Yemmie was only 4 foot 11 ¾ inches so they definitely looked like an extreme version of the 'Odd Couple'. What 'Yemmie' lacked in height he more than made up for in character and charisma. Here was a man that didn't hold with prejudice against race, culture or colour of any kind. Vince had made such a good comrade in 'Yemmie' that he felt compelled to transfer into the RCT in the hope that they would be posted to the same unit after Basic Training. Neither Vince nor 'Yemmie' fully understood the army system in the early stages of their training though. At the end of their JTR training together Vince was posted to 1 Squadron RCT in Colchester and his friend 'Yemmie' was sent out to BAOR (British Army of the Rhine) in West Germany. The bond of friendship they made in Rhyl was a relationship that a lot of soldiers make with comrades at some stage in their career, but 'Yemmie' took it a step further, he asked Vince to be his best man at both of his weddings. When Vince had completed his first three months of Basic Training he travelled to Kirkby-in-Ashfield and stayed with the Yemm family for a whole week of his leave. "They really looked after me in that week," says Vince. "They all made me felt like I was a member of their family. 'Yemmie' and I remained best friends for over forty three years until he died of cancer on 28th August 2014."

Boxing training had always figured large in Vince's life since he'd arrived in the UK but he'd never actually taken part in a competitive bout. His first ever boxing match was against another Junior Soldier at Rhyl called Junior Lance Corporal Andy Harvey, Andy was in the Royal Signals and because he was a big tough rugby player most of the trainee's and senior staff considered him to be a hard-man. A hard-man who would be able to shut Vince Rollock's mouth either in, or out of the boxing ring. At the time Vince was a mouthy teenager but no malice was ever meant because it was all just banter and bravado. When the bell rang and their fight started, Vince started prancing around the ring and he did a Muhammed Ali shuffle in front of Andy, but it really was just showmanship because Vince thought he was in for an arse kicking from Andy Harvey. Within the first round Vince had busted Andy's lip wide open and Andy pleaded to the referee for the fight to be stopped, "It was probably the easiest fight I've ever had," says Vince, "But Andy and I became great friends afterwards". Vince also had a boxing match against Dave 'Paddy' McCracken who had joined the Royal Military Police, Dave was a 6 foot 6 inches Rugby and Basketball playing athlete who eventually had a very successful career in the APTC (Army Physical Training Corps). Like most of Vince's fights, he beat him as well.

Other challenges took a lot more out of him though, especially when he took part in the Welsh 3000 competition. Only the fittest of Junior Tradesman took part in this gruelling struggle against nature which involved climbing, unaided, to the top of fifteen mountains within a twenty four hour period. This meant officially covering a distance of 26.5 miles but that was extended to over 30 miles if you included getting to and from the start and finish points. Competitors also had to physically carry tents, rations, water and all other sundry items up hill to the start point because no access roads were available. Vince's training for this monumental task involved living in the hills of

Snowdonia for several months and he celebrated every single day he spent out there.

Not every challenge was enjoyable for Vince though and he explains some of the problems he came up against at Rhyl, "I never looked for trouble in the army but somehow it just seemed to find me when I wasn't expecting it." In every army unit around the world you can expect a fight to break out in a barrack room at any time of the night or day. It's what soldiers do because they have to live in frustrating situations with very little privacy, they also have all of that testosterone pumping around their bodies. After getting into a couple of brawls during his training Vince was called into the Platoon Office to have a 'chat' with his Platoon Sergeant who was a member of the Green Howards Regiment. Sergeant Dave Stoddart told him, "Rollock, we need to have a chat. I think you would be a great Junior NCO but your Platoon Commander seems to think you're just a loudmouth. I think you are one of the fittest soldiers I've ever seen in my life and you also have a great attitude when you're competing. You'd be a great leader if only you could stay out of trouble. I've told the Commanding Officer that I'd like to promote you straight to Junior Corporal. If you can stay out of trouble until the end of this term then those two stripes are yours for the taking."

Vince was determined to have those two stripes on his arm and prove to the DS (Directing Staff) that he was a good leader of men and not a trouble maker. Unfortunately, several weeks later in Rhyl's local chippy, two civilian Welshmen walked into the fish-shop just as Vince had been handed his bag of chips and he was about to start walking back to camp whilst eating the takeaway. The local men were in their mid-twenties and obviously looking for trouble even though Vince had said nothing to them. They made some offensive comments and started getting physical with Vince who had by now been backed into a corner. Whilst being pushed and jostled Vince thought, "I could walk away from this but these tosser's will think I'm a soft git," and with that thought still in his mind he took care of them. With just a couple of punches he simply knocked the pair of them out. Vince was hauled in front of the Commanding Officer when the incident was reported to the camp and he was given a proper dressing down but no charges were actually brought against him. The chip shop owners tried to help Vince's case when they gave a statement declaring that Vince had done nothing wrong and that the two local men had started the trouble by pushing and provoking him. After Vince's 'interview without coffee' Sergeant Dave Stoddart told him, "You've let me down Rollock. I asked you not to get into trouble and that's exactly what you've done." No protestations were accepted and Vince wasn't promoted during his stay at Rhyl, a similar travesty of justice would be repeated later in his career when Vince was posted into the famous 10 Regiment RCT boxing team in Bielefeld.

After completing his Trade and Driver Training at the RCT Depot in Buller Barracks, Aldershot, Vince was posted to 1 Squadron RCT at Roman Way Camp, Colchester. Within a month of arriving in Colchester ('Collie') Vince was told that the entire Squadron was deploying to Belfast on a 6 month operational tour and that he would be based with their Headquarters in Moscow Camp. The tour for Vince was extremely frustrating and boring and he ended up getting into fights with soldiers from his own, and other units. The OC jailed Vince for 7 days in Palace Barracks nick for fighting and after he was released the Squadron Commander told him, "I know why you are behaving this way Driver Rollock and I think I may have a solution for you. For the rest of this tour in Belfast you will be exempt all duties and you have my permission to do boxing training every day if you so wish, but you are not allowed to do any heavy drinking and your energies must be channelled into purely hard Physical Training. If you let me down Driver Rollock then the deal is definitely off and you can go back to jail." Vince stuck to the agreement and the rest of his tour passed without further confrontations.

After his post-Northern Ireland leave, Vince returned to Colchester and was told that in a couple of weeks he, and the rest of his Troop, would be deploying to Cyprus. Using Bedford RL three tonners, the Troop was going to be involved in moving vulnerable refugees from areas where the Greek Cypriot and Turkish armies were fighting, and moving them into safer areas. The RCT Troop was flown in an RAF Hercules C130 aircraft from RAF Lyneham and straight onto the camp where they were going to be based at, RAF Akrotiri. On arrival Troop members were somewhat surprised to discover that they were going to be accommodated in tents for the next four months. Within weeks the work started to dry up which resulted in Vince and his RCT mates becoming increasingly bored and frustrated. As a result of their disinterest they decided to write a letter of complaint to Her Majesty Queen Elizabeth II. The following is a faithful copy of the letter they wrote and covers just about everything that Vince and his mates told their Queen.

LETTER OF COMPLAINT

Dear Ma'am

We are writing you this letter from RAF Akrotiri in Cyprus after completing a four month operational tour in Northern Ireland. Our tour in Cyprus started within four weeks of finishing in Belfast and we are really fed up because we have been away from our family and friends for nearly six months now!

We can't wait to see you on the television doing your Christmas speech when we do eventually get back to dear old Blighty.

We remain,
Ma'am,
Your obedient servants
 Blah Blah Blah.

The letter was signed by Drivers Vince Rollock, Dave Coles, Terry Docherty and Michael McNamara. A copy was also sent to the Officer Commanding 1 Squadron RCT back in Colchester, incidentally, the lads did get a 'thank you for your letter', letter from the Palace. While these letters were winging their way back to the UK Vince tried to get himself posted home using another tried and tested method, an approach that had been previously used by Corporal Max Klinger of the 4077th Mobile Army Surgical Hospital on the TV comedy programme MASH. Vince started dressing up in women's clothing. Vince's Troop Sergeant made him report sick and sent him off to see the RAF doctor on the camp. The 'quack' knew that Vince was swinging the lead but offered to send him to see a Psychiatrist. Meanwhile back at the ranch, the OC of 1

Squadron RCT paid a surprise visit to his Drivers in Cyprus and suddenly announced that there would be a change in personnel within A Troop, some of the lads, including Vince, were going home to Colchester. The OC also verified that these changes had nothing to do with letters that had been written to Her Majesty the Queen, or the fact that Driver Vince Rollock had started wearing chiffon tops and sling back shoes.

During this period of Vince's military career his friend 'Yemmie' was serving with an RCT unit that was based in Herford in West Germany and Staff Sergeant Gary Fuller came to watch him in a boxing competition. Gary was so impressed with Driver Yemm's boxing skills that he invited him to join up with 10 Regiment RCT's boxing team. 'Yemmie' suggested to Gary that he'd come if a certain Driver Vince Rollock, who was at 1 Squadron in Colchester, was also invited to join the team as their Heavyweight boxer. It was a done deal and 10 Regiment RCT asked 1 Squadron to release Vince for a posting to Bielefeld. Vince had no idea that his new Regiment was already becoming one of the most famous boxing units in the history of the British Army. The Chief Clerk of 1 Squadron told him, "They're the elite of army and RCT boxing at the moment, your life will be much better for being posted to 10 Regiment." When Vince arrived at Catterick Barracks in Bielefeld, he was placed into 36 Squadron and was allocated a bed-space in their accommodation. The following morning Driver Lester Robinson, who also was a member of the Regimental boxing team, came down from the gymnasium to collect him from his room. When the two Drivers entered the Gym they were met by the QMSI (Quartermaster Sergeant Instructor) Staff Sergeant Gary Fuller and his assistant coach Sergeant David Flynn RCT, both of whom were in overall charge of the boxing team. Their jobs included monitoring their diet, their exercise regime, their personal problems, and they also had the final decision on anything that they decided the team should, or shouldn't be allowed to do. Gary was a hard task master and you played by his rules or you didn't play at all. Vince sauntered up to Gary whilst smoking a panatela cigar, shook his hand and said, "Hi, I'm Vince Rollock your new heavyweight boxer." Gary eyed Vince up and down but didn't say a word, he just picked up his telephone and rang Lieutenant Colonel Lee, the Commanding Officer. "Good morning Sir, our new heavyweight has arrived but he doesn't look much like one to me, he looks more like a middleweight." After hanging up Gary told Vince that the CO was on his way down to watch him do some sparring, he then introduce Vince to the rest of his team. The following names will roll off the tongues of anyone who has served in the Royal Corps of Transport and 10 Regiment RCT in particular, the team included, Zac Rene, Stevie Johnson, Mickey Gannon, Ted Dublin, Les Lawton, John Dwyer, Gussy Dawkins, Seamus O'Callaghan, (Fiery) Phil Lewis, Ron Eldrett and Keith Johnson to name just some of them. After watching Vince spar against Keith Johnson and big John Dwyer the Commanding Officer officially invited Driver Rollock onto the 10 Regiment boxing team. 'Yemmie' hadn't actually been posted into the team at this stage.

Vince thought he was supremely fit when he arrived in Bielefeld but after his first training session he was breathing heavily. "The guy's on the boxing team were extremely fit and with only four weeks to my first fight I needed to play catch up because we were fighting against the Para's in Berlin." The teams daily workout consisted of a 10 mile run first thing in the morning followed by a weigh in; after getting showered they all went for a NAAFI break where the only intake they were allowed was a pint of milk or orange juice. Sandwiches, sweets and fizzy drinks (this was in the days before Diet Coke) were definitely taboo and any food felonies were punished with yet another 10 mile run, two crimes and you were off the team. Next, the team did some serious circuit training before being split into two teams where the black boxers played games against the white boxers. The teams competed in either five-a-side football or basketball before doing some pad and bag work. After a strict lunch consisting of specially cooked steaks, fish and vegetables, the boxers had an enforced rest period before returning back to the gym for more runs, ball games, bag work and sparring.

Even the Team Manager Staff Sergeant Gary Fuller was subject to a strict daily diet that was punishable by the rest of the team if he strayed. In 1975 the controversial slavery film 'Mandingo' had recently been released and it was set in the Southern States of America just prior to the American Civil War, the whole film is about slavery and the sexual tension between the black population and their white Plantation bosses. Vince went to see the film with some of the other black boxers and he watched as a black slave was strung up in an X shape by his hands and feet, the actor was then whipped for a minor transgression. The following day Gary Fuller was caught by Vince and the boxing team drinking a mug of hot chocolate in the gym, this was definitely against the rules and had one of the boxers done this they would have been in deep trouble. Vince became an instant Judge, jury and executioner, he orchestrated the boxing team to lash Gary in an X shape to the gymnasium monkey bars using his hands and feet, he then had the miscreant's tracksuit bottoms pulled down so they could all paddle Gary's backside with a table-tennis bat until it glowed like a coal fire. Gary took his punishment from the boxers without a word of complaint.

Vince's first fight for 10 Regiment was five weeks later in Berlin where he was up against Lance Corporal Andy Palmer, a mixed race soldier from 3 Para who was also 6 foot 3 inches in height. Andy bore an incredible resemblance to Muhammed Ali and Vince hoped that he couldn't box like him. In the first round Vince caught Andy with a belter of a right punch (his first punch of the fight actually) and the Para fell to the canvas for fifteen seconds, Vince naively stood over Andy thinking, 'Fuck me this is easy.' During that 15 seconds Vince could hear Sergeant David Flynn screaming at him from his corner, "Get to the fucking corner Vince, for fuck's sake man, get to the fucking corner!" A downed opponent's count won't start until the other boxer stands in a neutral corner, it's one of the Marquis of Queensbury rules. After Vince moved to a corner of the ring the referee started counting to ten and he got to eight seconds just as Andy got back on his feet and so the fight continued. Had Vince immediately complied with Dave Flynn's instructions the fight would have been a one punch knockout for 10 Regiment RCT.

In the second round Andy hit Vince with an illegal blow and he dropped to the canvas, the fighters were in a clinch when the ref shouted, **"STOP"!** after which Andy caught Vince with that illegal punch. David Flynn screamed at him to stay down but Vince was so annoyed with his opponent that he got straight back up and was ready to continue with the fight. Had Vince stayed down then Andy would have been disqualified and the win would have been awarded to 10 Regiment. Lance Corporal Andy Palmer was given a warning but in the end he won the fight on a point's decision at the end of round three. After the fight Gary Fuller said, "Listen Vince, you could've beaten Andy Palmer twice tonight and he's probably the best Heavyweight boxer in the army at the moment, I would also like to point out that you're not even in peak condition yet." Sometime later Vince bumped into Andy in a pub in Aldershot and they shared a few laughs over a couple of beers, Andy would go on to become a Professional boxer who won most of his fights on knockouts. He tragically died of cancer at the age of just 47 years old. Over the next three years Vince fought twenty times for 10 Regiment RCT and only lost three of those matches on points. In that time he won the BAOR Heavyweight finals and the Army Lightweight finals. Vince's last fight for the British Army was against the Royal Navy and he fought a naval rating called Paul Greenacre, Paul was the Combined Services Champion at that time. Boxing team mate Stevie Johnson took Vince to one side and had a quiet word in his ear before the fight started, "Listen 'Buck', (The boxing team always called Vince 'Buck') I've seen this bloke fight mate and I don't think you're going to beat him, you definitely won't knock him out." Mickey Gannon added to Vince's tales of woe, "This bloke is bloody good 'Buck', you'll not beat him." Driver Vince Rollock of 36 Squadron RCT set about giving Paul Greenacre and the rest of the Royal Navy an important lesson on how to box. "I gave him a lesson on how to punch properly and dropped him in every round, it was the easiest fight I've ever had."

Driver Vince Rollock fighting in the BAOR Boxing Finals in 1975. His opponent is Lance Corporal Patterson of 1 Para who Vince knocked down several times, Vince won his bout on points and 10 Regiment RCT became BAOR Champions.

It wasn't all about boxing though because the boxers also had to play catch up on their military careers once the boxing season came to a close. This included doing Trade Training and promotion courses as well as taking part in Military Exercises. Some of the Senior NCO's in 10 Regiment held grievances against the so called 'mollycoddled' boxers, purely because of their own personal and poisoned philosophies of life. Staff Sergeant Dick Bennet was the SQMS

(Squadron Quartermaster Sergeant) in charge of running the Squadrons G1098 whilst on Exercise. The G1098 was a Squadrons tented facility used for cooking meals and dealing with other admin issues whist the unit was deployed into the field. Dick Bennett enjoyed the notoriety that the boxers bought to his Corps but he always showed disdain towards Vince in person. On one particularly hot Exercise Dick collared Vince and thrust a shovel into his hand, "Right Rollock, I want you to dig a shit pit for me right here, make sure it's deep." After Dick had gone back to his G1098 Vince dug three shovels of earth out of the ground and then laid down in the sunshine to rest.

Sometime later he woke up when he heard Dick's voice bellowing around the Squadron location, **"Where the fuck is Rollock, I'll bet that lazy bastard is skiving"!** Vince remained lying on his back and never uttered a sound as Dick and Lance Corporal Ray Ratcliffe came through the trees looking for him, "Look! The lazy twat is sleeping instead of digging my shit pit!" Ray Ratcliffe was a good friend of Vince's and he automatically went into a, 'covering your arse bro' mode, "Staff! I don't think he's sleeping, I think he's passed out because of working in the direct sunlight." As Ray feigned looking for a pulse in Vince's neck, his 'casualty' started moaning and groaning, "Oh! Where am I….What happened?" Ray shouted, "Quick Staff! You'd better send for an ambulance. Don't worry, I'll look after him for you." After being taken to BMH (British Military Hospital) Rinteln, Vince was examined by a Doctor who was a Captain in the Royal Army Medical Corps. The 'quack' told him that he wasn't sending Vince back on the Exercise because as a black man he would absorb more heat from the sun than any of the white guys in the unit. He instructed Vince to go back to barracks and rest up for a couple of days. That night whilst the rest of the Squadron was out on Exercise, Driver Vince Rollock was downtown Bielefeld drinking beer and dancing with young German ladies at Sloopy's discotheque.

At other times Vince could be as determined and focused as the very best of soldiers but the subject matter had to be of interest to him. Vince was given a place on the next available JMQC (Junior Military Qualification Course) which was a gateway to being promoted to the giddy heights of Lance Corporal and Corporal. Without this qualification soldiers in the RCT couldn't be promoted above the rank of Driver. Vince came tied top of his course with Driver Pearson and things were looking Rosy in the Rollock garden because his OC, Major Rutherford, convinced Vince that he would be promoted on the next Promotions Board. He persuaded him to retract his recent request for a discharge from the army. Unfortunately the status quo wasn't going to last that long. Vince had also recently married a local German girl and they'd had a son who they called Sebatian, the marriage was a sham though and Vince became very unhappy with his life. The unhappy couple separated and Vince moved back into barracks where he went onto a lifestyle that was blurred by alcohol. Things came to a head one night at the Women's Royal Army Corps (WRAC) bar in Ripon Barracks.

Whilst dancing Vince accidently knocked a WRAC girls drink over and she punched him in the back shouting, "You clumsy bastard!" Vince apologised, "I told her I was really sorry and that I didn't know I'd done it. I offered to buy her another drink but she wouldn't have it and she continued to whinge and whine. I started to get angry and kicked her table of drinks over and shouted in her face, "Now that's what I call being clumsy." Up steps her 6 foot 6 inch rugby playing boyfriend who was obviously going to defend her honour. One punch later and Vince had quickly and efficiently dealt with his second overconfident rugby playing opponent. Driver Lester Robinson grabbed Vince by his shoulders and said, "Let's get the fuck put of here man." They drove out of Ripon Camp and were stopped at Seiker traffic lights by the local Polizei who breathalysed Vince and told him, "We're going to have to arrest you," to which Vince replied, "You're not going to arrest me." It took five Polizei vehicles and twelve Polizei Officers to place Vince in handcuffs, after a combined and concentrated effort the German Civil Police finally managed to arrest him. Within a few days Vince's wife turned up at the RMP (Royal Military Police) Post at the back of Ripon Barracks where she handed in an illegal firearm that she said belonged to Vince. The SIB (Special Investigation Branch) cautioned Vince and he told them on interview that his wife had bought the pistol for him. "She asked me to kill myself because she was so unhappy." Vince was never going to oblige her.

Vince thought his wife was having a relationship with a member of the local Polizei and he went to talk to her about that and the recent surrender of the illegal firearm. It all kicked off outside his wife's house and she suddenly started screaming, "Help! Help! Someone call for the Polizei!" A German (possibly an off duty Polizei Officer) came to her immediate rescue and Vince did his usual party trick and knocked him out. As a result of these and other felonies Vince was going to be Court Martialled, but miraculously all of the charges were dropped including the assault outside his wife's house. There has never been an explanation as to why all the charges were dropped but Major

Rutherford told him whilst on Orders, "I think it might be a good idea for you to leave the British Army at this time Driver Rollock," and that's exactly what he did.

Vince lived at home with his parents for a while before going on holiday to Barbados for a couple of weeks. He moved into some rented accommodation after working as a bus conductor, a 'bouncer' on the doors of nightclubs in Wakefield and doing some HGV deliveries for Express Dairies in Huddersfield. It was whilst working as a nightclub bouncer that Vince met a man called Les Carr who is an 8th Dan Karate expert and a British, and twice European champion fighter. Vince describes Les as a "Lean, mean and mysterious fighting machine." After watching Les fight in Bradford one evening, Vince decided to go training with him and see how he compared to this other athlete. "My body had never been in so much pain as after I'd been training with Les Carr, it was the best and most intense training I've ever done. In the 10 Regiment Boxing Team we were extremely fit and could easily run rings around any soldier in the British Army, but Les took physical training to a whole new level." Vince studied full contact Karate under the guidance of his new friend Les Carr and they both worked together as nightclub bouncers and to this day remain good friends. Vince eventually got involved in operating his own company.

When Vince enlisted into the army he thought his mum and dad just wanted him out of the way. "I thought my parents wanted rid of me but mum told me many years later that she couldn't sleep after I'd joined the army. There are things that your own kids don't know about within their own family and they will sometimes incorrectly assume the worst." When Vince dropped his own son off at Sheffield University, the big hard man broke down and cried like a baby in his own car. "It was very hard for me and I cried to my mum on the phone when I got home and she told me they'd both done the same after I got on that Train to Rhyl. I never knew how they felt." When Vince's sister Carolyn died of cancer at the age of 39, Vince and his wife Zena took her son Kedesh into their own family and became his legal guardian.

Vince is the proud father of Lisa, Sebatian, Natalie, Taurean, Javan and Benaiah and he is now a very successful motivational speaker.

Lance Corporal Ray Ratcliffe – ATO Driver with 9 Squadron RCT on the Belfast tour in 1976.

Ray 'Rat' Ratcliffe was always going to be a man of action in one form or another. He was born into a military family on 22 September 1956 at the Maternity Wing of the Cambridge Military Hospital in Aldershot. His dad, Sergeant Geoffrey Charles Ratcliffe, was serving in the RASC (Royal Army Service Corps) at the time of Ray's arrival into this world. Sergeant Ratcliffe was based at the RASC Depot in Buller Barracks Aldershot as a Drill Pig. It was his job to beast all of the Depot's recruits around the parade ground and start shaping them into something useful that the Corps could use. The recruits had to be transformed from the silly spotty faced adolescents that had arrived six weeks earlier, into the men that the British Army needed.

In 1972 Ray told his dad that he wanted to join the British Army as a Driver in the Royal Corps of Transport (the RCT had succeeded the RASC in 1965). Geoffrey Charles Ratcliffe was by now a civilian and living in Portsmouth but he was proud of the fact that his youngest son was following in his tradition of becoming a soldier, even more so that he was going to serve in his old Corps. It was probably inevitable that Ray would enlist into the British Army because he'd really enjoyed his time in the Army Cadet Force (ACF). In 1972, several months after being attested at his local Army Recruiting Office, Ray left home and headed off to the Junior Leaders Regiment RCT at Norton Manor Camp just outside Taunton in Somerset to start his Basic Training.

The Junior Leader Regiments of the British Army recruited young lads from the age of 16 years old. These teenagers were then put through eighteen months of military training in the hope that they would become the future NCO's and Warrant Officers of their own particular Corps. The military training covered a multitude of subjects such as weapon training, first aid, NBC (Nuclear Biological and Chemical Warfare), map reading, drill and plenty of fitness training. The young soldiers also had to attend academic lessons in Military Calculations (Maths), Communication Skills (English) and an Army in the Contemporary World (Military/History/Political) syllabus. It was only after each Junior Leader had been trained and qualified in all of the military subjects that they progressed onto Driver Training. Each Junior Leader could only leave Taunton after attaining a Land Rover, motorcycle and Heavy Goods Vehicle class III Licence, when they would be posted to their first Regular Army unit. During their eighteen months training at Norton Manor Camp all J/Dvr's (Junior Drivers) could be promoted to a higher rank if they showed the necessary leadership skills. Those ranks were J/LCpl (Junior Lance Corporal), J/Cpl (Junior Corporal), J/Sgt (Junior Sergeant), J/SSM (Junior Squadron Sergeant Major) and finally, only the best of the best could attain the slot as J/RSM (Junior Regimental Sergeant Major). Within the Regiment there were only three J/SSM's positions (one for each squadron) and one J/RSM, so the competition to get to the top slot was challenging to say the least.

Ray was tall for his age and because he was also good looking with blonde hair and blue eyes, he was also incredibly self-confident. He breezed through his training and was promoted very quickly. After just a couple of terms into his eighteen months training, Ray had already been promoted to Junior Squadron Sergeant Major of C Squadron. It looked like he was definitely going to reach the principal rank of Junior Regimental Sergeant Major, the only thing that would stand in his way was if he catastrophically fucked up, and that's exactly what Ray did. He'd made friends with J/LCpl Martin 'Skin' Keane and J/Dvr Royston 'Chalky' Proffit and the three of them decided to leave the camp without permission and go on the piss in Taunton, they were essentially AWOL (Absent Without Leave) for twelve hours. When the RMP's (Royal Military Police) arrested the lads they were already walking back to camp and Ray had just stolen a bottle of milk from a doorstep, it was only after taking a mouthful that he realised the milk had gone sour.

After being charged and put on CO's (Commanding Officers') Orders, Ray and 'Skin' were busted down to J/Dvr and the terrible trio were all fined, resulting in money being deducted from their end of term credits. The following statement is hard to believe; but Ray was such a great and charismatic soldier that within the next two terms he was again promoted back up to J/SSM of C Squadron. Unfortunately though, Ray's misdemeanour with 'Skin' and Royston ultimately barred him from receiving the top slot as J/RSM.

After completing his Driver Training at Taunton, Ray Ratcliffe then progressed on to his Trade Training, Ray had decided he wanted to be an RCT Air Despatcher. The training for this was done at 55 (AD) Air Despatch Squadron RCT based at RAF Thorney Island in West Sussex. In 1974 the training to become a qualified RCT Air Despatcher took about six weeks to complete, and it wasn't an easy course to pass. The lessons taught RCT NCO's and Drivers how to prepare vehicles, stores and equipment for delivery by parachute, using cargo planes and helicopters. Once the kit was made ready and strapped onto pallets, the cargo was loaded onto an RAF C 130 Hercules aircraft and it was despatched out of the rear of the aircraft. After the parachutes had deployed the cargo would hopefully land safely in the right place on a designated Landing Zone (LZ). Ray's Air Despatch training at Thorney Island was a complete waste of time because although he loved the practical side of the course, he absolutely hated the classroom work and after six months he washed out. In Ray's own words, "I was more interested in beer and women," he spent most of his spare time at one of his favourite watering holes down at Emsworth fishing village not far from Thorney Island.

After being rejected from 55 (AD) Squadron RCT, Ray was sent over to West Germany and posted into C Troop, 9 Squadron, in 10 Regiment RCT at Bielefeld. It was there that Ray caught up with his old mates from Taunton, 'Skin' Keane and 'Chalky' Proffit. 'Skin' and 'Chalky' had already been posted from the Junior Leaders Regiment straight into C Troop. Ray was allocated a room next to his old drinking buddies on the top floor of 9 Squadron's accommodation block. Both 'Skin' and 'Chalky' introduced Ray to all of the best watering holes in Bielefeld, the Quelle, the Drug Store and Hans Meyers to name just a few. On one particular night the three of them were having a great night out in Ripon Barracks NAAFI (Navy Army Air Force Families Institute) which was just a couple of miles up Detmolder Strasse. The NAAFI Bar in Ripon was much nicer than the pigs bar in 10 Regiment, not least because the furniture hadn't been smashed during the previous night's drunken inter-squadron bar fights, that and the Ripon bar was also used by female soldiers of the WRAC (Women's Royal Army Corps). Beer, women, and good mates on tap, Ray couldn't have been happier. On this particular night Corporal Dougie Allen was also in the same bar, he was a barrel-chested and dark haired full corporal who was also serving in C Troop. Dougie was a big punchy tough guy who was armed with a massive black bushy moustache that wouldn't have looked out of place on Thomas Magnum PI. Ray heard a fracas starting in the corridor just outside the NAAFI bar and went to investigate. He spotted Dougie giving his mate 'Chalky' a hard time, Ray intervened by shouting, "Oy! Fucking leave him alone", at which point Dougie started coming the strop and he turned his attention towards Ray. After blocking a couple of punches, Ray head-butted Dougie and broke his nose which brought the argument to a swift conclusion, it was a win win situation really, the lads were left alone and Dougie was given a week's sick leave. When Dougie Allen came back to work he wore a large white dressing on his nose and he also sported two beautiful shiners. Nothing was said about the incident in the NAAFI bar at Ripon because Corporal Dougie Allen was a man's man, he accepted the result of the fight and practised the old soldier's unwritten code, "Whatever happens in the bar, stays in the bar."

Ray passed his Heavy Goods Vehicle Class II test in a Mark 1 Militant (Mk II Millie) which was commonly referred to as an old knocker, with no power assisted steering and a crash gear-box. These post World War Two 10 Ton trucks could be a cow-son to drive. But Ray was a natural heavy goods driver with good upper body strength, at low speeds most RCT Drivers struggled to turn every corner in an old knocker, but Ray never broke into a sweat, he drove these old war horses like they were an Austin Mini Clubman Estate. In the mid 1970's, 10 Regiment RCT controlled a freight system from Bielefeld and Ray was assigned to some of these details. He would pick up and deliver all sorts of equipment from camps around North Westphalia, it was a dream job for any RCT Driver and Ray really enjoyed it, until something more interesting came along and distracted him. Usually women and beer!

During an Easter stand down period Ray was detailed to drive a Mk III Millie up to Fallingbostel. The truck had a tank engine on the back which needed delivering to an Armoured Workshop in Northern Germany. Ray was distracted and he decided not to complete the detail, instead he decided to join his mates, 'Skin' Keane, 'Chalky' Proffit, Chris Idden and Ray 'Pluck' Campbell, who were all buggering off to Paris for a few days. In 1975 most soldiers based in BAOR didn't possess a passport and they travelled using their Identity Cards and/or a NATO Travel Order instead. One country that wouldn't allow British soldiers to cross their borders using this method was France, the French weren't a part of the NATO setup and so British soldiers could only enter France using an ID card if he was also in possession of a NATO Travel Order. These special documents were kept under lock and key in the Chief Clerks office and they had to be filled in and signed by the Admin Officer to make them valid. None of the lads had a passport or a NATO Travel Order so Ray 'misappropriated' one for them all. After putting all of their details onto the form he then signed it Captain Rat and then rubber stamped the form with a 9 Squadron Admin Officers' seal of approval. The lads then headed off to Bielefeld Bahnhof (railway station) and got on a train bound for Paris, where the five of them had a brilliant weekend in the French Capital and Ray even hooked up with an English girl, who also had a great time. Enough said. What of the military detail though? Well, as in most of 10 Regiments' melodramas, someone stepped up to the mark and completed Ray's detail for him, they also covered up for him so that he wasn't dropped in the shit.

During his posting to 10 Regiment, Ray completed three tours of duty in Northern Ireland with 9 Squadron. Two in 1975, then the last tour during that wonderful hot summer of 1976. Ray felt that the training prior to deploying was adequate in regards to army tactics, driver training, and carrying out foot patrols, but he would have liked more political information about why the British Army was patrolling the streets of the UK with loaded weapons. That sort of lesson was probably deemed to be over the heads of Drivers though and so the majority of 9 Squadron RCT deployed without knowing exactly why they were going to the Province.

Ray's first tour was over the winter of 1975/1976 at a location called Brown Square in Belfast. It was a ram shackled outpost where the RCT Drivers accommodation was located on the top floor, Ray's bed-space was situated below a broken skylight. The accommodation was spartan to say the least and because the lads were only provided with a bedframe and mattress but no bedding, they had to use army sleeping bags. Apart from the bed, no furniture was provided and so the lads all had to live out of their suitcases and kitbags. During one of his off duty periods Ray went to bed and woke up several hours later feeling very cold, his teeth were chattering and he was shaking from head to toe, he was borderline hypothermic. A blizzard was raging outside and the snow was falling through the skylight above his bed and had completely engulfed Ray and his sleeping bag. The misery and suffering in Northern Ireland wasn't all about bullets and bombs. Ray recalls that 9 Squadron was operating in support of the Queens Own Highlanders (QOH) in Belfast and the majority of his time was spent driving the Jock's around on mobile patrols in a Humber 'Pig' Armoured Personnel Carrier.

His next deployment to Ulster was on **Operation Spearhead** which was an emergency tour. The British Army required extra boots on the ground and Ray, this time, was sent to Lisburn in South Armagh. On this six week tour Ray was accompanied by his best mates 'Skin' Keane, 'Chalky' Proffit, Colin Webber and Pat McCloud who Ray describes as, "A really good soldier." The Royal Marines they supported came from 42 Commando and according to Ray they all seemed a bit jumpy, but that was probably because some of their unit had already been killed by snipers during 42's deployment. Ray said, "They were really good lads though."

Ray's last tour of Northern Ireland was during the summer of 1976 where once again he deployed with C Troop 9 Squadron RCT, but this time he was located in Albert Street Mill as a Driver on the Ammunition Technician Officer's (ATO) bomb disposal team. Albert Street Mill was just a stone's throw away from the infamous Falls Road and Divis Flats area and the location was sited in one of the oldest buildings in Belfast. The outpost in Belfast was located in an old linen weaving factory, built in 1834. The British Army had converted the building into accommodation for roulement troops deploying in Belfast. The Albert Street Mill location was shared by a resident Infantry Company and an ATO team, consisting of RAOC (Royal Army Ordnance Corps) soldiers who dealt with the explosive devices, and their RCT Drivers who drove their adapted armoured vehicles. This was a plum job for any RCT Driver on an operational tour of Northern Ireland and Ray was probably selected because he'd already served on two other Tours. Only the best and most experienced drivers were given such a prestigious and responsible job. Every time an ATO team was called out onto the streets of Belfast it was usually with all blue lights flashing and Klaxon horns blaring, Ray's mate 'Chalky' Proffit was also selected to be one of the ATO teams Drivers.

Lance Corporal Ray Ratcliffe standing on the top of Albert Street Mill.

There were twelve RCT Drivers allocated to each ATO team location and they were split into four shifts consisting of:

Alfa (front line duty).

Bravo (those on 10 minutes notice to move).

Charlie (vehicle and equipment maintenance).

Delta (day off).

Every time a team went on a 'shout' they deployed in two vehicles which consisted of a Saracen and a Humber 'Pig.' On Ray's Alpha shift the lead vehicle was driven by Driver Adrian 'Posh' Edwards who spoke with a plum in his mouth and he was accompanied by the ATO Bomb Disposal Officer, an RAOC Private, an infantry soldier as escort and the wheelbarrow. The second 'Pig' was driven by Ray whose vehicle was loaded with all of the other equipment required to deal with any explosive device, this included detonators, wire, explosives and all sorts of other kit. Ray was accompanied in his 'Pig' by an RAOC junior NCO and an infantry escort. In 1976 those RCT Drivers who were selected for driving ATO vehicles weren't giving any extra pre-deployment training to prepare for the job, driving for ATO was all 'on the job training.'

The Europa Hotel in Belfast is famous for being Europe's most bombed hotel in recent history. During his tour as an ATO Driver, Ray was called out to deal with several possible car bombs outside that very hotel. On arrival at each incident they would turn up with blue lights flashing and Klaxon horns blaring. The ATO Drivers would be ushered through the Infantry cordon and pointed towards the suspect device. After parking up their vehicles at a safe distance from the bomb, the ATO Officer and his team would start removing the wheelbarrow from the front vehicle. The wheelbarrow was a small remotely controlled track vehicle that allowed the ATO team to deal with any suspect device from a safe distance, the idea was conceived by Peter Miller (a retired Royal Tank Regiment Lieutenant Colonel) who was working at the Bomb Disposal School in 1972. Peter went to his local garden centre and came away with an electrically powered wheelbarrow to start his research and development of this iconic piece of army equipment. This is why the remote controlled bomb disposal equipment is always referred to as a wheelbarrow.

On arrival at the scene, Ray would get out of his 'Pig' and climb into the back of his APC and start prepping a Pig Stick ready for use on the wheelbarrow. The Pig Stick was a metal tube about a foot and a half long and the circumference of a scaffold pole, the device was loaded with water and an explosive charge before attaching it onto the wheelbarrow. After confirming where the bomb was located on the suspect vehicle, the wheelbarrow would be remotely driven up to the car and the Pig Stick fired at the explosive device, this explosively propelled water would hopefully destroy the circuitry of the bomb rendering it ineffective. This procedure meant that the ATO Team could disarm a device with the minimal risk of detonation and injury to the bomb disposal team. On a few occasions Ray mischievously substituted the water in the Pig Stick and the bombs were disabled using his own piss. Sometimes he didn't even get the chance to prep the Pig Stick though. Ray had just got out of his 'Pig' on one particular shout to the Europa Hotel when the car bomb exploded. The force of the explosion knocked Ray off his feet and the team were lucky that no-one was killed or injured during that explosion. The ATO team also had a Q vehicle (civilian style Commer van) at their disposal and the team often hand painted it a different colour so its identity always remained covert to the IRA. On one trip to Lisburn, Ray drove the van whilst its paintwork was still wet. Ray enjoyed his trips to Lisburn because he'd become 'very good friends' with a WRAC (Women's Royal Army Corps) soldier called Isabelle, he often had permission from the ATO to stay over-night before returning back to Albert Street Mill.

On other shouts there was a lot of hanging about and Ray got chatting with some of the Belfast Firemen who were also in attendance at every suspect device. (The author apologizes to any politically correct feminists', but in 1976 they were called Firemen, not Firefighters) The Firemen chatted about their duties and Ray thought a career in the Fire Brigade just might be the way ahead for him. Life in the RCT was fun for Ray and he'd made some fantastic friends, but he also wanted something more out of life, like a more permanent and prolonged future career. For the rest of his tour Ray pondered over what the Belfast Firemen had told him and after returning to Bielefeld he signed off and applied for a discharge from the army. Over the next twelve months Ray patiently waited for his discharge to come through and 9 Squadrons' OC promoted him to Lance Corporal at the same time. Those in authority obviously saw the potential in Ray and they may well have been offering him promotion in an attempt to retain him in the army. Such was Ray's popularity that all of his mates tried to get him to change his mind, they thought he would eventually have reached the Rank of Warrant Officer.

Ray was discharged from the RCT at Buller Barracks in 1978, but unfortunately had to wait for three months until the fireman's strike had ended before applying to enlist into the Hampshire Fire Brigade. After completing his three month fire-fighting course Ray served at Southsea Fire Station and he eventually became the watch fire engine driver. His continued interest in women led to three marriages and four children (Bernard, Harry, George and daughter Hannah). His eldest son Bernard runs his own business in London and in 2014 he married the actor Sean Bean's daughter Molly. After twenty two years in the Fire Service doctors sadly diagnosed Ray with having Multiple Sclerosis which in short means that he'd developed lesions on one side of his brain. The disease unfortunately manifested itself in a multitude of symptoms, not least of which is pain, fatigue, and the loss of strength in his arms, hands and legs resulting in paralysis. Although Ray is now bed-bound and requires a measure of medical and social services support, he remains incredibly upbeat and displays the same courage, charm and wit that the author remembers of him from his service days in 10 Regiment RCT.

To a degree Ray regrets not listening to his friends about remaining within the Corps back in 1978. Lance Corporal Ivan Greenaway RCT, who went on to become a legendary RCT Squadron Sergeant Major, remains a good friend of Ray's and he feels there is no doubt that Ray would have eventually achieved Warrant Officer rank had he continued with his military career.

Authors note: Not only was Ray Ratcliffe the first RCT hero that I idolised when I initially arrived in C Troop 9 Squadron 10 Regiment RCT way back in 1975, but I was also his co-driver on my first long haul convoy from Bielefeld to Sonthofen which took two full days of driving just to get there. I learnt so much from Ray in the few years that I knew him as a Trog/Trogg and was honoured that he let me interview him for this book, Ray, you were an inspiration to me all those years ago when I was so young and naïve, but my respect for you was never more so than it is today my friend.

24274523 WO Ricky Lodge RCT
1971 – 1994

L-R Captain Terry Cavender RCT Margret Cavender Renate Lodge and Sergeant Ricky Lodge RCT at an 8 Regiment RCT Sergeants Mess function.   Maggie Cavender is Ricky's older sister.

Ricky Lodge was born in Edgeware General Hospital in Northwest London in 1953, he was bought up by his parents in Wealdstone which was just up the road.   Ricky was a bright lad at school and even though he wasn't really interested in any of the academic subjects he did manage to pass his Eleven Plus examination.   The Eleven Plus paper was a test taken by some school pupils who were in their last year of their primary school education, if they were intelligent enough to pass the exam they could then be offered the chance of being taught at their local Grammar School.   The education at Grammar schools has always been thought to be of a higher standard than most Secondary Modern establishments.   In 1964 any students who were a borderline pass on the Eleven Plus test were given an interview with a Grammar School Head Teacher to consider if they really were intelligent enough to fill in the gaps of the Grammar school register. Ricky explains, "I sort of talked my way into Grammar School really. My test results were nearly good enough and on interview I obviously came into my own and they granted me a place purely because of my verbal skills. It was all a mistake really because although I was quite clever, I wasn't actually clever enough." Had he gone to a Secondary Modern School, Ricky believes he would have been in the top 10% of the schools' brightest students even if he'd only coasted through the curriculum, but at the Grammar School he struggled and remained in the lower half of achievers, mainly because he couldn't be arsed to do the work. He was pretty much the same at sports and even though he loved playing football he wasn't really bothered whether or not he was picked for a game. If 11 boys had been picked from a line up to represent a school team, then it could be guaranteed that Ricky would have been the very next one to have been chosen.

After leaving school with a couple of O Levels and a slack handful of GCSE's, Ricky went to a Marine and Technical College where he wanted to train as a Merchant Navy Radio Officer. When given the option of going to a College in Lowestoft or South Shields, Ricky asked which one was the furthest away from Tydd St Giles where he lived. Ricky's sister Maggie was two years older than him and she'd escaped the village at the age of seventeen and Ricky followed suit two years later. Ricky remained at South Shields College for about a year and started running up a few debts because his grant of £305 a year wasn't covering even his basic monetary outgoings. In today's modern world students will probably scoff at a few piddling debts amounting to £200, but back in 1970 this was equivalent to over £3000 and Ricky wasn't even covering the rent for his digs and utility bills, and this was before he'd even thought about feeding himself. Student loans aren't anything new. Ricky eventually had to drop out of college, he then worked on a building site in Cambridge before heading back to London where he worked as a butchers mate, and finally he got a job at a builder's merchant yard in Kenton before deciding to enlist into the British Army.

The staff at the Army Selection Centre in Sutton Coldfield dissuaded Ricky from enlisting into the Parachute Regt which was his first choice of army career. The Sutton Coldfield staff steered him towards a career in the Royal Corps of Transport (RCT) because at that time there was a shortage of Drivers within the ranks of the RCT. Ricky unhappily agreed with their decision but only because they told him he could eventually get posted to 63 (Parachute) Squadron RCT after finishing Basic Training, in 63 Para he would still be able to qualify as a paratrooper, but as an RCT one. They also explained that the Airborne RCT unit was located just over the road from his would be Training Depot in Aldershot. Ricky started his Basic Training at Buller Barracks in Aldershot just before New Year's Eve in 1971 and soon discovered that there were a variety of RCT instructors at the Depot, some could be extremely unpleasant and cruel whilst others, like Sergeant Raine, were not only encouraging and enthusiastic but they could also take a joke. Ricky's recruit squad was assembled over the Christmas period and this may have had some bearing on why his Passing Out Parade was the smallest ever in RCT history. In fact when Ricky and his mates 'Passed Out' of Buller Barracks, their squad had to borrow soldiers from previous intakes to make up the numbers on their Passing Out Parade otherwise the parade would have amounted to only twelve men. During his Basic Training Ricky had been doing some extra runs every weekend whilst carrying heavier and heavier weights in a borrowed Bergen rucksack. He still wanted to become a paratrooper with 63 (Para) Squadron RCT. As with most things in the army though, they never turn out the way a soldier usually predicts them.

On completion of Basic and Trade training, Ricky's squad was held in Holding Troop with other soldiers anticipating their first posting. It wasn't until June 1972 that this amalgamation of trainees was eventually sent on their way. By this time Sergeant Raine had discouraged Ricky from requesting a posting to 63 Para and instead encouraged him to apply for a posting to 8 Regiment RCT which was based in Munster, West Germany. Apparently he would get all of the benefits that a BAOR posting would provide (Local Overseas Allowance and wonderful German Beer) and he'd also gain a bit more soldiering experience before taking on the exacting experience of going through P Company. Ricky took his advice and was eventually flown to RAF Gutersloh on a Tri-Star aeroplane, it was the first time he'd ever been on an aircraft of any kind. When the planes undercarriage touched down rather heavily at RAF Gutersloh Ricky nervously watched its engines from his window seat, a loud noise suddenly erupted outside the plane and the tremendous vibrations seemed to confirm that the aircraft was starting to fall apart, Ricky nearly shit himself. A huge piece of the massive engine just appeared to be breaking off the fuselage in front of his very eyes and Ricky thought his life was about to end. Not knowing anything about modern aircraft reverse thrust braking systems made Ricky feel a bit of a tit after the plane had safely rolled to a stop.

Every soldier travelling to BAOR in 1972 did so wearing their Number 2 Dress uniform, bulled boots and Twat Hat. Whilst wearing this parade ground garb and carrying their army suitcases, Ricky and four other Nigs (New In Germany) reported into the Guardroom at Portsmouth Barracks, Munster on a sunny Saturday morning. The Orderly Sergeant told them to book in at 27 Squadrons Duty NCO bunk and a Lance Corporal would issue bedding and show them where their accommodation was located. As the lads followed the directions they'd been given at the guardroom they fortuitously passed 27 Squadrons bar which was also on the ground floor but nearer to the Guardroom than the Duty NCO's bunk. They were cordially invited into the crowded bar and offered a bit of alcoholic libation. It would have been rude to say no and after a quick litre of German beer the other three lads dutifully headed off further up the road to the Duty NCO's bunk, but Ricky stayed for just one more beer. A bit later 27 Squadrons' furious Duty NCO turned up in the bar and gave him a bit of an earhole bashing. Ricky explains, "I wouldn't mind but I was only about an hour or two late before he had to come and find me." After making up his bed and unpacking his suitcase, Ricky caught a bus from outside the front of the barracks and headed off to have a good look around his new German home town. Several hours later he wanted to head back to camp but couldn't remember which number bus he'd travelled on, and so using his RCT initiative he popped into a busy local bar to ask for directions in his politest, and put on quintessentially English accent:

Ricky: "Excuse me! But can anyone in here speak English?"

An eight year old German lad stepped forward as all of the adults in the bar turned towards Ricky but didn't say a word.

German boy: "Yes I speak English, how can I help you?"

Ricky: "I'm terribly sorry but I'm lost, please can you tell me how to get back to camp from here?"

German boy: "Which camp?"

Ricky: "The Army camp."

German boy: "Which Army camp?"

Ricky: "The British Army Camp."

German boy: "Which British Army camp?"

Ricky: "You mean there's more than one?"

German boy: "Yes, I think there are at least four British Army Barracks in Munster. Do you know the name of your kaserne…sorry I mean barracks?"

Ricky: "Erm…no."

German boy: "That really isn't very helpful for giving you directions. Was it Oxford Barracks?"

Ricky: "Erm…I don't think so."

German boy: "Ok then, maybe it was York Barracks?"

Ricky: "Erm….possibly but I'm not really sure?"

German boy: "Could it have been Portsmouth Barracks then?"

Ricky: "Doesn't sound familiar I'm afraid. Got any other ideas?"

German boy: "Herr Englander we would now appear to be, how do you say in English…clutching at the straws I think."

Ricky: "Hmmm."

German boy: "Can you remember anything about the camp at all?"

Ricky: "Oh! I think it's near a place called Coerde."

There followed a discussion around the bar that included men, women, children and a locally produced tourist information map that someone had dug out of a newspaper rack. After a couple of minutes the young lad turned to Ricky:

German boy: "My father knows where you have to go. Come, we will take you back to your camp in our car."

Ricky thought to himself, 'what nice people, I think I'm going to like it here'.

When Ricky reported to 27 Squadron Headquarters on Monday morning, he was briefed that 8 Regiment RCT was the only RCT unit in the world to be protected by its own personally assigned Infantry Regiment. The Regiment's 'bodyguards' in 1972 was 1st Battalion Irish Guards, a mechanised Infantry Battalion equipped with AFV 432 Armoured Personnel Carriers (APC's), based in Oxford Barracks in Munster. 8 Regiment RCT was afforded this personal protection because since 1964, the unit had assumed the role of Special Weapons Transportation and they were the only RCT unit allowed to move Britain's nuclear arsenal in BAOR. When 8 Regt RCT deployed in the field on Exercise or if the balloon ever went up for real, their personal Infantry Regiment went along as their guard force. The Mick's would secure a secret location 'somewhere in West Germany' providing convoy and location security as 8 Regiment out-loaded all of the nuclear missiles and shells used by units of the Royal Artillery. This system remained in place until 1981 when someone at the MOD realised that using a battalion of Infantry to baby-sit an RCT unit, albeit in a nuclear role, just wasn't cost effective when they could easily provide their own security in the field. This would then free up the designated Battalion for other deployments around the world. The 'RCT Convoy Escort' task was eventually taken over in 1981 by ten Platoons of RCT and Royal Pioneer Corps (RPC) soldiers employed in the Infantry role. This unique job, carried out by 8 Regiment, was disbanded in 1988 along with the close support Platoons who returned to their principal duties.

When Ricky first arrived at Munster the preferred tactical nuclear weapon of choice for NATO Forces was the 'Honest John' nuclear Missile. It acquired its name in the 1950's during the trial period in the United States. The accuracy of this new unguided weapon system was thought to be overemphasized and these worries nearly saw the whole project cancelled. Colonel Holger Toftoy was overseeing the development at the time and he met a Texan who was always making wild and over exaggerated statements that no-one believed. The overconfident Yank always referred to himself as, "Honest John" and so the new missile was christened thus. 'Honest John' missiles stayed in use with some NATO forces up until 1985, eventually being superseded by the Lance Missile. Ricky was involved on a live in-load during this change over period and he drove down to a clandestine railway siding somewhere near Paderborn to collect the new missiles.

In 1972 the RCT took charge of all the transport and driving responsibilities on the streets of Northern Ireland during **'OPERATION MOTORMAN'** which included working side by side with the roulement infantry battalions. The task needed professional Drivers because Infantry MT drivers simply weren't doing the job properly and a lot of vehicles were breaking down because of poor maintenance. When word got around 8 Regiment RCT that the Corps was trawling for Drivers to deploy to the Province, Ricky was one of the first to knock on his Squadron Sergeant Major's door begging to go. Poor young Ricky was laughed out of the Headquarters because there were plenty of more experienced Drivers who were available and also wanting to see a bit of action. The following year 27 Squadron started doing some Northern Ireland training in Munster in preparation for a tour of South Armagh, and this time Ricky was definitely going. He hated driving the lumbering 'Pig' Armoured Personnel Carrier because it was like driving a wallowing steel whale but like every RCT Driver since time immemorial, he adored screaming up and down the road in an Alvis Saracen. There really is nothing quite like hearing the high pitched whine of an Alvis Saracens' eight cylinder Rolls Royce engine as it's being pushed to the limit through each gear. When the Squadron arrived in Northern Ireland, Ricky's Troop was sent to Newry and he was accommodated in an old Ulster Defence Regt (UDR) Barracks. The vehicles handed over to 27 Squadron were still in an appalling state, the twelve months since relieving the Infantry from their MT responsibilities wasn't sufficient time to bring every vehicle back up to scratch. Both the Commanders and Drivers front and side visors were missing and if the hatches needed closing in an emergency the Driver had to actually get out of the vehicle and remove a split pin to allow it to close - not a good idea if someone was shooting at you. The 'Pigs' were badly battle scarred and covered in a multitude of paints that had been thrown at them during numerous riots, they'd obviously seen plenty of action.

27 Squadron RCT initially operated in support of the Royal Hampshire Regiment for two weeks before D Company of 2 Para took over from them. On the 28th of February 1973 Corporal Francis Foxford of the Hampshire Regt shot Kevin Heatley, a 12 year old boy, who was sitting on a wall chatting with his friends in Main Avenue on the Derrybeg Estate. The soldiers involved in the incident declared that they had been fired upon by a small person and Corporal Foxford had simply returned fire. This claim was rejected eight months later during the court case and Corporal Foxford was found guilty of unlawfully killing the lad and he was sentenced to three years imprisonment. The verdict was later overturned on appeal and Foxford returned to serve with his Battalion. This sad and unfortunate death made the IRA determined to kill at least one of the Royal Hampshire Regiment soldiers before the Battalion finished their tour

of duty in the Province. During Ricky's first fortnight in Newry he didn't get a complete night's sleep because of the backlash of violence from Kevin Heatley's death. When the Paras took over from the Hampshire's they inherited the same level of violence every single day and D Company's Commander decided to try a tactic that might stop at least some of the locals enthusiasm for rioting. One of Ricky's duties was to drive around the Derrybeg estate throughout the night with metal dustbins attached to the back of his Saracen. The noise kept the local residents awake every night and they didn't seem to have the energy for violence the following day. Things eventually quietened down.

At night Ricky and the other RCT Drivers in Newry had to drop off members of Charlie Company at the top of the estate so they could melt away into the countryside. The Infantry would then set up covert Observation Posts (OP's) and monitor any suspicious activities on the massive Catholic housing estate. After the Infantry had debussed, the RCT Drivers then had to drive through the Derrybeg Estate on their own, in what can only be described as a rickety old army vehicle that couldn't be battened down properly and armed with only a 7.62mm Self Loading Rifle, ten rounds of ammunition and an army radio that could only broadcast up to the end of the street. Even though the local inhabitants wanted to drag them out of their vehicles and kick them to death, the RCT Drivers weren't worried because as Ricky explains, "We were young and confident RCT Drivers who were full of bravado."

Between April 1973 and 1978 Ricky ultimately completed six tours of duty in Northern Ireland and the US Forces in West Germany complained about how much time 8 Regiment was spending there. Our NATO Allies dictated that Squadrons from 8 Regiment RCT could no longer be sent on an OP BANNER tour because it wouldn't be able to meet its nuclear role commitments. So after the 27 and 13 Squadron tours had been completed, 8 Regiment RCT was no longer allowed to provide full Squadrons for subsequent tours. The Regiment was, however, given 'permission by the US' to provide one troop of RCT Drivers to supplement other RCT unit OP BANNER Tours. From 1973 onwards, 8 Regiment continually had at least a one Troop presence in Northern Ireland.

Twelve months after his tour in Newry, Ricky returned to Northern Ireland on another two tours of Belfast with 3 Tank Transporter Squadron. On his 1974 tour he was based in Dunmore Park (a TA barracks) and worked in support of Mike Company, 42 Commando. Things hadn't improved in Northern Ireland since Ricky had left a year previously, in fact the situation had got progressively more violent and bloody. When 3 Tank Transporter Squadron RCT arrived at RAF Aldergrove the Drivers were taken around the different Belfast locations in an unarmoured army bus. In the short period of time between Ricky's arrival at Aldergrove and him eventually getting into his location at Dunmore Park, the IRA had exploded numerous bombs around the City. The 1974 tour proved to be a tough one. The Dunmore Park RCT accommodation was abysmal to say the least, the RCT accommodation was only a small room and it had to billet eight RCT Drivers and four other Drivers from 42 Commando's MT Section. The bunk beds were stacked three high and there was barely enough room to store everyone's army suitcases let alone their helmets, rifles and flak jackets. Ricky ironically described the tour as being a good one, "We were always kept busy because there were so many bombings and shootings, and in fact 42 Commando lost one of their guys in a shooting in North Belfast. We also had a couple of weapons and ammunition finds in Belfast and I've lost count of how many riots we were involved in, every riot was always good fun though."

In 1976 Ricky was once again back in Belfast but on this occasion he was attached to 9 Squadron, 10 Regiment RCT, Ricky and the other lads from 8 Regt were formed up as their own Troop for the tour. Every one of his Belfast tours was at Dunmore Park, except for a short detachment with an independent Royal Artillery Battery in Carnmoney Mill on the outskirts of North Belfast. During this detachment Ricky started to realise that RCT soldiers were better trained for tours of Northern Ireland than some of the other troops patrolling the streets. On one particular occasion he was left with his 'Pig' and another Gunner whilst the patrol had to briefly go and deal with another situation. The Bombardier briefed Ricky before leaving, "Listen, I know you're an RCT Lance Corporal and this bloke is only a Gunner, but I'm putting him in charge because he's probably more suited to this sort of thing than you are." Ricky didn't mind or argue the case but he was a bit annoyed when the Gunner couldn't operate the radio or use proper voice procedure. Ricky eventually took charge of the radio until the Section Commander returned to the vehicle.

There were six Sangers built around Carnmoney Mill location and not one of them was manned in the entire time Ricky was there. The Gunners had barely enough soldiers to patrol their very large area of operations let alone put sentries in guard towers. The Gunners often bluffed their way through the problem by always manning the front gate and making soldiers put in an appearance in the towers during the changing of the guard. The detachment was provided with two RCT Drivers and a couple of Land Rovers to do their mobile patrols. It was another very successful tour for Ricky and he in fact went back out to Belfast six months after the tour had ended, he had to give evidence in a Magistrates Courts not far from where a nearly fatal incident happened. Ricky had to give evidence against some rioting bad boys with whom he'd become embroiled in some hand to hand combat during the tour. The incident was very scary at the time and was initiated by some sort of 'Rent-a-mob' Belfast firm. Whilst out on a co-ordinated mobile and foot patrol on the Bawnmore Park estate, the foot patrol entered their target area whilst two mobile Sections circled the region to catch any suspects trying to escape capture. The 'footsie' put out a call to the mobile patrols that they were doing P checks on some suspects and requested back-up at an illegal drinking hole called, 'The Boundary Bar.' The mobile patrols de-bussed as soon as they met up with the footsie and they deployed onto every street corner, this unfortunately spread their manpower a little thin on the ground.

The Boundary Bar began to empty and a riot started within minutes. Ricky noticed that everyone in the patrol wasn't able to re-act as a cohesive unit, mainly because they were simply trying to avoid getting their heads kicked in by the drunken Catholic hoodlums. Ricky received a pretty good kicking from a group of heavies who were actually getting in each other's way and were hampering each other in the violence they were trying to dish out. He was hit over the head by 'Paddy' Riley who used a Pye radio microphone like a sort of medieval ball and chain flail. Ricky fell to his knees but remained conscious and continued to fight off his assailants for a few minutes. As he struggled back to his feet Ricky noticed that 'Paddy' Riley had shifted his attention onto the Radio Operator who was part of the footsie patrol. The Gunner was dealing with Mo McLaughlin as well and the two thugs were trying to wrestle the Artilleryman's rifle away from him, which would have been bad news for everyone in the patrol. Ricky kicked and battered his way out of his own attack and ran over to the brawling Gunner, he thrust the muzzle of his weapon into 'Paddy' Riley's shoulder, and then cocked the rifle and took the safety catch off. Ricky screamed in Riley's ear, "Fucking drop it!" which the Irishman rather sensibly did.

Riley and McLaughlin were the ringleaders of this particular jamboree and after Ricky had bounced them down the road to his vehicle and they were taken out of the picture, the riot seemed to lose its impetus. The patrol members re-grouped around the army vehicles where they started distributing riot sticks and Federal Riot Guns (FRG's) amongst the lads. The soldiers involved were a bit peeved when told to retreat because they wanted to give the rioters a bit of payback. Ricky blithely said, "I suppose it was a bit fraught at the time." The whole sequence of events seemed to defy all aspects of time for Ricky because some of the action seemed to be in slow motion and at other times it all went past in a blur. On interview the author asked Ricky if he would have pulled the trigger had Riley not let go of the Gunners rifle, he answered in all sincerity that he probably would have done but it was a moot question because Riley had done the sensible thing and saved his own life. Riley and McLaughlin legged it later that night and were picked up a couple of days later in a dawn raid, along with a load of other rioters involved in that riot. Ricky actually arrested McLaughlin and his father which he found quite satisfying.

Eight months later Ricky and his mate were dropped off outside the locked Magistrates court by an unarmoured army coach from Moscow camp; they were wearing civilian clothes and neither of them were armed. The two lads were greatly relieved when the doors were opened and they were admitted into the relative safety of the court. When the case was heard, Riley and McLaughlin were found guilty and given a six month prison sentence each. When 10 Regiment returned to Bielefeld after the Belfast tour Ricky happily went back to 8 Regiment in Munster for a couple of well-deserved weeks leave, his German friend Manfred gave him some exciting news. "Ricky, you have to come and meet this beautiful girl called Renate, she's a trainee nurse and I think I am in love man." Ricky and Renate fell in love at first sight but because of nursing training and nuclear warheads they didn't get married for another eight years. Ricky would like to publicly apologise to his German friend in this chapter, "Sorry Manfred, but the better man won!"

Ricky had been at 8 Regiment for six years and had completed five tours of duty in Northern Ireland (he completed another tour later) and yet he was still only an acting Lance Corporal. It was the way of things at that time because the Corps was very undermanned and consequently lacked the necessary Junior NCO's and Drivers on the ground. The thought of doing a stint with the MT Troop at 22 SAS Regiment in Hereford really appealed to Ricky. A lot of 8 Regt RCT had previously volunteered to work for the Special Forces unit and he wanted to follow suit. On arrival at MT Troop 22 SAS Regiment, Ricky immediately recognised a soldier who he'd previously served with in 8 Regt RCT, Lance Corporal Taff Lloyd. The beauty of serving with the Special Forces was that everyone worked hard and the RCT soldiers were all treated like adults. The RCT troops were simply given a task to complete and then left to get on with it. There never seemed to be time to catch his breath in Hereford though because everyone was always doing something in double quick time. The support troops took part in plenty of Admin Exercises doing physical stuff like running up and down Pen Y Fan whilst completing map reading exercises and honing their own military skills.

The SAS also ran their own pre para courses at Hereford and Ricky took up the challenge that he'd originally set himself at Buller Barracks six years previously. The training was tough despite the fact that he was really fit at the time. Lance Corporal Andy Mayhew (another 8 Regiment RCT soldier) and Ricky did the Pre Para training, and the Parachute course at RAF Brize Norton together, they both successfully qualifying as army paratroopers. Ricky didn't have one decent jump on the Parachuting Course at RAF Brize Norton, he either badly exited from the RAF C130 Hercules or his rigging lines became twisted after the parachute had deployed. He was the last man in the stick on his fifth training jump over Salisbury Plain and because of high twists on his rigging he was the first to land on the DZ. Ricky knew he was in trouble because whilst spinning he could see the DZ crew running towards where he was about to hit the ground, with seconds to spare Ricky freed his rigging lines and he landed rather heavily, but safely.

After completing his jumps, Ricky went on an Exercise to Canada with B Squadron 22 SAS, the units' vehicles leaving the UK by ship 6-8 weeks before the Exercise started. Before leaving for Canada Ricky recommended Lance Corporal Keith Harris RCT, who he also knew from 8 Regiment, for his Para Course, what are mates for? Ricky flew to Canada with a REME Vehicle Mechanic to collect the vehicles from Vancouver Port and then drove them 720 miles to the Canadian Airborne Centre in Edmonton Alberta. The SAS Troop was to be based in Edmonton during the Exercise and this was where Ricky and the other lads prepped the vehicles before the 'Super Troopers' arrived in Canada. It was an easy deployment in Canada and Ricky found time to do a motorbike course and qualify for his Canadian para wings. The Canadians never jumped from lower than 1200 feet (British paras usually jump from 800 feet) which Ricky loved because it gave him more time in the air to enjoy the view. The Canadians also did a lot of ramps jumps out of their RCAF's C 130 Hercules aircraft which Ricky really enjoyed, not even he could do a bad exit with an opening that size. Within two years Ricky was picked up for promotion to full Corporal which was just before he was posted to 1 Squadron RCT at Colchester. Regrettably he was posted just before getting the chance to go with a support troop out to the Jungle Warfare Training School in Brunei.

Ricky was made a Section Commander in 1 Squadron RCT where he spent a lot of time working with the Royal Engineers based at Waterbeach Barracks in Cambridge. Whilst with 1 Squadron he also completed two United Nations (UN) tours in Cyprus (one on a later posting when he was a Staff Sergeant). "We worked hard out in Cyprus but because of the mid-day heat the Squadron usually stood down at lunchtime, and then we all headed off to the beach with some beers. Another posting was looming for Ricky after he'd completed a couple of years at 1 Squadron and he requested a posting back to 8 Regt. He and Renate planned on getting married and after one year back in Munster they had a quiet registry office ceremony. The Irish Guards had moved on by this time and the nuclear convoy protection was being done by ten platoons of Royal Pioneer Corps and RCT soldiers acting in an Infantry role. Ricky was posted into H Troop which was the same troop he'd been in previously but was now re-designated as 'Convoy Escort Troop'. He was appointed Section Commander of the Security Alert Team and was allotted his own Land Rover and Trailer. Ricky and his team would put an inner cordon around the nuclear warheads in the field and protect them from sabotage by Russian Spetsnaz (Russian Special Forces) troops. To help him and his men achieve their aims, they were equipped with General Purpose Machine Guns (GPMG's) which is a predominantly Infantry issued weapon. RCT Sections were normally issued with Light Machine Guns (LMG's) which were in essence a thirty round magazine fed Bren Gun. The Gimpy had a higher rate of fire and used 200 rounds of link belt ammunition. The fire power of the GPMG was worlds apart from anything normally issued to RCT Troops. For all training and advisory purposes the Infantry soldiers, who were initially from the Hampshire Regt, remained permanently attached to 8 Regiment. The Royal Pioneer Corps Platoons attached to 8 Regiment were solely responsible for the outer cordon of defence when nuclear warheads were deployed into the field.

Nuclear Convoy Protection was a role that Ricky eventually became synonymous with in 8 Regt and he also went on to become a Nuclear Biological and Chemical Warfare (NBC), Skill at Arms (SAA) and Helicopter Handling instructor. The CO of 8 Regt RCT took the role of Convoy Protection Team so seriously that he negotiated for two Corps soldiers from his unit to attend the Long Range Reconnaissance Patrol (LRRP) School Course in Baden-Wurttemberg. Ricky and a Royal Pioneer Corps NCO from 8 Regt were both nominated for the month long Course which was normally the reserve of Special Forces soldiers only. The Course was geared towards RAF aircrew and 'Stay Behind Troops' like the SAS and Royal Artillery Gunners. The Special Forces would go to ground after the Russians had invaded parts of West Germany, they would be dug into concealed Observation Posts and remain behind the Russian Army lines. These clandestine soldiers would then pinpoint and report specific Russian targets and relay their positions to units that had an option of using eight inch nuclear shells. After seven days of intense classroom work, the course went onto the practical phase before doing the Escape and

Evasion (E & E) Exercise. Each individual had to remain undetected for seven days whilst achieving certain goals. Everyone was captured in the end and they all had to go through the dreaded Resistance to Interrogation (R to I) phase of the Course. Ricky explains, "The E&E and R to I phases were the real deal, no punches were pulled."

The Staff who ran the Course had an inkling that Ricky was working with, or was actually serving in, Royal Artillery units and when they asked for his rank he correctly told them, "Corporal." But the interrogators incorrectly kept pushing him into admitting that he was really a Bombardier. Ricky realised their legitimate mistake and this helped him keep focused on giving nothing away. The Royal Pioneer Corps soldier who attended the course with Ricky failed the R to I phase of the Course. During Ricky's debrief after being interrogated he was asked by the staff if he'd had any hallucinations whilst being grilled. He pointed out to the staff that, "Hallucinations by their very nature are in fact real to the one having the hallucination, so how would I know if I was hallucinating?" Authors note: Sometimes Ricky, you can be such a smart arse! It wasn't until a few days after returning to 8 Regt that he suddenly remembered planning to escape from his captors with a Chinese gentleman. The problem was that there definitely weren't any soldiers from China on the course so he more than likely had hallucinated. Ricky describes the incredibly intense and gruelling LRRP Course as being fun.

Once he was back in Munster, Ricky was promoted to Sergeant and he applied to go on what he describes as "The hardest course in the World." Senior Brecon is an Infantry Platoon Sergeants Course and Ricky was attempting it as a Corps soldier and without having done Junior Brecon first. "Everything I did on that Course I had to think about it first, and that was even when I didn't have a Command Appointment. The Infantry candidates went through a lot of the drills automatically because they did them every day of their working lives, but I had to really think about the Infantry stuff before making any crucial decisions. Intellectually, Senior Brecon was very difficult for me and physically it was even worse because when I did the Course in 1983, the Brecon Beacons suffered the worst winter they'd seen for years." Eighty candidates started the Course but only forty made it to the end, and not all of them passed. After Senior Brecon Ricky spent three years working in the Training Wing at 8 Regt and he enjoyed every single minute of it, "There were over one thousand soldiers in 8 Regt at that time and they were a mixture of nearly twenty different cap badges. I wrote most of the training programmes that covered everything from Induction to the Regt's NBC role, to the Pre Brecon Courses. It was very challenging work but I loved it." The training involved making sure that every Driver who went on Exercise scrimmed up (camouflaged) their truck to the highest possible standard, "We even had access to some reconnaissance photographs from RAF aircraft that were trying to find us when we deployed in the field. They were brilliant training aids."

Ricky was made substantive Sergeant whilst running 8 Regt's high profile Training Wing and at the end of his posting his Manning and Records Office (MRO) gave him a posting to the Princess Marina College at Arborfield. PMCA was a high profile Army Apprentice College where future Artificers of the Royal Electrical and Mechanical Engineers (REME) would start their military training and careers. When told of the posting Ricky went to see his OC and told him that he thought it wasn't a good move for him, "Sir! I'm currently running a Training Wing for a Regiment of one thousand soldiers in a specific role and I'm not only instructing, I'm also writing entire courses and running complicated Exercises. Now Manning and Records expect me to go to Arborfield, be given a timetable and just turn up and give a few lessons, how can this be growth for me, Sir?" The OC agreed and wrote a letter to MRO explaining Ricky's complaint, the Major received a shitty letter back in reply, "It is a real honour to be given this post at the Princess Marina College but if Sergeant Lodge doesn't want to be there, then the College will feel he isn't the sort of instructor the college requires." Ricky did want a posting to the South of England though and MRO granted his wish by posting him to 144 (Para) Field Ambulance whose Headquarters was based in Chelsea, London. 'Lovely Jubbly' thought Ricky. But MRO obviously felt snubbed by Sergeant Lodge and someone vindictively posted Ricky to a 144 (Para) Field Ambulance detachment in Glasgow instead.

The OC of Ricky's detachment was a top Maxillofacial Surgeon in a Glasgow Hospital and on the rare occasions he turned up for Drill Nights he usually did some admin and then buggered off again. Ricky wasn't met on arrival at the barracks and didn't see anyone from the unit for three days. Some of the TA soldiers did give Ricky a hand with his furniture because it had been delivered to the drill hall and not his Married Quarter in Anniesland. To thank the lads Ricky took them to a nearby pub for a drink and as they walked down Mary Hill, he couldn't help but notice that the walls were covered in IRA slogans. One of the lads pointed out a particularly quiet public house where they wouldn't be bothered. Halfway through their first quiet pint Ricky witnessed the

'Bouncer' being carried out on a stretcher. The whole TA system rubbed against the grain for Ricky, he never signed for any of the meagre stores in the barracks and he didn't get a signature for them when he left, it all seemed very slap dash. Over the years Ricky and Renate both worked hard but didn't spend much money and as a result they'd accumulated a substantial amount of funds in their joint bank account. They decided to buy a yacht and sail it around the Scottish Canals whenever they had any spare time. After eighteen months at 144 (Para) Field Ambulance Ricky was posted back to 1 Squadron in Colchester and at his leaving do the TA lads, who he got on very well with, presented him with a ships bell for his yacht. After the farewell party Ricky was walking back to his Married Quarter when one of the accompanying TA lads sidled up to him:

TA Para: "I went and collected the bell for you from the shop Sergeant."

Ricky: "Thank you, it's a fantastic present."

TA Para: "You like it then?"

Ricky: "Of course I do, it will look great on my Yacht."

TA Para: "I got you something else that you might like Sergeant."

Ricky: "What's that then?"

The Para handed over a brand new and very expensive hand bearing compass.

TA Para: "I nicked it from the counter whilst the shop keeper went out the back to get your bell. Do you like it Sergeant?"

Ricky was touched by the well thought of gift, but slightly concerned that a Police Officer was going to put a hand on his shoulder every time he took it out of his pocket.

Ricky and Renate took three weeks leave and decided to sail their yacht down to Essex before taking up his post as SQMS in 1 Squadron. Although Ricky had previously done some sailing in Germany, this trip involved sailing from one near disaster onto the next even nearer disaster. After being stuck in Berwick upon Tweed for nearly a week because of bad weather, they eventually made it to Whitby before running out of time and so they moored the boat up and left it in Whitby harbour, completing the journey to Essex by train. His promotion to Staff Sergeant was a big boost in wages but Ricky hated the job of SQMS and he thought the SQMS Course at Blackdown was dire. Staff Sergeant Keith Harris RCT (from the Exercise in Canada) got violent with his annoying Troop Commander one day and the OC swapped his job with Ricky. Ricky was a happy bunny once he was put back in charge of soldiers. He and Renate decided they needed to get on the property market and so they sold their yacht and used the funds to put a deposit on a house in Colchester, unfortunately they bought at the wrong time and they were to lose a lot of money when they sold it later.

Whilst enjoying tea and toast in the Sergeant's Mess one morning Ricky was summoned to see the Squadron Sergeant Major, "Ricky, do you fancy a six month trip out to Namibia?" Without thinking Ricky said, "Yes". He knew Renate wouldn't mind because if she objected it would be like trying to cage a wild animal. Ricky reported down to Warminster and met up with the other team members before they actually flew out to the formerly German South-West African colony. The British Military and Advisory Training Team (BMATT) were deploying to help organise a Namibian Defence Force which was to be an amalgamation of, The People's Liberation Army of Namibia (PLAN) and the South West African Territorial (SWAT Force). These two military organisations had previously been fighting each other in a thirty year war so it was going to be an uphill struggle to try and organise them into a cohesive army, the new government was mainly run by PLAN because they were the largest group. On the day the BMATT team arrived in Africa the Namibian Parliament had only just been sworn in and so an Army Act hadn't even been written up yet, and because of that the team had nothing to work with, no budget or authority was available to the British Team and they simply bluffed they're way through the next six months.

Ricky and one other RCT Staff Sergeant were there to establish an MT (Mechanical Transport) school for the new army and they hadn't got one vehicle to their name. They had to beg, steal and borrow everything they needed. For the Infantry Wallah's on the BMATT team, collecting up spare weapons wasn't a problem, let's face it, this was Africa and there was an abundance of weapons available on every street corner. Vehicles were a more difficult shopping list of items to acquire though, in the end Ricky obtained some cast offs from South Africans fleeing the country. They eventually gathered together numerous 4x4 Toyota pick-up trucks, minibuses, several buses and a 7 ton truck (that was later stolen). When the BMATT team returned to the UK, Ricky reported back to 1 Squadron just in time for Saddam Hussein to invade Kuwait. He had no sooner got home when he had to get involved in the outloading of ammunition depots for the First Gulf War. He then received his third posting to 8 Regiment where he trained Drivers of 12 Squadron RCT in preparation for their deployment out to Saudi Arabia. He taught them about the possible Chemical threat they might face and how to soldier in a hot and dry environment. Ricky also put the Battle Casualty Replacements (BCR's) through an intense training programme to prepare them, should they be required. All good stuff, but Ricky was unhappy because he would rather have deployed out to Saudi Arabia with the Squadron itself.

When 12 Squadron returned from Saudi Arabia the MOD reduced the overall size of 8 Regt and disbanded 27 Squadron RCT. For most of 8 Regt it didn't make much difference because every unit in the British Army was undermanned and they all adopted the same re-structuring system. The shortfall in 12 Squadron RCT was simply made up from those Drivers in the disbanded 27 Squadron. Redundancy notices were flying all over the place in the British Army and Ricky avoided them by taking a posting as a Transport Control Warrant Officer (TCWO). He only took the job for two years though so that he would be guaranteed an army pension in the rank of WO 2. It was a good job with an annual budget of over £1.5m and he oversaw the transport movement of 20 Squadron RCT and the Royal Baggage Vehicles. Ricky was still running around like a mad thing even though he was now in a strictly administrative job and he took part in an Army Cross Country Championships near Aldershot. He instructed his 'Light Vehicles Manager' to make sure he was given an automatic vehicle from the hire firm because his knees would be in rag order after the race. The keys were put on his desk after it was delivered and when he went to find it he found he'd been issued a brand new top of the range Mercedes Benz! For a brief second he felt guilty about issuing many Senior Officers with a Nissan Micra to keep the car hire costs down…he only felt that guilt for a brief second though.

By the time Ricky was due to leave the Army, Renate had returned to Munster to care for her terminally ill mum. Ricky had to stay in their own home in Essex because they had a dog. He was unemployed for a long time before getting a few driving and security jobs before working for Motability for six years. After buying a few old houses and modernising them, Ricky and Renate got themselves out of negative equity and bought another yacht which they lived on and sailed around Scotland. They have both recently sailed through the French canals and returned back to Essex by skirting the Bay of Biscay. After doing some maintenance and repairs to their boat, they will be heading off again this coming spring.

24316562 Sergeant Bill Baker
RCT 1974 – 1994

Driver Bill Baker

On the 5th May 1974 Bill Baker arrived at the Junior Leaders Regiment RCT at the same time as the author and they were both allocated bed-spaces in room 6 of Dalton Troop, the two of them were separated by just four bed-spaces. As far as personalities and confidence were concerned they seemed to have come from opposite ends of the universe not opposite ends of the room, though this was mainly because the author didn't have a personality or any confidence. Bill, on the other hand, was both loud and brash and gave the appearance of being the most confident young man in the twelve man dormitory. Little did the author know at the time, but this was all bravado and Bill was just as nervous as all of the other anxious recruits. The difference was that Bill had a knack of bluffing his way through life and generally had the luck of the devil when things went awry, even when the 'shit that hit the fan' was his own.

Although Bill came from Portsmouth, he spoke like the actor Jack Wild playing the part of the Artful Dodger in the 1968 film 'Oliver', in fact the similarities didn't end there. Bill could also think on his feet and he usually had an answer for everything. When he did drop himself in deep shit, he nearly always came out on top, or at least, on toppish. After leaving school without an exam result to his name, Bill set off for the Army Recruiting Office with his best mate Steve (Jim) Hawkins. When the recruiter asked Bill what he wanted to do in the army he replied on a whim, "Dunno really, I wanna drive Lorries I suppose," and on that impulse both Steve and Bill signed on the dotted line, enlisting into the Royal Corps of Transport (RCT). When he arrived back home, Bill proudly informed his dad that he'd joined up and that he was going to serve in the British Army. Bill explains his dad's response, "My dad went totally ballistic, he was absolutely fucking furious, I shouldn't have been surprised really because the old man had served in the Royal Navy for 37 years."

It wasn't a long train journey from Portsmouth to Norton Manor Camp in Taunton, Somerset where the Junior Leaders Regiment RCT was based, but travelling with his mate Steve (Jim) Hawkins even on that short trip probably made the apprehensive journey a lot less worrying. On arrival at Taunton Railway Station all the young recruits were encouraged by an RCT Sergeant to climb into the back of a Bedford RL truck, "Come on you lot! Fucking move yourselves, we haven't got all day"! Bill thought 'Oh gawd blimey, 'ere we go.' The Women's Royal Voluntary Service (WRVS) club was being used as a reception centre for the new recruits and it was here that Bill and Steve were separated because Steve was placed into B Squadron. An RCT clerk issued Bill with his individual regimental number on a piece of paper and told him to memorise it. He also told him that he was being placed into Dalton Troop which was in C Squadron. His Troop Sergeant, Sergeant 'Rock' Reed was waiting outside for him. 'Rock' Reed was a bull of a man who typified a cartoon image of a British Army Sergeant from the 1940's, his boots gleamed and his heavily starched uniform seemed to creak every time he moved. He also had a Drill voice that was comparable to a 100 Decibel fog horn. But he wasn't the one that Bill should have been worrying about.

Junior Squadron Sergeant Major (J/SSM) 'Scouse' MacDonald was a bully in every sense of the word. At the age of 17 ½ years he was coming to the end of his training in Taunton and would soon be posted to a Regular Army unit as a Driver. MacDonald had a private bunk that was attached to Room 6 in Dalton Troop and everyone in that room was deemed to be his personal slave. His boots were bulled for him and cigarettes were provided by the recruits, without question, for any of his sycophantic, arse kissing Junior Corporals (J/Cpl) and

Junior Sergeants (J/Sgt) that visited him in his lair. The occupants of Room 6 found out the lie of the land within weeks of their arrival at Taunton. MacDonald regularly made every recruit in Room 6 line up and stand to attention in the middle of the dormitory, he then approached each recruit individually and told them to brace their stomach muscles while he punched them in the stomach. If a recruit tried to ride the punch they would have to go through the same process until they did exactly as instructed. After administering the punch, MacDonald would then ask the recruit if it hurt and they had to shout, "No Sir!" When asked why it didn't hurt they had to confirm, "Because I'm in your Squadron, Sir!" And so it went on down the line of Junior Leaders until he'd had the fun of punching them all whilst hiding behind the security of his Junior Warrant Officer rank. When he came to Junior Driver Phil Crossland he carried out the same routine and again asked if it hurt, to which Phil shouted, "Fucking right it did sir!" for his outburst Phil received a sharp slap across the face. Next in line was Bill, who thought to himself, 'I ain't going down that road, that's a two for one.' Bill, like the rest of us, didn't ride the punch and gave the requisite answer. Several weeks later Bill was admitted to the Medical Reception Station (MRS) for a week because of an unaccountable injury he'd suffered to his ribs, from an unaccountable person.

Each Wednesday afternoon every Junior Leader had to take part in a sport or hobby and whichever one they signed up for, they were stuck with that afternoon pastime until the end of that term. There were only a limited amount of places for each interest, the subjects ranging from Motorbike riding, Judo, Orienteering, and even Model Making whilst stuck in a stuffy old classroom. Bill quickly grabbed one of motorbike slots, which enabled him to pass his motorbike test even before anyone else had started their Driver Training phase. In the Motorcycle Wing the lucky few were trained to ride and maintain the BSA 350cc standard British Army motorbike (meanwhile, the author was making a fucking 1/72nd size plastic model of a Supermarine Spitfire whilst stuck in a stuffy old classroom). On the test day, all students were given the route to take and Bill led the convoy of six riders under examination. The last motorbike was ridden by a Qualified Testing Officer (QTO) who kept a keen eye on all of the students to see if they made any mistakes. Depending on the severity of their faults, and how many, hinged on whether or not a student passed or failed his bike test. To gain a pass on the test it was mandatory for everyone to complete the route within the constraints of the law and the national speed limit. As the convoy travelled through Taunton Town Centre, Bill was the only rider who got through a set of traffic lights while they were still on green, the rest of the convoy had to stop after the lights turned red and they all lost sight of Bill. It was too good an opportunity for Bill to miss. He cranked up his bike and shot round the rest of the route whilst travelling at a questionable speed. He was standing to attention at the Motorcycle Wing when everyone else returned. The QTO was quizzical but said, "Well, in all honesty I didn't see you make any mistakes but that's because I didn't see you for the majority of the journey, so I suppose I'll have to give you a pass." Bill was then granted his motorbike licence.

Senior Troop had some more unpleasant experiences for Bill that were not dissimilar to the bullying he'd seen and suffered in Dalton Troop. The Junior Leaders now held the rank of Driver (Dvr) and some deemed themselves to be Regular Army soldiers and they did as they damned well pleased. The same sort of bullies thought that being in Senior Troop gave them the right to be even more unpleasant and sadistic. Bill was witness to one Senior Troop Driver who was tied face-down on his bed and a very hot iron was held near his face; the tormentors told him they were about to press the iron into the middle of his back. As the iron was moved behind him a very cold metal mess tin was pressed into his back, which made him scream out loud, a very cruel joke that was common practice in Senior Troop. *Note: (The author would like to point out that both he and Bill thoroughly enjoyed their time at Taunton and that the incidents in Dalton and Senior Troops were isolated and rare instances, carried out by just a few sick individuals).*

At 0800 hours on the first day of his new posting to 10 Regiment RCT, Bill reported to the Headquarters of 17 Squadron RCT as instructed by the fearsome Sergeant in the Guardroom. The majority of the Squadron were out on Exercise at the time though and so 17 Squadron Headquarters looked a bit like a ghost town but Bill continued to look for someone in authority. He could hear some laughter coming from behind the closed Admin Officers door and as there didn't seem to be anyone else around he headed in that direction. Captain 'Nobby' Hall was inside his office with several other soldiers and Bill was certain he could hear an 8mm cine projector whirring away behind the door. After knocking on the door, Bill entered a very dark and smoke filled room where he heard someone shout:

Captain 'Nobby' Hall: "Shut that fucking door will you!"

Bill: "Sorry sir, I'm looking for the Admin Officer."

Captain 'Nobby' Hall: "Well you've found him, what do you fucking want?"

Bill: "Well Sir! I'm Driver Baker from the Junior Leaders Regiment in Taunton and I was told to report to the Headquarters of 17 Squadron RCT."

Captain 'Nobby' Hall: "Well get in here and shut that fucking door will you! You're blurring the film, grab a chair, sit down over there and watch the film. I'll deal with you later."

On that Monday morning Bill sat with a handful of other RCT Drivers and watched a German pornographic film for twenty minutes before being processed into the unit, even though Bill didn't speak any German he soon picked up the intricate plot of the film.

Bill passed his Heavy Goods Vehicle (HGV) Class II test in a Mark III Militant, but he wasn't put into one of the Squadrons Troop Sections, instead he was sent up to the Motorcycle wing and told to report to Lance Corporal Bill Buckley. Bill Buckley was the British Army's version of Evil Knievel and there wasn't a thing he didn't know about motorbikes or how to handle them, (it was a popular myth within 10 Regiment RCT that Bill came out of his mother's womb riding a Raleigh chopper bike). The Motorcycle Wing had between 20 – 30 BSA 350 army motorbikes and these were evenly divided between each Squadron when the Regiment deployed on Exercise. In the 1970's there was always a shortage of spares for all types of vehicles in 10 Regiment and the Motorcycle Wing was no exception. Tyres, wheels, brake cables and even indicator and headlight bulbs were always in short supply. Cannibalisation was the buzz word of the decade and Bill Buckley did an exceptional job of keeping the majority of his fleet on the road. Bill Baker joined the Motorcycle Wing and learned a lot from his new boss, even down to stripping the engine of an old B 40 bike just so they could use its piston.

It wasn't just the mechanics of a motorbike that Bill was learning about either because he also had to learn about the Standard Operating Procedures (SOP's) of being a 'Don R' (Old army phonetic spelling for a dispatch rider). Whenever Bill Baker went on Exercise he was usually riding a BSA 350 motorbike and leading a convoy of trucks to their Squadron hide. After leaving the camp he would have to speed ahead to the next junction where he'd park up and point his bike in the direction the trucks would have to turn and then after the last truck went through that checkpoint, he'd have to race up to the next junction and repeat the same procedure. It could be an exhausting job that was fraught with dangers, even on narrow country roads Bill and the other Don R's would have to overtake every truck they were shepherding and get ahead of the front truck before they got to the next road junction. Bill explained, "You had to have your wits about you because some of those German drivers were nutters and they weren't shy about using their right foot on the old accelerator." But as far as

Bill was concerned he had the best job in the RCT and even though he was kept busy on Exercise there was an element of freedom with the job. When not guiding a convoy or tearing up and down the Main Supply Route (MSR) trying to find a lost section of trucks, he often pulled off the road and into a quiet Gastatte where he enjoyed a nice Bratwurst, some pommes frites and a cool glass of Herforder Pils bier. Bill was pretty good at the job as well and as a result he was promoted to Lance Corporal by the Officer Commanding of 17 Squadron RCT.

Things came a bit unstuck for Bill on Exercise Crusader in the early 1980's because he lost a 9mm Sterling Sub Machinegun, 'somewhere in BAOR.' Because the weapon kept getting in his way whilst riding the bike, Bill used to tuck it away in one of his side panniers. "The fucking thing must have fallen out when I was travelling over some rough ground in a wood. The powers that be even shut down the whole Exercise for a while and a massive effort was made to try and find the damned thing. The weapon was never found though and the monkey's (Royal Military Police) believed that a 10 Regiment truck had probably driven over the gun and pushed it down into the mud." Bill was put on Commanding Officers Orders after the Exercise and Lieutenant Colonel Benton RCT relieved him of the heavy burden on his right sleeve. Bill was busted back down to Driver rank and given a hefty fine to pay. Bill stated, "To be fair I was just pleased that I wasn't going to Collie, (Colchester Military Prison).

During his time in the RCT Bill did several tours of duty in Northern Ireland. He served in Londonderry, Belfast and South Armagh at locations like Fort George, Moscow Camp, Bessbrook and Newton Hamilton. Bill was responsible for the 'Squirts'- water cannons in Moscow Camp on his first tour of Belfast. These large trucks had a crew of three, an RCT driver, an RCT cannon operator and an infantry soldier who provided protection. The weight of water in the tanks of these vehicles put an extra strain on the truck and this invariably led to the drive shafts snapping rather too often, the other problem with these riot control assets was the fact that the water cannons simply didn't work. Bill deployed onto the streets of Belfast in 1976 and his crew thought they were going to use the water cannon for the first time in restrained anger. When they got into position the 'squirt' again failed to work and they disappointedly had to return back to Moscow Camp.

Every week a unit disco was organised in Moscow Camp and transport was sent down into Belfast to pick up some of the local lassies so the soldiers wouldn't have to 'dance' with each other. Bill chatted up a very beautiful girl and offered to walk her home after the transport had dropped everyone off when the disco had ended. He would be unarmed and without any means of communication with the Security Forces, which was an incredibly stupid thing for a British soldier to do in Belfast in 1976. Bill escorted the girl to a Catholic area and after being invited into the house they both went upstairs. Just as things were heating up for Bill and his conquest, he heard a commotion downstairs as five men burst through the front door. The new love of Bill's life said, "Oh don't worry, that'll just be my brothers and their mates." The girl slipped downstairs in her dressing gown to see what the lads were doing and Bill was left upstairs for the next 40 minutes 'shitting a brick'. After the lads had gone and the girl returned to the bedroom you'd think that a clever soldier would have made a very rapid exit and returned to camp, not Bill though, oh no, he stayed for the rest of the night and did the dishonourable thing, he then hitched a lift back to Moscow Camp on a milk truck.

On Bill's second tour of Northern Ireland he was placed into an RCT Section in Bessbrook location which was on the border of South Armagh and the Southern Ireland Republic. That little hotspot of the world was commonly called 'Bandit Country' by the British Army and Bill was going to be a witness to the reason why it deserved that nickname. 17 Squadron RCT were operating in support of 2nd Royal Green Jackets (2 RGJ) whose Commanding Officer was Lieutenant Colonel Ian Douglas Corden-Lloyd. On 17th February 1978 the CO flew out from the Bessbrook location in an Army Air Corps (AAC) Gazelle helicopter, accompanied by a SNCO bodyguard called Sergeant Ives. The flight headed towards an RGJ Observation Post (OP) that was situated very near to the border. The soldiers in the OP were engaged in a fire-fight with the IRA who were firing, with supposed impunity, from the Southern side of the border The Southern Irish Police (Garda) were witness to this attack. Lieutenant Colonel Corden-Lloyd had heard on the net (Military radio network) that his boys were under fire and so he immediately flew out to support his troops on the ground. The army helicopter crashed into the ground after the IRA had fired directly at it whilst it overflew the incident at Jonesborough. The RGJ CO was killed as a result of the crash but both the pilot, Captain Philip Schofield and Sergeant Ives, although injured, survived the disaster.

Bill Baker and his Green Jacket friend, Bluey, were manning both a .30 Cal Browning Medium Machinegun and a Gimpy (General Purpose Machinegun) in the Sanger that was overlooking the helicopter pad. They both saw the three men run out, get into the helicopter and fly off towards the incident point just a couple of miles away. They heard the gunfire in the distance and the sound of someone nearby taking a pot-shot at the Bessbrook army outpost. Bill and Bluey both cocked their weapons and returned fire. It was some time later that

Bill witnessed the 2 RGJ CO's body being taken off another helicopter that had been sent out to retrieve his body. A few days later a local farmer in Bessbrook submitted a claim to the British Army for the three cows that Bill and Bluey had accidentally shot and killed.

After returning from South Armagh, Bill did a Transporter, Tanker, Fuel (TTF) and Petrol Oil and Diesel (POD) Operators course in 10 Regiment, which qualified him to drive large and small fuel tankers, he also got his Lance Corporal tape back on his arm and with it a posting to 7 Signal Regiment at Herford. Bill found Exercises with the 'Bleeps' very boring because after filling up his 22,500 litre Foden tanker with fuel he'd then have to wait until the end of the day for the 'Sigs' to come to him for re-fuelling. On one particular Exercise at Dummer See (Dummer See was a man-made lake to the East of Hamburg) Bill got so fed up with waiting around all day that he headed off to watch some of the civilian windsurfers on the lake. By the end of the day he'd managed to fall off a hired board several hundred times, windsurf out into the middle of the lake, and even managed to get back to the shore again in time to refuel the 'bleep' vehicles. "I was so chuffed with myself that I went out and bought all the gear and took up windsurfing with a vengeance." Bill eventually passed the RYA courses at 3, 2 and 1 levels for windsurfing on inshore lakes and the same for Open Sea Windsurfing, he also managed to pass the RYA courses at Level One. Bill went on to become an army instructor in the sport and was lucky enough to be sent out to Belize on three tours, not tramping around a steamy jungle carrying a rifle though, oh no, Bill was living in a seconded bungalow just off St Georges Quay trying to teach drunken squaddies how to windsurf. His daily uniform consisted of some brightly coloured tee shirts and shorts.

Bill was promoted to full Corporal on leaving Herford and was sent to the RCT Depot and Training Regiment RCT at Buller Barracks, Aldershot as a Skill at Arms Instructor The Training Wing at Buller Barracks consisted of two sergeants who taught the recruits and the Senior Military Qualification (SMQC) courses, and it also had two full corporals on the staff who instructed the Junior Military Qualification Courses (JMQC). After a couple of years teaching 'guns' to the JMQC courses, Bill got his chance to become a bonafide British Army Drill Instructor. He was promoted to Acting Sergeant and sent off to the Guards Depot at Pirbright where the world's best army drill instructors would teach him how to beast recruits around a drill square. "It was the hardest fucking course I'd done in the army" said Bill, "The Guards are in a world of their own, they run on a tangent to everyone else. On the All Arms Advanced Drill Instructors Course we were bounced around the drill square all day by a Guards Sergeant who thought he was God Almighty. The same bloke jailed us several times a day and then the Regimental Police (RP's) took a turn at giving us a hard time. It was a life of relentless harassment and bullshit." It was important for Bill to pass this course though because he'd grown fed up with "Rubber tyres, scrim nets and digging shell-scrapes." Bill thought the life of a 'Drill Pig' in the Training Wing was an easy option, "All I had to do was march out and inspect each Course as if I was God Almighty, pick them up for a few faults, bounce them around the square for 40 minutes and then go back to my office for a cup of coffee whilst one of my 'Full Screws' (Corporals) did something else with them." After passing the Drill Course, Bill was promoted to Substantive Sergeant and he became responsible for a bit more than just doing a 40 minute drill period every so often. He also had to teach the Phase One recruits how to make their beds, press their uniforms, the art of field-craft and virtually how to wipe their backsides properly. "It was like a sausage machine in Buller Barracks. Every 12 weeks my Training Wing Staff had to turn thirty useless young men into something resembling half decent squaddies." It must have been a good job though because Bill carried on doing it for ten years, his career at the Depot, however, could have ended quite abruptly on the ranges one sunny afternoon.

Bill was commanding forty recruits at a Falling Plate shooting competition on Ash Ranges one beautiful sunny afternoon. The lads were knocking down the heavy metal plate targets on the 200 metre range using a Light Machinegun (LMG). At the same time Rod Pailer was on a business trip from London and he turned up on the range hoping to visit his Brother-in-Law, Bill Baker. Rod turned up wearing long hair and a pin striped suit, complete with waistcoat and briefcase. On seeing the LMG's being fired at the metal plates, Rod asked Bill if there was any chance of him having a go. Bill was in charge and so he said, "Yeah, I think I can sort something out for you Rod." One of the full Corporals from the Training Wing was told to closely shepherd Rod, **'a civilian,'** through firing a full magazine of thirty rounds from this lethal weapon. As Rod was walking down to the 100 meter point, carrying the LMG and a magazine full of live ammunition, Bill's Officer Commanding (OC) and Squadron Sergeant Major (SSM) turned up on the ranges to see how the recruits were enjoying their day. The OC immediately spotted something was wrong because Rod was **'a civilian'** businessman and he was sauntering onto the firing point with one of the OC's LMG's and a magazine of live ammunition. The following conversation is how Bill remembers his army career about to disappear down the toilet:

SSM: "Sergeant Baker!"

Bill: "Oh fuck me, that's torn it."

OC: "Sergeant Baker, Would you be so good as to explain to me exactly who that civilian gentleman is?"

Bill: "Which civilian gentleman would that be sir?"

OC: "The one in a three piece suit that is now firing one of my LMG's on the 100 meter point."

Bill: "Oh him sir! He's my Brother-in Law, sir."

OC: "Oh good, I'm so glad you clarified that for me Sergeant Baker. That of course makes everything abundantly clear."

Bill: "His name's Rod Pailer sir."

OC: "Yes, I see, slightly irrelevant though don't you think Sergeant Baker?"

After blatting off a full magazine of 7.62 mm ammunition Bill's Brother-in-law stood up on the firing point and shouted:

Rod: "Hey Bill! That was fucking brilliant mate! Can I have another go?"

It was at this point Bill's OC turned to his Squadron Sergeant Major and said:

OC: "Sarn't Major…I think we ought to return to Buller Barracks before we see anything untoward, don't you?"

SSM: "Yes sir, I definitely think we should! Goodbye Sarn't Baker."

Bill stood to attention and saluted his OC as the Major climbed back into his Land Rover and headed back to Buller Barracks. Incredible as it seems, nothing further was said about the incident, which either proves Bill was deemed to be a very important member of Buller Barracks Permanent Staff, or he was just one of the luckiest bastards on this planet. More than likely he was the latter.

In the autumn of 1982 Bill applied through District Council Instructions (DCI's) to be attached to 1st Battalion of the Parachute Regiment for six weeks when they deployed out to Kenya on **Exercise Grand Prix.** He would be instructing the Paras how to windsurf on Lake Naivasha during the Rest and Recuperation (R&R) phase of their deployment. The Paras worked very hard on the Exercise doing both direct, and indirect live-firing exercises as well as some serious jungle warfare training, so they definitely needed some down time. During his six weeks with 1 Para Bill did about one day's work because the Paras simply weren't interested in poncing about on a lake during their R&R. They were more interested in getting pissed out of their tiny skulls. As a result Bill did a lot of windsurfing and sunbathing on his own but during the evening he'd meet up with the Paras in the local bars and join them in getting totally trolleyed.

In 1992 Bill took a £56,000 voluntary redundancy package from the MOD and headed off to a life in Civvy Street where he became a screaming pisshead. After using £2,500 of his redundancy package to put a deposit on a house near Portsmouth, he literally pissed the rest of the money up against the wall of said house. The last thing he heard his ex-wife say was, "If you walk out of that door again, I won't be here when you come back." Bill got on with his drinking when he came back from the pub because, as promised, his wife wasn't there when he got home. After his wife had walked out and the money started drying up Bill came to the conclusion that he needed to get a job. He did some HGV 1 driving jobs for MFI before they went bust and eventually ended up working for the MOD in their Civilian Guard Service. The work was so boring that Bill transferred to the MOD dog section and in due course he was promoted to Section Commander. He was then put in charge of a ten man team at Longmoor Training Camp near Bordon in Hampshire. On one particularly night the weather was so foul that Bill said to the lads in his section, "Listen boys! It's a shitty night out there so let's have a night in front of the telly in the guardroom." The next thing Bill knew was everyone was sound asleep in front of the television, and that included the guard dogs. Unfortunately someone in authority from the Guard Service paid a surprise visit and found them all snoring away. Bill was vocally reprimanded and everyone on the guard was warned that they were being put on a fizzer, a Board of Inquiry was set up to deal with all of the transgressors and a court date was duly arranged.

Half way through the military court of inquiry Bill stood up and told the President of the Board, "Listen! I've had enough of this bollocks. I should be held responsible for what happened because the lads in my Section didn't do anything wrong, I was in charge at the time. I resign here and now and you can shove your job wherever you like." Bill advised the men in his Section to do the same because they would at least preserve their pension rights, they didn't resign though and in the end they were all sacked for gross misconduct, Bill was the only one that night to retain all of his pension rights.

Bill and his second wife went over to the Isle of Wight for a weekend break and fell in love with its quality of life there. They bought a house, but eighteen months later it felt like they were living on Alcatraz. During their time on the Island, Bill and his wife celebrated his Father-in-Laws 60th Birthday party in a local pub. Bill drove to the pub and was pissed as a rat by closing time, but he'd pre-booked a taxi to get himself, Hayley and her parents back home after the party. That night a torrent of rain was lashing down as they left the pub and so Bill suggested they all wait in his car for the taxi to arrive. Within five minutes Bill saw some headlights approaching the pub car park and so he turned to his wife and in-laws and said, "Taxi's here, let's go." He stumbled out of the car and clumsily fell onto the ground just as a Police Officer got out of the now parked police car.

Policeman: "Good evening sir, and what do we think we're doing?"

Bill: "Well I'm waiting for a taxi, I thought you were it."

Policeman: "Well, we're not a taxi firm sir, we are policemen. Would you mind blowing into this bag for me please."

Bill: "Now wait a minute, I'm not drink driving, I just told you, I'm waiting for a taxi to take us home."

Policeman: "Of course you are sir, but would you just indulge me for a couple of minutes and blow into this bag before we commence with this conversation?"

Bill: "Oh shit!"

The landlord at the pub and the taxi driver both submitted affidavits to Bill's solicitor stating that Bill wasn't going to drink and drive and that he'd done everything in a responsible manner. The judge on the following court case sympathised with Bill and told him, "In this case I'm afraid the law really is an ass, Mr Baker, although you weren't guilty of driving under the influence of alcohol and you did absolutely everything right, you were still guilty of being drunk and in charge of a motor vehicle. However, I'm not going to take your licence off you but I have to fine you £150.00 with court costs and 10 points will be put onto your driving licence, I'm afraid that is what the law insists I do."

Bill applied for another HGV driving job but with those extra 10 points on his licence the interviewer told him that he didn't think he had much of a chance getting the job. He had three other candidates to see and told Bill, "I can't see you getting this job Mr Baker because of those 10 points, I'll telephone you after I've completed all of the other interviews. Thank you for coming today." As it happened the other three candidates didn't turn up for their interviews and Bill Baker got the job that he's still doing today.

At the end of the interview for his chapter in this book, the author asked Bill if he had any regrets about his time in the RCT. He told the author that he was disappointed that he'd not been awarded a Long Service and Good Conduct Medal (LS & GC Mil) and that he'd appealed to the MOD against the charge that prevented the award. "When I asked if there was any possibility of me getting a medal the Warrant Officer at the Ministry of Defence said, "You've absolutely no fucking chance Mr Baker!"

<u>24316568 Sergeant David Hand</u>
<u>RCT 1974 – 1994</u>

Corporal Glenn 'Doc' Savage and Driver Dave Hand on 404 Troops' Vehicle yard in Airport Camp Belize. They were just about to set off for Mountain Pine Ridge.

Dave Hand never was a scholar in his formative years at school and so he lists his Senior School Educational Qualifications as, "Fuck all." He unconditionally states that the reason for his poor education was because, "I was a bit of a twat in class." Things changed considerably after he left home in Manchester on the 5th of May 1974 and arrived at the Junior Leaders Regiment RCT in Taunton, Somerset where as a Junior Leader in the Royal Corps of Transport he would have to knuckle down and become disciplined and studious if he wanted to make a career in the Corps. The military training really suited Dave and he enjoyed his time in Carter Troop, A Squadron. He even made an effort on the compulsory educational courses in Maths (Military Calculations) and English (Communication Skills). Where Dave really excelled though was in the Skill at Arms lessons and on the firing range where he seemed to have a natural ability when it came to stripping, assembling, and shooting army weapons. Later in his career this talent would win him an award when he outshot an SAS (Special Air Service) trained soldier in Cyprus.

When it came to driving skills Dave also surpassed every other trainee Driver in Senior Troop at JLR Taunton. He passed his HGV (Heavy Goods Vehicle) III test after only 24 hours dual training in a Bedford RL truck, he even beat Junior

Regimental Sergeant Major 'Geordie' Lejeurne's extraordinary time of just 30 hours training. Dave's prize for this outstanding achievement was the Regimental accolade of 'Best Driver' at Taunton in 1975 and his name was added onto a commemorative shield in the unit cinema, he was also given an atlas book to remember the occasion. Dave would have preferred a magnificent jewel encrusted trophy that he could have taken away with him, a massive silver cup inscribed with the words, 'Driver Dave Hand RCT – Dog's Bollocks of a Driver' would also have been acceptable. 'Geordie' Lejeurne's prize for becoming Junior RSM and runner-up best Driver was the chance to complete his HGV II test before leaving the Training Regiment, a prize that Dave Hand would have appreciated much more than his, "Crappy atlas book."

Because Dave had passed his driving test so quickly he was offered the chance of being posted to a Tank Transporter Squadron in BAOR. He was dissuaded from doing this by his Senior Troop Instructor Corporal 'Para' Young. Pete Young told him, "Don't take the posting, you will spend the next three years just changing tyres on a Tank Transporter just so someone else can drive the fucking thing." Dave subsequently found out that this bit of information wasn't quite true and that he could have acquired his HGV I licence very quickly at a Tank Transporter unit. In the end Dave was posted to 9 Squadron, 10 Regiment RCT in Bielefeld, West Germany which he believes was a penance for cold-shouldering the first, and most prestigious offer.

A posting to 10 Regiment RCT was described by most Drivers in the Corps as a punishment posting and the place was mockingly called "10th Penal Battalion," (A reference to the very popular series of books written by Sven Hassel at the time). Hassel's books describe the activities of a German tank crew serving in 27th (Penal) Panzer Regiment during World War Two, each character in the book had been either Court Martialled or was some sort of political agitator who opposed the Nazi regime, the main characters were therefore deemed to be an undesirable and expendable Nazi military commodity. On his first visit to the NAAFI Bar in the regiment, Dave was witness to a punch-up and he remembers Driver Dave Ledbetter hitting himself on the head with a fire extinguisher. The violence escalated into a massive brawl and the scene did resemble several passages from a Sven Hassel book. Dave thought to himself, 'Fuck me! What the hell have I done to deserve a posting to this mad-house?' It wasn't all bad news though because his new boss in A Troop turned out to be a very good Senior NCO, Staff Sergeant George McAllister RCT put Dave straight onto an HGV II driving course which he passed with ease. Dave even remembers his driver training trucks' registration number, 37 EP 83 which was an AEC 10 Ton 'old Knocker.'

It wasn't long before Dave started getting into bad company in 9 Squadron, but to be fair virtually every Driver in 10 Regiment was a bad influence on someone. Dave got into a spiral of spending most of his time and money on drinking and getting into minor misdemeanours which eventually came to the attention of the Commanding Officer of the Regiment. Within his first year in the unit Dave was put under close arrest for three months by Lieutenant Colonel Benton RCT because 10 Regiment RCT had a bad record of soldiers being Court Martialled at this time. By putting Dave under close arrest for three months the CO could ultimately give him a sentence of less than 28 days in the nick which meant no embarrassing Court Martial for one of his Drivers. The CO could then avoid having yet another of his soldiers doing time at the MCTC (Military Correction Training Centre) in Colchester. Lieutenant Colonel Benton's credibility at the time had been chipped away at because of his 10 Regiments poor discipline record and the Brigadier at HQ 1st British Corps was pressuring him into doing something about it. During his time in the guardroom Dave was put in the custody of the RP Staff (Regimental Police) and their boss Sergeant Jimmy McMahon, Jimmy Mac was a short, tough, and fearsome Scottish soldier who had served in 63 (Parachute) Squadron RCT and he'd also been a very successful 10 Regiment RCT boxer. Whilst under arrest in the guardroom Dave was dragged into the toilets by Jimmy and they had the following encounter:

Sergeant McMahon: "So you think you're a bit of a hard case do you Hand?"

Dave Hand: "No Staff!"

Sergeant McMahon: "Well let's see how hard you are then…hit me."

Dave Hand: "You what Staff?"

Sergeant McMahon: "Are you fucking deaf Hand? I said hit me."

Dave Hand: "You've got to be joking Staff, I'm not going to hit you."

Sergeant McMahon: "I'll tell you what, you can hit me three times and I'll only hit you the once, that's more than fair."

Dave Hand: "I'm not going to hit you Staff."

Sergeant McMahon: "Listen Hand, you might as well take a shot because I'm going to fucking hit you anyway."

Given this fait accompli Dave sighed and punched Jimmy in the stomach as hard as he could. His fist simply bounced off a wall of solid muscle and Jimmy never moved an inch.

Dave Hand: "Oh shit!"

Sergeant McMahon: "Ok, let's have punch number two now."

After Dave took all three of his shots Jimmy still stood ramrod straight with a grin that stretched from ear to ear.

Sergeant McMahon: "Ok, now it's my turn."

Dave was near to shitting a brick at this time but he remained stood to attention and closed his eyes so he couldn't see the inevitable punch that was coming his way. It was like a soldier facing a firing squad after being given a blindfold. The punch was so hard and fast that Dave flew backwards and ended up in one of the toilet cubicles, retching and trying to regain his breath. Sergeant Jimmy McMahon simply turned on his heel and strode back into the guardroom.

One evening in the cell area Dave and several other prisoners were standing to attention outside their cells waiting to be inspected by the Orderly Officer yet again. Inspections were repetitively carried out during the day and night and the inmates usually had their immaculate cells and pristine equipment degraded and wrecked by someone in authority. In accordance with SOP's (Standard Operating Procedures) the orderly officer arrived at the Guardroom at 2200 hours and he inspected soldiers on Restriction of Privileges (ROP's), next he was ushered through to the cell area at the rear of the Guardroom to give the incarcerated soldiers a discerning review. Dave was first up and he stated, "24316568 Driver Hand, I have no requests or complaints Sir". The orderly officer was obviously in a rush to get back to the Officers Mess because he simply sneered and carried on to the next cell where he encountered Driver Smith (name changed to protect the guilty). Driver Smith was a well-known gob-shite in 10 Regiment and he was a very quick witted soldier. The orderly officer stood in front of him while he delivered his short speech and inspected his attire. He looked him up and down and said, "You haven't polished those boots have you Smith?" Driver Smith relied, "No". The orderly Sergeant went ballistic and shouted, "NO WHAT SMITH?" Quick as a flash Driver Smith's repartee was, "No polish Sergeant." Cue Sergeant McMahon to have another quiet physical interaction in the bogs! Dave and the other 'guests' nearly pissed themselves laughing."

During his time at 10 Regiment, Dave also had a very short and disastrous marriage that was always doomed to failure. His wife was so unhappy that Captain (Phil) Gosling RCT offered Dave the chance of a posting to 2 ADSR (Armoured Division Signal Regiment) in Lübbeck. By getting away from 10 Regiment, Dave and his wife could hopefully sort out their personal problems and save the marriage. The new posting only seemed to make matters worse though because Dave was away on more Exercises with the Royal Signals than when he was with 9 Squadron in Bielefeld. Dave and his wife agreed that she should go home to England whilst he was away on Exercise and that she'd come back to Lübbeck when the manoeuvres had finished. Unfortunately, once Dave's wife got back home with her family she refused to come back to Lübbeck. Dave went off the rails, drinking heavily and getting into fights with both soldiers and civilians alike. He also wrapped his Audi 80 car round a lamp post one night. After being breathalysed by the German Polizei they told him that fortunately he was just under the legal limit. Dave hated it at 2 ADSR and even serving alongside other great ex-10 Regiment soldiers like Corporal Dave North and Driver Kev Randle didn't help much. At the end of his three year tour with 2 ADSR, Dave was posted to 8 Squadron, 27 (Logistic Support) Regiment RCT in Aldershot. His 'enlightened' comrades in 2 ADSR warned him that it would be a shit posting, but Dave wasn't bothered.

As it turned out, the posting to Aldershot was one of the best of Dave's career, which only goes to prove that most soldiers will say anything just to piss on someone else's bonfire. Dave got to drive modern Foden trucks for the Army Freight System and after picking up stores from the COD (Central Ordnance Depot) at Bicester he would deliver them all over the UK. The freight system at 27 Regiment RCT also involved collecting containers from Bicester and delivering them to military units in BAOR, some details took over a week to complete because of the great distances involved. On these occasions Dave would collect the load and then drive it down to 17 Port and Maritime Regiment

RCT at Marchwood Military Port. On arrival at the Military Port he would be guided onto an LSL (Landing Ship Logistics) which would then set sail for Antwerp docks. After the ship docked Dave would then drive his vehicle and load off the ship and head for whichever BAOR depot needed his load. Before heading back on the same route, Dave would pick up another container that needed transporting back to England. It was the sort of job that most RCT Drivers could only dream about.

On Friday 2nd April 1982 Dave's Troop had just returned from an Exercise in Wales and they were all going through the usual RCT Endex (End of Exercise) routine. Weapons had to be handed into the armoury, wagons had to be refuelled, scrim nets and tool kits had to be returned to the stores before heading to the wash-down to clean the trucks. Their Sergeant briefed the whole Troop, "Ok lads, hand in your scrim nets and weapons but leave your tool kits on the vehicles. I want you to fuel up but don't bother washing down the vehicles. When you've done all that, line up your wagons and parade back here on the vehicle park."

Somewhat bemused the Drivers did as instructed and when they formed up the Troop Commander gave them another briefing, "Bad news I'm afraid lads, no-one will be standing down for the foreseeable future. Some Argentine Forces have seized control of the Falkland Islands and the MOD is sending a task force down there to restore them back to its rightful owners." He continued, "Our job will be to assist in the out-loading of every ammunition depot in the UK and then deliver those munitions to Marchwood where they'll be loaded onto an RFA (Royal Fleet Auxiliary) ship. During this operation I want the correct coloured flags used on trucks. Blue is to identify the convoy commander, Green is for the last vehicle in the convoy, yellow is to signify a mechanical breakdown and red flags must be displayed on all vehicles carrying live ammunition. I want you all to remember your convoy drills and maintain convoy discipline at all times. Also, make sure you stay within the relevant speed limits and let's make this a professional undertaking, let's show our Country what we, the Royal Corps of Transport, are capable of doing. Any questions?" One of the lads piped up and asked, "Yes Sir. Where the fuck is the Falklands?"

After the Troop Commander headed back to his office the Troop Sergeant had a last minute word with the boys before they started their first run, "Last one to Hilton Park Services on the M6 gets the teas in." Over the next four days Dave and his mates drove around the clock, picking up and delivering tons and tons of live ammunition from both CAD (Central Ammunition Depot) Longtown in Cumbria, and CAD Kineton near Birmingham. They worked incredibly long hours which was only possible because each wagon had a co-driver and they took rotated turns of either sleeping or driving.

One of Dave's convoy's turned up at Southampton with yet another cargo of ammunition after they'd already completed two days of solid driving. They arrived at the dockside mid-morning and were briefed that the ship wasn't due in till the next day so they might well get some shut eye in their vehicles. The Drivers hadn't had a shower or shave for over 48 hours and the last decent hot meal they'd enjoyed was the previous afternoon. They were tired, hungry and slightly whiffy. Dave asked permission to go into town so he could draw some money from his bank account and his Troop Sergeant agreed with the proviso that he was back at his vehicle by 11 o'clock. In Dave's defence the Sergeant didn't specify whether that was 1100 hours or 2300 hours.

After drawing his money from the bank, Dave was accosted outside a pub by a gorgeous young woman. She threw her arms around his neck and gave him a passionate kiss telling him that he was wonderful and that she wanted to buy him a drink. At the time all of the media coverage of our, "Wonderful and heroic servicemen" was on overload, and the nation believed that anyone in an army uniform was going off to die for them and win a Victoria Cross. Dave apologised and said, "Sorry love but I haven't done anything brave, I've just driven some stuff here in a truck, I'd love to stop for a drink sweetheart but I've got to be back at my wagon before eleven." In Dave's defence he mitigates that the young woman was persistent and that she was particularly gorgeous. At 2245 hours a very pissed Driver Dave Hand reported back to Staff Sergeant 'Paddy' Docherty with two newly tattooed eyes on his arse, the Troop Staffie wasn't amused and when Dave pointed out that it wasn't even 11 o'clock yet, he nearly exploded with frustration. Dave was ordered to sleep it off in the cab of his truck. He woke up the next morning with the mother of all hangovers, fortunately no disciplinary action was taken against him.

Before Dave actually got back to the port and faced the furious Staff Docherty, he decided to pop into a tattoo parlour (you already know how this ends) and enquire as to how much they charged for their wares. When given a quote of £10 Dave exploded into a pissed and outrageously comical performance, "TEN FUCKING QUID TO HAVE TWO FUCKING EYES TATTOOED ON ME

ARSE! I'M NOT FUCKING MADE OF MONEY PAL!" The tattooist looked at Dave and said, "Put it this way mate. I'm not tattooing your sweaty squaddie arse for less than a tenner." Dave admitted on interview, "To be honest I'd not even had a wash for a couple of days and it wasn't exactly going to be a pleasant job for him." Dave bent over a couch with his combat trousers round his ankles whilst the tattooist's wife knelt down and held Dave' Gluteous Maximus steady while the tattooist quickly did the job. The door of the parlour cubicle suddenly burst open and a bloke walked in, after witnessing what he thought was a strange sadomasochistic ménage et trois he departed very quickly saying, "Sorry lads, I didn't mean to intrude!" Dave shouted after him, "No hang on mate, it's not like that!"

After the Falklands out-load was completed the unit resumed its normal routine and after yet another freight run Dave was summoned by the Admin Officer. Apparently an RCT Driver who had volunteered to do a tour of Belize in Central America had just been prosecuted for drunk driving. Dave was offered the chance of replacing him on that tour and he seized it with both hands. Serving at 27 Regiment RCT gave Drivers plenty of opportunities to pick up brilliant and obscure postings around the world, the morning Dave left for Belize he was casually offered the chance of other short tours of duty to either Cyprus or Canada. Dave flew to Belize from Brize Norton and soon after his arrival at 404 Troop in Airport Camp he was detailed to drive a minibus for the members of a CSE (Combined Services Entertainment) show on a week-long tour. Most of the Drivers avoided this duty because it meant they couldn't drink alcohol for the whole seven days, Dave wasn't bothered though and he thought it might do him some good to give his liver a bit of a breather. The CSE show was made up of an ensemble of comedians, singers and beautiful dancing girls who toured the world and entertained the British Army in far-flung and remote countries. Dave enjoyed giving them the orientation tour of Belize after which he was at their beck and call for the week. He had such a great time with them that he volunteered to be minibus driver for the next troupe who flew out two months later. After their plane landed, Dave and the RCT baggage truck driver were waiting together for the cast/company to step off the plane. The very first passenger to descend down the steps of the aircraft was Candy Davis who played the busty and sexy personal assistant to Mr Grace in the comedy series 'Are you being served.' She was wearing fishnet stockings and her ample breasts were definitely trying to escape from her low cut blouse. The baggage Driver's mouth dropped open and he turned to a smug looking Dave and said,

"You jammy fucker Dave!" Dave replied, "It's a tough job, but I'll get through it somehow."

Driver Dave Hand roughing it with the girls from the CSE Show in the Belle Vue hotel in Belize City. "It was hell but someone had to step up to the plate and take one for the boys".

After his six month tour of Belize came to an end, Dave flew back to the UK and re-joined 27 Regiment in Aldershot and within a couple of months he was sent out on a Squadron UN (United Nations) tour to Cyprus where his OC detailed Dave to represent the Squadron in a UN shooting competition. Dave was allocated a place in the SMG (Sterling Sub Machine Gun) 9mm category and he would be up against soldiers from every arm of the UN forces, including the Infantry. Dave came first in his class of shooters, scoring 94 out of 100 shots. The runner up was a CSM (Company Sergeant Major) serving in the Queens Lancashire Regiment who scored an almost as good 93 out of 100. At the prize giving parade Driver John 'Geordie' Elrick RCT noticed the CSM was wearing SAS (Special Air Service) wings on the top of his right sleeve and he didn't look very happy with his second placed certificate. The absolute cream of Britain's fighting forces had just been beaten in a shooting competition by a scruffy army truck driver. The lads in the Squadron started crowing that Driver

Dave Hand RCT had unbelievably trounced one of Britain's finest in a skill of which they were supposed to be the masters. From that point onwards Dave was nicknamed 'Sass' for the rest of his time in the unit. After the Squadron returned to Aldershot everyone was sporting magnificent sun tans when they went on the piss in town. One of the RCT Drivers shouted across the pub to Dave, who was standing at the bar, "Hey Sass! Get me another pint in will you?" A couple of very attractive young girls who already knew Dave sidled up to him:

Girl: "Hiya, your names Dave isn't it?"

Dave: "Er, yeah."

Girl: "Why's he called you Sass then?"

Dave: "Oh it's just a nickname they gave me."

Girl: "Ah right, so are you in the SAS Regiment then?"

Dave: "Fuck me no! I'm just a truck driver in the RCT."

Girl: "Oh, we understand."

Dave: "Understand what?"

Girl: "You're not allowed to tell anyone."

Dave: "Tell anyone what?"

Girl: "That you're in the Special Air Service."

Dave: "But I'm not in the Special Air Service, I'm a fucking army lorry driver."

Girl: "Don't worry we know how it is, we won't tell anyone."

Dave: "Oh for fuck's sake! Listen to me girls, there's nothing to tell, I am not now, nor ever have been, a member of the Special Air Service."

Girl: "You have to tell everyone that, we saw it on a telly programme once. Nice sun tan by the way, been anywhere exotic lately?"

Three hours later when Dave was pissed out of his head, he turned to his idolising entourage and said:

Dave: Lishen girls, I shouldn't be shaying thish to anyone but I know I can trusht you two. When I wash sherving in the junglesh's of Vietnam…"

A notice was published on Part One Orders just before the Squadron returned from Cyprus stating that the unit was looking for volunteers to put their names forward for a six month tour of the Falkland Islands. Dave's mate Driver John Elrick asked him if he fancied doing the detachment as it might be an interesting tour because of the war back in 1982. There wasn't a chance in hell of Dave volunteering though because as far as he was concerned, "There's no fighting going on down there now and the place is just cold and covered in sheep shit. They can stick a posting down there right up their own jacksey's." So that was an emphatic, **"No!"** from Dave, he definitely didn't want to go down to the Falkland Islands for six months. Just before the unit returned to Aldershot another inclusion on Part One Orders read, 'The following volunteers have been selected for a six month tour of the Falkland Islands', Dave Hand's name was on the list. He stormed into the Squadron Headquarters and remonstrated with the Chief Clerk.

Dave: "Hey Chief! What the fuck is this all about, I didn't fucking volunteer for the Falklands tour, how come my names on the list?"

Chief Clerk: "Your mate Elrick said you wanted to go."

Dave: "Well I don't, so can you take me off the list please?"

Chief Clerk: "We can't do that I'm afraid. It's too late to change the list now."

Dave: "No it isn't Chief, just put a line through my name and tell them I'm not going."

Chief Clerk: "Too late Driver Hand, you're going!"

Dave: "Where the fuck is that bastard Elrick?"

Dave went hunting for his mate and found him in the NAAFI bar drinking a nice cool pint of lager. As soon as he clocked the look on Dave's face he took off like Linford Christie with Dave in hot pursuit. The escape route used by John took him into the Royal Signals bar where he stopped and bought Dave a pint to apologise, they left the bar a couple of hours later laughing about their forthcoming tour in the Falkland Islands.

The Tristar from Brize Norton left in mid-December bound for Senegal in West Africa as a refuelling location before heading for Ascension Island, from Ascension they boarded the LSL (Landing Ship Logistics) Sir Percival and took a wonderful 10 day ocean voyage to Port Stanley, the ship arrived at the Falkland Islands on Christmas Eve and docked in the bay for the evening. Dave spotted the Rapier missile systems situated on the high ground above Port Stanley and he decided it might be a good idea if he switched on for the rest of the tour, it looked like he might have to do some proper soldiering for the next 4 months. This illusion was shattered when he disembarked the following morning and spotted two unconscious Royal Engineers passed out on the dockside holding onto a couple of empty vodka bottles.

Dave was taken to the RCT troop office on the edge of Stanley and was briefed by Sergeant Lofty Barnes RCT, during the briefing a steady stream of Drivers turned up with all sorts of goodies including beer, cigars, beer, biscuits, beer, soft toys and more beer. Dave later discovered that the troop office was in the middle of the route from the dock to the NAAFI and the items were "liberated" for the use of the lads at troop "social gatherings" every Friday night. He also noticed that soft toy penguins were included in the freight arrivals and soon all the RCT vehicles had them dangling off their rear view mirrors with the drivers smoking King Edward cigars, most tried to look like Clint Eastwood in the film 'Pale Rider'. Someone in the Troop noticed that the penguins were made in Britain and it seemed strange that a soft toy made in the UK would be shipped all the way to the Falklands where a squaddie would buy it to take home to his mum or girlfriend as a souvenir from the Falkland Islands. The Troop Commander in Port Stanley received complaints from the NAAFI Manager asking how the RCT vehicle cabs were displaying stuffed penguins before they'd actually been put on sale in his shop.

Dave had signed off during his four month tour in the Falkland Islands and was posted to 40 Squadron RCT in Catterick Garrison to see his time out before leaving the army. Before his time was up Dave's OC at 40 Squadron told him that if he signed on for another 3 years he'd get a £3000 bonus. The boss also promised to promote Dave to Lance Corporal and give him a three month posting to Jurby Camp on the Isle of Man, and during his tenure on the IOM he'd have to wear civilian clothes every day and would be responsible for only a small MT Section. The vehicles were located at an army adventure training centre and they consisted of six civilian minibuses, four civilian cars (Dave was allocated one of these for his own personal use) and four military TK trucks. The job was so easy and laid back that Dave felt it was like being on holiday. Next door to his office block was a pub called the Jurby Arms and so after allocating vehicles at about 0900 hours Dave went next door and read the newspaper sport pages while supping a couple of pints, he was living the dream. HQ North West Command at Preston were so impressed with the job Dave had done that they gave him an outstanding report and the OC decided that he wanted Dave to be a part of the Transport Office Staff. Dave started to switch on big time and the OC promoted him to full Corporal. Before his five year posting to Catterick was concluded, he also got married to his beautiful girlfriend Isabel.

In 1989 Dave was posted to Berlin where he and Isabel were allocated a Married Quarter right next door to the 1936 Olympic Stadium. Dave's Troop Office was located in the stadium itself and his unit was involved in Flag Tours. Brixmis (British Mission) and Soxmis (Soviet Mission) were both British and Russian Liaison units that operated behind the Iron Curtain in East, and West Germany during the Cold War and the Flag Tours operated in East Berlin. 'Officially', their job description was, 'To maintain liaison between the Staff of the two Commanders-in-chief and their Military Governments in the Zones.' In reality these clandestine patrols operated in marked civilian cars and were there to gather military information about what their opposing forces were doing. Flag Tours did pretty much the same sort of stuff but they were restricted to operating in East Berlin only and were a lot more overt. Dave, however, often took Intelligence units into East Berlin so they could have a good shufty around and see what the 'bad guys' were doing. Dave states, "Brixmis was a far better organisation than us because they got to stay behind the lines for days at a time and they had the run of East Germany, we only got to play in East Berlin. They were gathering info on what tanks, vehicles and weapons the Soviets and East Germans were using and all this information was passed onto Headquarters Berlin Infantry Brigade."

Another outstanding Confidential Report saw Dave recommended for promotion again but he wasn't picked up on the promotion board, instead he was sent to 26 Squadron RCT at Lisburn, Northern Ireland, as a full Corporal. However, after about 4 months in Lisburn the Corps Promotions Order came out and Dave was picked up for his 3rd stripe. Unfortunately, there wasn't a vacancy anywhere in 26 Squadron or the rest of the Province for an RCT Sergeant. 10 Regiment RCT was in the process of moving back to the UK and Dave was offered the chance of re-joining his old unit but he turned the offer down and reluctantly took a posting to an MT section at HQ Scotland in Edinburgh. He only took the post because he didn't want to lose his promotion to Sergeant through being finicky about the postings he'd already been offered. After two boring uneventful years in Scotland Dave applied for an MOD redundancy package and was selected for Phase 3 redundancy.

After leaving the British Army, Dave got a job working for a company that imported and exported freight through the soon to be opened Channel Tunnel. He loved the job but in 2003 the company folded due to clandestine immigrants using the tunnel to gain entry to the UK. He got back in the cab and did some long distance HGV driving and he also worked for a Transport Distribution Company in Milton Keynes. Whilst working there he became aware of slight but expensive accidents being caused by poor procedures carried out within the firm, so he wrote some potential directives and presented them to the Transport Manager. The firm adopted Dave's plans and he eventually became the driver trainer until 2012. Dave now works as an Application Appraisal Manager for a company called JAUPT dealing with Driver CPC (Certificate of Professional Competence) Legislation. His office is only a ten minute walk from his house in Milton Keynes where he lives as a very happy and contented bunny (his words, not the authors).

24357695 Driver Ken Blake
RCT 1976 – 1986

Sergeant Ken Blake when he was serving with the Territorial Army at Grantham.

The Blake family have definitely 'done their bit' of serving within the ranks of the British Military, Tony Blake and all five of his sons have served more than their fair share of time wearing various cap badges of the Armed Forces. Tony enlisted into the Royal Navy in 1941 as an Electrical Engineer Artificer and he served on HMS Enterprise, a D Class Light Cruiser, almost until the end of the Second World War, and in that time he saw action out in the Far East, took part in **Operation Stonewall** in the Bay of Biscay blockading German Merchant

Marine imports, and he also supported the US Landings off Utah Beach on D Day 6th June 1944. On 24th December 1943 during **Operation Stonewall**, Tony's ship was involved in a search and destroy operation against a German blockade breaking ship called 'Alsterfuhrer', this blockade runner was heading for France after collecting an essential load of cargo from Japan. But an RAF (Czechoslovak) B 24 Liberator from 311 Squadron bombed and destroyed 'Alsterfuhrer' before HMS Enterprise and other ships could be engaged. However, the blockade Task Force did sink five other Kriegsmarine ships in the Bay of Biscay that were sent out to escort 'Alsterfuhrer' home, this was the last sea battle to take part in the Atlantic Theatre of War in World War Two. In 1945 Tony was posted up to Scotland where he joined the crew of HMS Theseus, a recently built Colossus-class light fleet aircraft carrier, it was planned to sail the carrier out to the Far East in the final fight against the forces of Japan, but the war ended before the plans were confirmed and Tony didn't have to go.

Tony's eldest son Roy served in the RASC (Royal Army Service Corps) and RCT (Royal Corps or Transport) and Chris his second eldest son served in the RA (Royal artillery) and RHA (Royal Horse Artillery). Chris Blake was serving in 156 (Inkerman) Battery of 94 Locating Regiment RA when his good friend Gunner Robert Curtis was killed in Northern Ireland, Robert was the very first soldier to be shot and killed during the 'Troubles' that had flared up in 1969. Gunner Curtis was taking part in a riot control operation in the New Lodge area of Belfast when he was shot by an IRA gunman firing a reported Sterling Sub Machinegun. The ricocheted shot tragically killed Robert instantaneously after it had passed through a gap in his flak jacket vest and pierced his heart. Sidney, the third born son, hated his name so much that he insisted on everyone calling him by his middle name of David, and Norman the fourth son, was nicknamed Joey in 1962 by the Blake family because he'd allowed the family budgerigar to escape from their flat (Cockney humour- you can't beat it). Both David and 'Joey' served in 2 RGJ (2ND Battalion of the Royal Green Jackets) where David also saw the tragic after effects of violence in Northern Ireland when he was serving with his Battalion in Londonderry during 'Bloody Sunday'. All witnessed details are not printed out of respect for David and the other infantry soldiers involved in this incident. After leaving the army David was unfortunately killed in a head on car crash in 1982 whilst driving home from his job as a Civilian Prison Officer, the crash was the result of a young tearaway driving on the wrong side of the road, David was just 28 years old.

So bearing in mind the brothers combined experiences in the British Army, it was no wonder that all four of them tried to prevent Ken from enlisting into a teeth arms branch of the forces. As he walked through the door of the Marble

Arch Recruiting Office on the Edgware Road, Ken could still hear the voices of his brothers ringing in his ears, "Don't join the Infantry Ken, get yourself a trade", "Bruv, listen to me, whatever you do don't join the Royal Artillery, I know what I'm talking about, you'll regret it if you do" and "Don't sign anything until we've had a chance to look at what they try to talk you into". Ken did very well on his selection tests and the Recruiting Sergeant told him, "You've done very well young lad and we can now offer you a place in the Royal Tank Regiment, however, at this particular moment in time my own personal Regiment, the RRF (Royal Regiment of Fusiliers) are looking to sign up potential Sergeants like yourself into its ranks." When Ken told the Sergeant that he wanted to consult with his brothers first the recruiter told him that this was a one-time offer and that the chance might not be on the table when he came back, Ken stuck to his guns though and presented the options to his brothers. David had previously worked in an Army Recruiting Office and so he knew what the Sergeant was trying to do, all Recruiters try and pressurise the best potential soldiers into signing up for their own Regiments. Both Royal Green Jacket brothers took one look at the paperwork and shouted, "What's this fucking Fusilier shit all about, we told you, you're not going into the fucking Infantry bruv." Roy, Chris, David and Joey all agreed that Ken would be better off joining the Royal Corps of Transport where he would have the chance of gaining a trade that he could use after being discharged from the army. There was a problem though, Ken really did want to go into the Infantry where he'd have the chance of carrying and firing the famous Gimpy, the 7.62mm GPMG (General Purpose Machine Gun) which was, and still is, the main fire support weapon used by all Infantry Regiments, most Corps units rarely use this weapon unless attached to an Infantry Battalion.

As a compromise the brothers agreed that Ken should join the 5th Battalion of the Queens Regiment, a Territorial Army Infantry unit that was based at Burnt Oak in London, and if he didn't like his time in a Rifle Platoon he could leave without all the hassle of having to give any kind of notice. After a wonderful two and a half years of training with the famous Gimpy and carrying it around various Training Areas in the UK (including on Junior Brecon), Ken came to the conclusion that his brothers were right and that any time spent in the Infantry was going to be fruitless, Ken was 20 years old when he left the Territorial Army. It wasn't long before he followed his brother's advice again and he enlisted into the Regular British Army joining the Royal Corps of Transport, he kept his original Service Number that he'd been issued by the TA.

The training staff at the RCT Depot in Buller Barracks were very different from Ken's instructors in the Territorial Army, "I know the staff at Buller weren't all the same but my Troop Sergeant and his Corporals were evil bastards, they were particularly cruel and vindictive for no other reason than taking great pleasure from inflicting misery on their recruits." Whilst on a Field Craft Exercise Ken and his fellow recruits were made to mix the contents of their ration packs into one of their mess tins, this including steak and kidney pie, rice pudding, biscuits, chocolate bar and coffee powder, once thoroughly mixed they were then forced to eat the whole nauseating sundry of ingredients. Ken can still remember his malevolent Sergeants' words after everyone had complied with his instruction, "Now eat and enjoy." Ken refused to eat the disgusting concoction and he tipped it all onto the ground, it would cost him a good private kicking during a visit to the local pub at the end of the Exercise. The Troop Sergeant had been drinking for a while and he followed Ken into the toilets where he beat him up and told him, "I'm making you a stronger character", the pub landlord threw them all out of his pub.

Ken felt a great sense of relief when he progressed onto the Driver Training phase at Leconfield in Yorkshire, although the training staff treated everyone with a great deal of discipline, they also treated every trainee with respect. The Driver Training came easy to Ken and after one day of driving a car and Land Rover, he was put onto driving a Bedford TK 3 ton Truck. He completed his dual Driver Training and passed his HGV III driving test on his first attempt. He did his Combat Training on Driffield Training area and learned about cross country driving and how to tactically drive and camouflage a Bedford MK truck. On completion of their Driver Training phase in Yorkshire the trainees returned to Buller Barracks in Aldershot to await their first posting. The Troop Commander privately read out the individual recruits end of course reports to them, Ken stood to attention in front of his Officers' desk and quietly listened to what the Training Staff thought of him, the following reports are permanently etched into Ken's brain.

Final Basic Training report on 24357695 Driver Blake RCT.
64 Training Squadron Buller Barracks Aldershot.

Driver Blake is an uninspiring soldier who seldom does anything useful, and when he does it is usually of a low standard.

Final Driver Training Course report on 24357695 Driver Blake RCT.
Army School of Mechanical Transport Normandy Barracks Leconfield.

Driver Blake has excelled in everything he's done on his Driver Training here in Leconfield, in particular his time spent in Combat Troop.

When asked by his Troop Commander how he felt about the two final reports Ken said, "I feel just great about them sir, it says absolutely everything about this place and the instructors in it, don't you think…**Sir**!"

The future postings were published on the Squadron notice Board and Ken spotted he'd been posted to 36 Squadron in 10 Regiment RCT in Bielefeld, he chuckled to himself when one of the other Drivers started chanting, "Driver Ken Blake…dead man walking."

Ken flew to RAF Gutersloh in West Germany where he met other Drivers destined for 36 Squadron, Mick Studley, 'Baz' Bassington and Nat Dervish, had also just arrived from the RCT Depot in Aldershot. On arrival at their Headquarters the four Buller Boys were processed into the Squadron with three other Drivers who'd also just arrived but from the Junior Leaders Regiment in Taunton, they were told to make their beds up and sort their shit out because they would be going on Exercise in the next couple of days. For the next three weeks Ken and the other Nig's (New in Germany) would be attached to various Troop G1098 admin trucks because they didn't have an HGV II driving licence and they wouldn't be allowed to drive a ten ton truck. They'd be working in either the 'Dixie Bash' (Pan scrubbing for the cooks) or doing guard duties and most of the menial work around the Troop location. The Sergeant in charge of Ken's G1098 was a borderline alcoholic and during the Exercise he became very abusive towards the newly arrived Drivers, when he started getting a bit physical with them Corporal Vic Northover came into the cook's tent and shouted, "I wouldn't do that if I were you Sarge, fucking leave them alone! I suggest you go to bed and sleep it off or I'm going to put you to bed myself." Although junior in rank to his Troop Sergeant, Vic was an accomplished 10 Regiment RCT boxer who could easily have 'tucked the Sergeant up', the Senior NCO did the sensible thing and backed off before Vic gave him a thick ear.

By the time Exercise Crusader started in 1980 Ken had passed his HGV II test and he was driving an AEC Mark III Militant ten tonner, Corporal Geoff Marley was his Section Commander and he accompanied Ken in the cab of his truck. During the Exercise, day and night, a constant glut of military vehicles swamped just about every road and autobahn in BAOR, it was a massive NATO Exercise and so the British army was working alongside the Dutch, German and American armed forces. On one particular night Ken was driving the fourth truck in his Section on a single carriageway road heading for Sennelager Training Area, it was a dreadful night because the rain was pelting down and another convoy of army trucks was heading in the opposite direction. The front three trucks in Geoff Marley's Section had pulled over and were driving slowly on the hard shoulder so Ken could overtake them and reassume the lead position in the convoy. The oncoming military headlights and the rain splattering on Ken's windscreen slightly muddied his vision at the time, but he could still quite clearly see some headlights coming towards him on his side of the road. A German civilian owned red Opel Kadett car was heading straight towards Ken and his military truck, inside the car was a 21 year old male driver and his 17 year old girlfriend who was facing and sitting astride him. Evidence later proved that the two lovers were heavily under the influence of alcohol and drugs at the time. A fully laden Millie with simulated ammunition on the back weighed in at about 24 tons and the two vehicles were approaching each other at a combined speed of at least 120 Mph. The car seemed to slide underneath the Millie's front bumper and forced the trucks engine up to the roof of the cab, at the same time the collision lifted the 22 ton truck off the road and partially turned it back on itself. Ken remembers hitting his head on the top of the cab and a sleeping Corporal Geoff Marley, who was resting his head on the engine cover, was thrown through the passenger side window of the cab. Within minutes of the accident a shocked Ken got out of the cab of his truck and started directing traffic in the pouring rain, he was confused at the fact that the small red car that had hit his vehicle seemed to have disappeared entirely. Due to the combined speed of the vehicles when they collided the Opel Kadett had been compacted into such a small size that even the emergency services couldn't find much trace of the car, or it occupants. A befuddled Geoff Marley was found wondering around the trees at the side of the road with a broken collar bone, he was apparently searching for the rest of his Section and trying to piece together exactly what had happened. When the military and civilian emergency services turned up at the RTA (Road Traffic Accident) both Ken and Geoff were placed into an RMP (Royal Military Police) car and were automatically afforded diplomatic immunity by the British military coppers, they were advised not to say anything to the GCP (German Civilian Police). The occupants of the Red Opel Kadett were found guilty of causing the accident whilst under the influence of drugs and alcohol, Ken was released without charge. No-one in the convoy wanted to attend the young couple's funeral because they didn't know them personally and they also didn't want to be photographed by the German press who'd try to make the British soldiers look guilty or flippant. A smile can be interpreted as a smirk and a frown can be seen as an admission of guilt.

Innocent of the horrific RTA on Exercise Crusader Ken wasn't overwhelmed by the accident, but nonetheless, he was still involved in a very traumatic experience which resulted in the death of two young people, his luck didn't seem to have improved several months later. After quite a heavy drinking session downtown in Bielefeld, Ken and his mate were arrested by the GCP (German Civilian Police) whilst they walked back to camp on Detmolder Strasse, they'd collared the pair of them because they apparently bore a remarkable resemblance to a couple of men seen causing criminal damage to some shops in a precinct. The damage amounted to about six or seven 8ft by 12ft shop windows being smashed and the perpetrators were seen to be dancing in front of the broken windows before running away. The Polizei lifted Ken and his friend and took them to the Monkey House (Royal Military Police Post) which was located at the back of Ripon Barracks. Under caution the two lads were informed about the accusations levelled against them and they replied, "We don't know what you're talking about, we haven't done anything." The monkey's (Royal Military Police) referred the case to their Commanding Officer who in turn recommended they be tried by Court Martial.

By the time the evidence had been collated Ken was serving in Girdwood Park in Northern Ireland where the British Army was under increasing pressure because of the Bobby Sands hunger strike. 36 Squadron RCT was providing transport support to all of the Belfast based units whilst 17 Squadron RCT, their sister Squadron, covered the Bandit Country down in South Armagh. Both Squadrons had bolstered their understrength ranks with Drivers drafted in from 8 Regiment RCT in Munster. The Drivers on 36 Squadrons tour in Belfast were put under increasing pressure by the RWF (Royal Welch Fusiliers) who were the roulement Infantry Battalion at that time, an escalation of violence at that time necessitated a lot of extra mobile patrols. The RCT Section in Girdwood Park was equipped with six Humber 'Pig' APC's (Armoured Personnel Carriers), four short wheel-based Makrolon armoured snatch Land Rovers, and a six wheeled Saracen Armoured Ambulance. These vehicles were used day and night 24 hours a day and in 1981 they took a great deal of punishment from the unfriendly locals. The RCT Section Commander at Girdwood Park was Corporal Tom Pate RCT and he was constantly under pressure from the Fusiliers to provide extra vehicles and Drivers that he simply didn't have, and he couldn't acquire anything extra from elsewhere. The REME (Royal Electrical and Mechanical Engineers) mechanic in location had a relentless battle trying to get parts to keep Tom's fleet of army vehicles on the road. One of the Saracen Ambulances' two tone Klaxon sirens wasn't working during this particular violent episode and the VM (Vehicle Mechanic) struggled to obtain a replacement part for it. Lance Corporal John Skinner RCT drove the battened down ambulance to pick up an injured soldier from the middle of a riot in the New Lodge area, BBC Belfast was there to record the incident and John saw the report on the 6 O'clock news later that day. Instead of the usual Klaxon siren sounds of:

Nuhr..nerr..nuhr..nerr..nuhr..nerr.

He recognised his own ambulance by its unmistakable sound of:

nerr......nerr......nerr......nerr.

John Skinner suddenly shouted out in the RCT room, "Fucking hell that's me and my ambulance." The GOC (General Officer Commanding) Northern Ireland was watching the same news report and shouted to his ADC, "Get that fucking vehicle off the road and get the damned thing fixed!" Girdwood Park's REME detachment received a new set of Klaxon sirens within twenty four hours, which only goes to prove that life moves in mysterious ways when a British Army General gets involved.

On Ken's very first mobile patrol he was working as a searcher on a VCP (Vehicle Check Point) in the White Rock area of Belfast, he and Driver 'Geordie Bolam RCT had guided a car into the search area between two 'Pigs' that were parked in the middle of the road. The very first car they stopped was driven by an elderly Irish gentleman who opened the boot of his car so it could be searched, 'Geordie' immediately noticed a powerful and unconcealed .22 calibre rifle with a telescopic sight attached, "What the fuck are you doing with this in your car feller?" The old Irishman replied, "Oy'll be shooten' rabbits wid it soir." The RUC were summoned to look at the weapon and interview the suspect, one of the Irish policeman immediately recognised the elderly gent and twatted him around the back of his head, "Seamus you silly man, how many fucking times have we told you not to bring that bloody rifle into the city with you, leave the fucking thing back at the farm. You're going to get yourself shot one of these days." They turned to Ken and said, "Sorry about that lads but he's a bit thick you know."

Note: By the 31st of December 1990 Driver 'Geordie' Bolam had been promoted to Full Corporal and was by now serving in 16 Tank Transporter Regiment RCT, on the eve of the first Gulf war starting he was sadly killed in an accident whilst loading a Challenger 2 Main Battle Tank onto his Tank Transporter.

Half way through the tour Ken and his alleged 'window breaking' mate were collected by the Squadron OC and SSM and they were transported to Hollywood Barracks where their Courts Martial was at last going to take place. Both men were locked up in the guardroom for a week to await their trial but they were soon returned to their relative locations because all hell had broken loose in Belfast. The death of Bobby Sands in the Maze Prison on the 5TH of May 1981 resulted in an escalation of the violence around the city and every pair of soldiers boots were needed on the ground. Through the visor of his 'Pig' Ken was watching a riot from the top of Lepper Street looking towards Piccadilly roundabout in the New Lodge Estate, it was dusk but in the half-light he could clearly see a group of RUC (Royal Ulster Constabulary) Officers trying to control the rioters. As one of the Officers ran from one side of the road to the other the Officer rather comically stumbled and fell over onto the tarmac, Ken laughed out loud because it reminded him of a Laurel and Hardy style gag. Some of the Officers' comrades picked him up and dragged him to the shelter of a doorway. As he laughed out loud Ken shouted, "He should be watching where he puts his feet the clumsy fucker"! An RUC Officer returned to the 'Pig' after getting a sitrep (Situation Report) on the riot, after telling the soldiers what was happening he then informed them, "That man you were all laughing at just now had just been shot dead", he then returned to the riot. Ken was silent and didn't know where to look so he hung his head in shame, during the deathly silence in his 'Pig' none of the Infantrymen had the courage to say anything either and they simply stared at their boots. Ken today still feels guilty for laughing at that RUC Officer, "When that copper told us what had happened you could have heard a pin drop in the back of my 'Pig', it was the last time I've ever laughed at someone else's misfortune".

All of the 'Pig's' 36 Squadron RCT were using on the streets of Belfast were old and decrepit because they'd originally been introduced into the British Army in 1952, because of their age they were prone to breakdowns and fuel blockages but until the new Saxon AT 105 came on the scene, they had to be endured by both RCT Drivers and the Infantry alike. The 'Pig's' had all been up-armoured which made them much heavier, but their braking system hadn't been overhauled or upgraded at all, and so the RCT Drivers were advised not to exceed a maximum speed of 20 Mph, mainly because the stopping distance at 30 Mph had increased from 30 yards to 30 days. These old battle buses weren't waterproofed either, so if it was pissing down with rain the Driver and Infantry Commander usually got a good soaking through the front and side hatches. The same problem arose when acid and petrol bombs were thrown at mobile patrols. On one occasion Ken was sitting next to an inexperienced 2nd Lieutenant from the RWF who was commanding the patrol, the naïve officer kept opening his front hatch to get a better view of the riot. Ken suddenly released the pressure in the hydraulic pump that opened the very heavy hatch and it clanged down into the closed position and knocked the officer backwards into his seat. Ken had seen some teenagers approach the left side of the 'Pig' with a collection of glass bottles and one shouted "NOW!" and the bottles were thrown at Ken's 'Pig'. The officer, who hadn't seen them, could hear the glass bottle hit his hatch after it had closed and he then sensed the smell of rotten eggs, he shouted, "What the bloody hell was that?" One of his soldiers in the back of the 'Pig' shouted "Its acid Sir! They're pelting us with acid bombs"! The youngsters followed up their attack with some petrol bombs and Ken's clothing caught fire as the flames dripped through his hatches and door, luckily a quick thinking RWF soldier in the rear of the vehicle quickly extinguished the flames before Ken was badly burned. It was because of these types of attack that each 'Pig' was equipped with three blankets, two 2kg fire extinguishers and a 20 litre water jerry-can. Ken was just 24 years old at this time and he loved the thrill of the violence and danger.

On another occasion Ken drove a 'Pig' to a bomb threat and parked his vehicle at the corner of the street, the Infantry soldiers de-bussed and staked out the area to stop anyone from entering the dangerous area. From his position Ken could clearly see the car bomb parked outside an office block in the City Centre, its doors and boot had been left open and the engine was still running. As some civilian workers came out of the office block front door the Security Forces screamed at them to go back into the building and try to find a rear exit, Ken looked around the corner of the building and was adding to the warnings when the bomb exploded. Ken explains what happened in his own words.

"As I turned and shouted for everyone to move back I saw a blinding flash of flames and heard a terrific boom as the car bomb exploded. Everything that happened in the next few seconds went into slow motion. I turned away from the bomb and a pressure wave hit me, I thought my head was going to implode so I opened my mouth to relieve the compression being exerted. By this time I was on my knees and thinking, 'This isn't good, I might be dying here'. The car's engine and other debris flew past me and I was engulfed by a choking smoke and dust cloud, the shock wave hit all of the windows in the near vicinity and glass went flying all over the street. What I didn't expect was the vacuum caused by the bomb and how it felt like my eyeballs and lungs were being sucked out of my body, during the outward phase of the explosion I couldn't breathe in because there just wasn't any air left to breath because of the overpressure. As I stood back up I saw a lot of injured people who were covered in shards of glass. A young girl about my age confronted me and asked for help but the Patrol Commander had received orders that we were to respond to a Rat Trap (the setting up of road blocks around the city at pre-planned junctions to seal off the city), he also said that the emergency Medical Services were en-route and there was nothing we could do anyway. There were several bombings all over the Province that day and although many people were injured, no-one was killed. I have often wondered what happened to that young girl back then but she obviously didn't die. I realised that one army field dressing was fuck all use when the shit hits the fan and I decided from that day on to hone my First Aid skills for the future".

A couple of days later Ken was escorting some locally employed women cleaners to New Barnsley Police Station on the Springfield road but they were being held up by more rioters who were blocking yet another road. Ken's 'Pig' was being escorted by two RUC Makrolon Land Rovers. Just before he turned into the police station Ken saw the leading and protecting Land Rover get hit in its main bodywork by an RPG (Rocket Propelled Grenade) warhead. Although the weapon exploded in the vehicle the police driver still managed to accelerate over the road junction and drive away, simply because he was cocooned in an armoured shelter within the vehicle itself. The RUC driver survived the attack but the two RUC Officers in the back of the Land Rover were killed instantly.

At the end of the tour Ken had mixed emotions about returning to Bielefeld because of the intimidating Courts Martial he'd face to try and disprove the charges against him, still, on the other hand, at least no-one would be trying to kill him in Bielefeld. During the Northern Ireland tour the Royal Welch Fusilier's recommended Ken for a GOC's commendation for services in Northern Ireland, the testimonial was for good leadership and staying calm and in control during a violent and stressful incident. Ken was surprised at the recommendation but hoped the endorsement might help his case in the military court room. At the time 10 Regiments Commanding Officer insisted that Ken and the other accused soldier weren't allowed to go on post Northern Ireland leave, they were to remain incarcerated in the guardroom until the trial started. The OC of 36 Squadron was furious at the CO's idea and his condemnation against it became so vociferous that the order was overturned. However, the two lads were only given permission to go on leave if they both, "Promise to come back again."

 The two lads did come back to Bielefeld after their leave and the trial was quite brief in comparison to the OJ Simpson case, the expensive Barrister the lads had employed spotted several discrepancies in the evidence presented against them:

a. The Polizei stated that the two lads had been arrested outside the shop windows that had been smashed but they'd actually been arrested four miles away and one hour after the incident.

b. The individual eye witness descriptions of what the two lads were wearing at the time didn't all match up in the various statements.

c. The Barrister also quizzed the RMP's that had dealt with them on the night at the RMP Post, "Did my clients have any traces of glass on their clothes and shoes?"

d. "I assume that if they were drunk whilst dancing in and out of the shop windows that they must have suffered a modicum of cuts and abrasions.

e. Did you inspect their clothing and shoes?"

The barrister started giving the two RMP's a hard time and sarcastically asked, "Are you sure you're policemen?"

Ken didn't do himself any favours at this point because someone in the court pulled a funny face at him and he started giggling, the giggles descended into guffaws of laughter and Ken was eventually ejected from the court room by the President of the Board and told to, "Sort yourself out man."

The inconsistencies in the trial evidence were brushed aside by the Senior Officers on the Courts Martial Board, both Ken and his mate were found guilty as charged and they were awarded 56 days detention and ordered to pay an astronomical amount of money in compensation to the store owners. Whilst waiting for the findings of the Court Martial to be confirmed by Brigadier Dixon, the two lads spent a total of 156 days in the Regimental jail at 10 Regiment RCT. The Brigade Commander listed his own notes on the Court Martial paperwork:

A. Why didn't the Commanding Officer of 10 Regiment RCT simply deal with this case himself?
B. There were too many inconsistencies in all of the evidence presented to the Courts Martial including eyewitness accounts.
C. It was time to bring this case to a conclusion because the whole thing had already cost the Ministry of Defence a lot of unnecessary expense.

The Brigadiers final notes stated that the Courts Martial was **'Not Confirmed'** because with all of the discrepancies he felt that both RCT soldiers were innocent of all charges. When Ken and his friend were summoned to appear on Commanding Officers Orders, the CO and RSM (Regimental Sergeant Major) venomously spat at them both, "We know you fucking well did it. But because the case hasn't been confirmed we're now instructed to give you what you want because of the time you've spent behind bars. We also need to get you both out of BAOR because the shop owners are still trying to get recompense through a civilian action" Ken requested a posting to Belize in Central America and his mate demanded a discharge from the British Army, both were given exactly what they wanted. It wasn't until Ken had started his six month posting to Belize that he suddenly thought, 'Why didn't I ask for a posting to Hong Kong? That would have been a three year posting! Oh bollocks!'

When his tour in Belize was over Ken was told to put in his preference of postings, his first choice was Hong Kong (Authors note: You've got to admire his blind cheek and fucking optimism), second choice was anywhere in the UK, and last choice was 26 Squadron in Northern Ireland. On receipt of his Posting Order to 26 Squadron the Chief Clerk told him, "You should never ask for a

Driver Ken Blake during his tour of duty in Belize.

posting to Northern Ireland on your preferences Driver Blake, because you're always guaranteed that's the one you'll get". After serving a two and a half year posting at 26 Squadron, Driver Ken Blake left the Royal Corps of Transport and was discharged from the British Army. In civilian life Ken worked as a Long Distance Lorry Driver and an Airport Airfreight worker at Heathrow Airport, he also enlisted into the TA Royal Corps of Transport after his discharge, in 1995 he eventually left the 'Territorials' after achieving the creditable rank of Sergeant. Ken now lives in Aldershot with his lovely wife Theresa who he married on 9th April 2009.

Before concluding Ken's interview for this book I earnestly asked him if he'd actually smashed those windows in the Bielefeld precinct, he just smiled at me and said, "Harry!   The Brigadier said he thought we were innocent of all charges."

24361322 Corporal George Redpath
RCT 1975 – 1994

Corporal George Redpath in his UBRE during the first Gulf War, this photograph was included in Maureen Lipman's autobiography 'When's it coming out'.

George Redpath's dad, (George Snr), joined the Royal Army Service Corps (RASC) as a boy soldier not long after the Second World War had come to a close. He enlisted as a clerk and George remembers his dad serving in Bulford, Aberdeen, and Nairobi in Kenya before being medically discharged in 1963 in the rank of Staff Sergeant. During his time in the army George Snr witnessed some of the grim realities of soldiering both in the Korean War and the Aden Conflict. His two brothers also served in the British Army, in the Black Watch and the Parachute Regiment. After leaving the army George's dad returned to Scotland where he initially worked for the Department of Social Security (DSS) where he doled out money to people who were out of work. He became angry that those receiving benefit payments were getting more money than he was earning in a Government Department, and so he left the DSS and went on the dole himself. However, George snr didn't like sitting at home all day and so he applied for a job as a Plant Maintenance Manager at Bogside Mine in the coal mining village of Oakley where he lived. Every piece of equipment that went down to the coal face had to be accounted for and safety checked before it was used, George Snr often had to go down the mine himself to check on the gear and either have it repaired or actually replaced if it had completely broken down.

In 1970 at the age of 15 years old, George Jnr told his dad that he wanted to join the British Army after leaving school, but his dad refused to sign the papers allowing him to enlist into the Junior Leaders Regiment RCT (Royal Corps of Transport). He'd only let him join-up in one of the following technical Corps, the REME (Royal Electrical and Mechanical Engineers), the Royal Signals or the Royal Engineers. George snr would only sign the entry forms if his son gained a trade from enlisting into the British Army. Unfortunately George Jnr had no interest in any of these trades and was hell-bent on being an army truck driver, he wanted to join the RCT and nothing less would do. For the next three years George Jnr worked in a garage as an apprentice panel beater and also laboured in a linen factory where he met his future wife Maureen. He joined his dad at Bogside Colliery in 1972 and after completing his training at Comrie worked at the coalface. It was during those three years that George decided he wanted to join his local Territorial Army (TA) unit which just happened to be 231 Squadron of 153 Highland Transport Regiment RCT in Dunfermline. In August 1974 he went all the way down to Bedford to do his TA Basic Training Course. George had joined the Army Cadet Force (ACF) as a schoolboy, which helped him coast through the Basic Training Course with relative ease. One thing he couldn't understand though was why they had to do Infantry training if they were going to be driving trucks for the army. His Troop Sergeant put him in the picture, "Listen son, everyone in the British Army is a soldier first, and a tradesman second. Every soldier, regardless of their trade, must be able to fight as an Infantryman."

When George finished his Basic Training he returned home and continued to turn up for every Drill Night and weekend Exercise. The unit continued to assess his attitude and commitment to the unit before putting him through his expensive HGV III Driver Training. After several months he learned to drive in a British School of Motoring (BSM) Austin Mini under the tuition of a civilian Driving Instructor, but his actual driving test was directed by an RCT Qualified Testing Officer (QTO) during one of the training weekends in barracks. George and the QTO had both jumped into an army Land Rover to begin his test when George turned to the invigilator and said, "How the fuck do I start this thing?" The Land Rover had an ignition key which turned easily enough but it would only fire up after the driver had pushed the starter button. The instructor halted the test and George had to wait for another four weeks before a Military Driving Instructor could take him through a conversion course. British Army Land Rovers then carried a spare wheel on the bonnet and a pint-sized George had trouble seeing over the top of it from the drivers' seat, so he purloined another seat cushion to raise his driving position, but this resulted in him being unable to reach the foot pedals. To solve the problem George reversed the Land Rover's sloping seat cushion so it was higher at the back and the additional cushion supported his lumbar region. He then simply removed the spare wheel for the test period during which he could clearly see where he was going (RCT Drivers were always improvising and adapting their vehicles for their own comfort and safety). George did his two week Summer Camp down at the TA Training Centre which had by now moved to Grantham in Lincolnshire, and during that fortnight he was put through his HGV III Driver Training driving a Bedford RL truck.

From the mid 1970's the National Coal Board (NCB) was being put under increasing pressure from the British Government because of the availability of cheap foreign coal imports, and George started to think about a career move out of mining and into the Regular British Army. He'd married Maureen in 1976 and their son Barry was born in 1979, but he was worried that if the British coal industry collapsed and he lost his job, he wouldn't be able to provide for his family. The Permanent Staff at 231 Squadron RCT handled George's enquiries about transferring into the Regular Army brilliantly, they answered all of his questions and the instructors encouraged him into making the move. The PSI's (Permanent Staff Instructors) even took their wives round to visit Maureen at home to explain what life was like for the Regular Army wives. Both Maureen and George had their eyes wrenched open about Regular Forces life both in the United Kingdom and on overseas tours, a few myths were also reassuringly dispelled during the advisory visits. The 'pros' side of life included postings to Germany, Cyprus, Hong Kong and Canada, the Local Overseas Allowance (LOA) meant that George's wages would be significantly higher when he was serving in the aforementioned countries, and the standard of Married Accommodation overseas was in the main, fantastic. But on the 'cons' side of army life were the facts that, firstly, the men in furry hats were on the other side of the Berlin Wall and if they attacked West Germany, then all hell would break loose in the British Army of the Rhine (BAOR) area of operations. Maureen would have to leave George in the firing line and high-tail it back to the UK with only the clothes on her back. Secondly, Maureen wouldn't get to see much of George because he would constantly be away on Field Exercises for weeks on end and when he wasn't doing that, then he'd more than likely be away on four month tours of Northern Ireland. George and Maureen had to make a decision. When George had started as a miner there were forty four working pits in the Fife area alone, but by 1980 there were only fourteen left. George and Maureen could see what was happening and they decided to transfer into the Regular RCT before the inevitable happened, it was a no brainer really.

George snr and the Bogside Colliery Manager both tried to talk George Jnr out of going into the Regular Army because he was due to go to university, the pit manager almost guaranteed George Jnr that he would eventually become a pit manager himself, "You have a real future in this industry George, you'd be better off staying with the National Coal Board." And the rest is history as they say. 153 Highland Transport Regiments' Commanding Officer, Regimental Sergeant Major and their Instructors were all Regular Army RCT and they couldn't have been more helpful and supportive to George had they tried. In August 1980 George handed in his notice to the National Coal Board and within a week he was down at Buller Barracks in Aldershot doing his Regular Army RCT Basic Training, George retained his TA Service Number throughout the rest of his Regular Army career. He was already trained on the SLR (7.62 mm Self Loading Rifle) and the LMG (Light Machine Gun), he knew how to march and what was expected of him as a soldier and Driver, and not least, he was already a fully trained HGV III Driver. Because of his previous TA experience Driver George Redpath was deemed to be a TSA (Trained Soldier Available), so after everyone had passed their usual Friday afternoon BFT (Basic Fitness Test) three mile run, the squad got ready for the following weeks weapon training whilst Driver George Redpath was sent home on leave for two weeks, the weapon instructors at Buller had nothing else to teach him.

After a relaxing two weeks leave, George travelled back to Aldershot and joined up with the rest of his intake. The recruits were being sent up to Grantham Training Centre to start on the Driver Training Phase of their military training (a few Regular Army Driver Training Courses utilised the Grantham TA Camp in an effort to try and keep the barracks open). The squad travelled up to Lincolnshire on a white 39 seater army coach. The first soldier George met at the TA Barracks was the QTO who had taken him on his HGV III test! The Warrant Officer said, "Hiya George, what the fuck are you doing back here?" After explaining about transferring into the Regulars, the QTO re-assessed George on the Monday morning in a Bedford RL and then sent him home on another weeks leave whilst the other lads continued with their Driver Training. George returned to Grantham after his leave and then travelled back to Aldershot with the rest of the recruits on another 'White Elephant' army coach. Whilst waiting for a posting order, George and another RCT Junior NCO from Buller Barracks were sent up to a Newcastle Police Station to collect and escort an RCT prisoner back to Buller Barracks. The Driver had been Absent With-Out Leave (AWOL) and he would eventually be sent to the Military Corrective Training Centre (MCTC) in Colchester. After handing his detainee over to the Regimental Police (RP) Staff at Buller Barracks Guardroom, George and the other soldiers on his Course were sent home on leave for two weeks prior to being allocated their first Regular Army posting. George thought to himself, 'This Regular Army stuff is great, I spend most of my time on leave and they pay me for doing it', when he turned up on the door at home Maureen said, "Good grief, are you home **again**"!

When he reported back to Buller Barracks two weeks later he was given a Posting Order to 11 Squadron RCT, which was part of 4 Armoured Division Transport Regiment RCT (4 ADT Regt RCT) based in Minden. The Chief Clerk said, "Here's a rail warrant Driver Redpath. I want you to go home on leave for three weeks." George was incredulous that the British Army was going to send him on leave for the fourth time in only three months. He reported to his local TA Centre in Dunfermline and collected some Military Freight Organisation (MFO) boxes. The storeman recognised George and enquired, "Hiya mate, how's things going in the Regulars?" George honestly told him, "It's fucking brilliant mate, they keep sending me on leave!" The Redpath's sold the majority of their electrical stuff like the washing machine and fridge and they also found a buyer for the family car because they were flying out to BAOR courtesy of a British Airways chartered flight. At the RAF processing Centre in Hendon, George met up with Driver Alex McNichol RCT who had been a recruit on George's Basic Training Course. It transpired that not only were they both heading for 11 Squadron RCT, they were also allocated Married Quarter flats opposite each other in Humboldt Strasse, Minden, West Germany.

A Corporal met the new arrivals at the unit Guardroom in Minden and took them to their apartments which a unit representative had already taken over for them. The NCO said, "Right, unpack your suitcases and then come round to my flat because my wife is cooking dinner for you all." On arrival at the Corporals' flat everyone was offered a nice cold beer from the fridge, this is Standard Operating Procedure (SOP) expected of soldiers whenever you visited them in their Married Quarter. Maureen refused the beer saying, "Oh no thanks, it's far too early in the day for me." The Corporal then came out with another SOP statement which always followed the refusal of beer in a BAOR Married Quarter, "Oh come on you miserable cow, have a drink." Apparently, if you call a women a Cow in Scotland it is tantamount to calling her a whore and Maureen naturally flew off the handle. The Corporal dived for cover as George stepped in between them and tried to explain to Maureen that it was purely army banter and that no offence was meant. It's a bizarre life in the British Army and it can take a while getting used to its strange customs and traditions. On the 14th of November 1980, George dutifully reported into the Headquarters of 11 Squadron RCT where he was told, unbelievably, to go on leave for another week in order to help Maureen settle into their new Married Quarter. When he got home Maureen said, "I don't believe it, you've been given more leave. Are you ever going to do some bloody work?"

The 11 Squadron RCT Christmas duty list was published on Part One Orders at least a week before the leave period began and George noticed his name had been put down for Guard Duty on Christmas Day. On Christmas Day morning after the Orderly Sergeant had inspected the guard, he asked if there were any married soldiers on duty that day. George proved (smartly lifted his right arm from the elbow) and said, "Yes Sergeant, I am." Because the British Army didn't want wives and children to be inconvenienced over the Christmas period it was general policy that all married soldiers didn't have to do any duties on this, the most holy of religious holidays. George was sent home on leave yet again. Some of the 'singlies' took a different view of this policy because it meant they would have to cover every duty on the camp whilst the 'Pads' had their feet up at home.

When the Squadron returned from their Post Northern Ireland leave, George was put into A Troop along with other soldiers who'd been on the Rear Party. Drivers 'Big Skip' Kilford, Sid Leather-Barrow, Keith 'Scouse' Lyons and Ian Biggins were all put on the next available Truck Tanker Fuel (TTF) and Unit Bulk Refuelling Equipment (UBRE) Course which was run by Staff Sergeant Roy Last RCT. These lads were going to be trained how to operate and drive the Squadrons refuelling equipment and vehicles. Prior to doing the TTF Course George did his HGV II Driver Training. On his test day George drove around Soltau training area in an antiquated Mk 1 AEC Militant which was loaded with an Eager Beaver on the back. The truck had been designed and built just after the Second World War and was affectionately referred to as an 'Old

Knocker' by all RCT Drivers. On the final part of his TTF Course George was taught how to drive a modern 12,500 Litre Foden Tanker which, after driving the 'Old Knocker', George described as, "Going from an old stock car to driving a luxurious Bentley." The Foden's were fast and had modern brakes, tilting cabs and powered steering. In comparison the 'Old Knockers' were at best sluggish, they also had immovable everything, leaking windows and cupola covers, and an unpowered and bench pressing steering system that felt like it exceeded 190 lbs in resistance. Over the next two years George did stints on Exercise, driving both TTF's and UBRE's, he also worked in the Squadrons' SQMS store and the MT Office before becoming an 11 Squadron driving instructor. The OC of the Squadron promoted George to Lance Corporal in quick time because of his maturity, confidence, bearing and previous TA experience and qualifications. (Note: Compare this to Staff Sergeant Les Reed's experiences when he joined the Regulars from the TA.)

In June 1982 George deployed with the rest of A Troop on the second of their six week detachments to British Army Training Unit Suffield (BATUS) in Canada where the Squadron was providing logistic support on Exercise Med Man 2. Driver Ronnie Drew RCT was George's co-driver on his allocated Bedford MK 4 tonner UBRE, George even remembers its Registration Number - 41 GB 41. On the 11th of June, Ronnie drove the fuel truck along Rattlesnake Road heading out onto the Prairie whilst George used his privately owned 8mm cine-camera to record some of his experiences on Exercise in Canada. Just after he'd stopped filming George noticed a low flying Gazelle helicopter from 3 Regiment AAC (Army Air Corps) flying overhead and within seconds he heard an almighty explosion as the helicopter plummeted into the crest of a hill. The aircraft crashed at an estimated 116 Knots (130 mph) and cart-wheeled before catching fire, the helicopter was carrying the Pilot, an Observer and 4 ADTR's very own Padré. The AAC Observer was sitting in the rear seat, allowing the Chaplain to sit up front in the left hand position next to the pilot, by doing this the 'man of God' would have a better view and experience during the flight, unfortunately he was killed when a detached aircraft battery hit him during the crash. The AAC pilot and Observer suffered from multiple injuries and after being hospitalised for many months they went through a lengthy recovery process.

The Padré wasn't the only fatality on Exercise Med Man 2 because Lance Corporal Louis Williams of the 1st Battalion Royal Welch Fusiliers was killed only the day before. On large scale military Exercises fatalities are a way of life for soldiers but the majority of them are due to Road Traffic Accidents (RTA's). Louis Williams was actually shot in the chest during a live firing Exercise whilst out on the Canadian prairie. This was apparently the first fatality of its kind on the BATUS Training Area and a Board of Inquiry fully investigated the incident to find out what had happened. Soldiering is a very dangerous profession even on Training Exercises which became evident whilst George was travelling in yet another 'replen' convoy out on the prairies. The RCT trucks were met as they approached the Infantry location by the units' Captain Quartermaster (QM), for safety reasons the QM was in constant radio contact with his own unit. The QM had to meet the convoy outside of his location because the area was protected by several live minefields, (the British Army doesn't fuck about when they play war games), and he was there to guide the truckies through the dangerous labyrinth. After climbing into the leading Land Rover the QM gave the RCT Driver directions on where he should and shouldn't drive, but after twenty minutes he became lost and had to radio his unit for guidance. As it turned out, the QM had guided the convoy into the middle of a live minefield and he gave shouted instructions for everyone to remain inside their vehicles. The average temperature on the prairies in Batus that year reached over 40 degrees and the Drivers on the convoy could do nothing but sit and wait for a Royal Engineer (RE) Mine Detection Team to mark a clear exit path for them. As they sweated it out in the cabs of their vehicles the lads spotted plenty of red topped safety helicopters and vehicles buzzing all around them. It took nearly four hours for the grinning RE Sappers to guide the ten RCT wagons out of the minefield, one at a time.

George asked for a couple of extensions to his posting in 4 ADTR and he eventually served in Minden from 1980 until 1986. His application for a third tour was turned down though and instead he was given a posting to 60 Squadron RCT in Catterick, North Yorkshire. A year prior to being given this posting, George had been sent on a Fire NCO's Course with the Defence Fire Agency (DFA) in Blackdown Barracks near Aldershot. The two week Course was held during the winter period and George was kindly invited to spend the weekend at Corporal Martin 'Willie' Rushton's Army Married Quarter in Willems Park, Aldershot. Martin's maisonette accommodation had been built in 1964 and it was just one of the appalling dwellings that soldiers and their families in Aldershot Garrison had to live, several murders had actually been committed near these unspeakably gloomy homes. The massive complex was drab and depressing to look at and even if the British Army had invested £10Bn on improving the development, it would still have remained a dreary and miserable slum. The weekend that George stayed with his RCT friend Martin and his wife Bianca, he noticed that the inside of the bedroom windows were covered in ice and he told his friend, "I hope that Maureen and I are never posted to this God forsaken place."

After packing up his Married Quarter in Minden, George was called in for an interview with 11 Squadrons Admin Officer (AO) who told him his posting had been cancelled. He was now posted to 8 Squadron, 27 Log Support Regiment RCT in Aldershot. George told his AO, "Oh bollocks! I'm not going there Sir, and anyway my boxes are already packed and addressed to go to 60 Squadron." George was given a couple of sweeteners at the same time though when the AO informed him that the posting included a promotion to full Corporal, and that his new Squadron would be doing a six month UN tour of Cyprus not long after he arrived. Several days later George was informed that he and his family had been allocated a Married Quarter on the second floor in Willems Park. He told Maureen, "You're not going to like this place love." George was quite right, Maureen hated the place and so his brother John helped move all their stuff into storage and she stayed up in Scotland whilst George was away in Cyprus. Despite his prolific qualifications and experience in the TTF and UBRE Role, George was assigned the job of Bus Driver by his Section Commander, Corporal Mo Yoseuf RCT. To qualify for this technically challenging post George simply had to drive a 55 seater coach up and down Nicosia airfield and around the local town for two days before gaining his coach licence. George says, sardonically, "I was awarded my United Nations (UN) medal for driving Forces children to school and taking soldiers on skiing trips up to the Troodos Mountains in an army bus, George always refers to the UN Medal as his Bus Drivers Badge.

George hated Aldershot with a passion and when the unit returned from Cyprus he volunteered to go on every available Exercise because Maureen was still up in Scotland with her parents. In 1987 the South of England suffered from a horrendous storm not long after 8 Squadron had returned from a post Cyprus Exercise. George gave up his free time to clear the roads of trees and other debris using one of the units JCB's (the JCB superseded the Eager Beaver fork lift truck before it went completely out of service). He also deployed on **Exercise Purple Warrio**r (See Corporal Ric Spur chapter, Ric did his last ever military parachute jump on this Exercise) which took place in South West Scotland and was designed to test out the military lessons learned from the Falklands War in 1982. It was the UK's biggest military training deployment since the end of the Second World War, involving all of the UK's Armed Forces. The Exercise incorporated the use of:

Corporal George Redpath – UN Bus Driver

Royal Navy (RN)
Apart from contributing 28 Royal Navy and Royal Fleet Auxiliary (RFA) ships the Dark Blue Jobs also provided:
12 Sea Harriers
29 Sea King Helicopters
6 Lynx Helicopters
8 Gazelle Helicopters

The Light Blue Jobs supplied the following aircraft.

Royal Air Force (RAF)
15 C130 Hercules Aircraft
6 Buccaneer's

6 Jaguar's
6 Harrier's
4 Phantom's
2 Nimrod's
2 Canberra's
2 VC 10 Airliners
4 Chinook Helicopters
3 Puma Helicopters

The real work was done by the ground troops, as usual, and they were made up of 5 Airborne, 3 Commando and 1 Infantry Brigades who were in turn supported by soldiers of the:
Royal Horse Artillery (RHA)
Royal Engineers (RE)
Royal Signals (Signals)
Army Air Corps (AAC)
Royal Army Medical Corps (RAMC)
Royal Army Ordnance Corps (RAOC)
Royal Electrical and Mechanical Engineers (REME)
Royal Military Police (RMP)
Royal Pioneer Corps (RPC)
and most important of all, soldiers of the Royal Corps of Transport (RCT).

To cut a long story short, 'This was a fucking big Exercise.'

The RCT and RE's provided nearly two thousand vehicles, ranging from Land Rovers and Heavy Goods Vehicles as well as Heavy Plant equipment. George did some re-fuelling work on the exercise helicopters and also collected the deployed parachutes after elements of 5 Airborne Brigade had landed on their Drop Zone (DZ). In the latter half of the Exercise, George and another RCT Lance Corporal were summoned back to Aldershot for OC's Orders. Neither of them had any idea why the Squadron Commander wanted to interview them. It was night-time before they arrived back in barracks and after pressing their kit and bulling their boots, the lads got their heads down ready to face the boss in the morning. Even though George knew he'd previously been recommended for promotion, he and the other Lance Corporal were still surprised when the OC congratulated them and handed over two sets of full Corporal stripes. The Major asked George, "Where would you like to be posted to Corporal Redpath?" George tried to wangle one of the usual dream postings of Canada,

Cyprus or Hong Kong but he eventually settled on a posting to 1 Armoured Division Transport Regiment RCT (1 ADTR Regt RCT) based in Bunde, West Germany. Maureen's brother, Driver Michael Ritchie RCT (later WO2 TCWO), was already based in Bunde with 33 Squadron RCT and the family ties were too strong to resist. 1 ADTR was made up of four RCT Squadrons, 2 Squadron, 4 Squadron, 33 and finally 74 Squadron, which was where George was sent as a Section Commander.

During his time in the army George was a conscientious supporter of the RAOB (Buffs) which is an organisation that contributes funds to charity, he took part in one particular fund raising event when he cycled from Hamburg to Bielefeld. The journey was over 150 miles long and ended when he and his fellow Buffs cycled into the 10 Regt RCT camp gates in Bielefeld, the title of this book says it all really, 'most roads do lead to 10 Regt'. Within two years George was getting bored of doing the same old Exercises over and over again and so he started looking for a different job. He'd already completed his Senior Military Qualification Course (SMQC) and Education for Promotion Certificate (EPC) Courses and was ready for promotion to Sergeant. Word got around the unit that the Regimental Provost Sergeant (RP Sgt) was being posted and the idea of his job really appealed to George. The post was a Monday to Friday appointment without having to do any night duties or Field Training Exercises, a piece of piss as far as George was concerned. His primary concern as 1 ADTR's Provost Sergeant was the security of the camp, the Regimental Policemen (RP's) that worked for him and any prisoners that had been placed in his custody. He would answer solely to the Regimental Sergeant Major (RSM) and would report to him every morning with the previous nights' Guard Commander. The duty personnel would deliver a verbal report on any of the previous night's incidents and George would be briefed on anything that was happening on the camp that day.

George had to attend a two week course at the Military Corrective Training Centre (MCTC) in Colchester before taking over as the Provost Sergeant. He was promoted to the rank of Acting Sergeant before leaving for the Course. In Colchester he shared a two man room with a Gurkha Corporal who wasn't very fluent in English. The Nepalese NCO struggled with the amount of information on the course syllabus and most evenings saw George and his room-mate going over their notes and reiterating everything they'd learned during the days' lessons. The Course in 1989 incorporated routines to be followed if a prisoner escapes from his cell, how to deal with female prisoners and the wives of prisoners, which prisoners should be segregated, how to deal with soldiers who are attending an ROP (Restriction of Privileges) Parade, what they can/cannot be made to do and how harsh they can be treated after eating a full meal (apparently a prisoner cannot be marched at double time for at least one hour after consuming a meal). Authors note: Yeah I know, I can hear every soldier who has ever done a bit of porridge laughing at that rule. The students on the Course also had to go through the process of giving a full body search to several inmate volunteers. Because the prisoners agreed to have a full body search for training purposes, their sentences were considerably reduced. Quite an incentive for having a finger shoved up your bum I suppose. It should be pointed out that the student was wearing a marigold glove daubed in lashings of KY Jelly before instigating the inspection. By military law an RAMC Medic and witness had to be in attendance during any full body search in a Service prison cell. Even the underside of a prisoners' foreskin was inspected and any sticking plasters removed in case drugs were concealed underneath them. If the plaster was covering a genuine wound then the RAMC Medic was on site to re-dress the wound. The Curriculum at Colchester was an All Arms Course that even Royal Navy and Royal Air Force personnel attended. All aspects of Queens Regulations and Military Law were covered in depth and George found this heavy going at times, his Ghurkha room-mate struggled quite significantly. At the end of the Course, four outstanding students were given the option of permanently transferring into the MPSC. George and another RCT Corporal from 10 Regiment RCT were two of them, George turned down the offer because it would mean being permanently based at Colchester Garrison.

On return to 1 ADTR George retained his Acting Sergeant's Stripe and took over the job as Provost Sergeant for about one year before the First Gulf War kicked off. Unfortunately George returned to his previous rank of Corporal and he deployed with 33 Squadron RCT in his war time role as a UBRE Section Commander. George was quite happy to go off and fight in an uncertain war that could easily have escalated into a chemical warfare scenario, he'd been trained to do a job and this was his time to prove his mettle. Over the years he'd repeatedly done the training and this was similar to a civilian doing a City and Guilds examination. It was a simple pass or fail exam to see if they could do what they had been trained to do, unfortunately some of the Squadrons' soldiers wouldn't be coming home alive.

The Squadrons' vehicles all had to be painted in desert camouflage colours. Three spray-teams were set up to work in eight hour shifts to get the job completed, plenty of sand coloured paint and paint brushes were also made available so Drivers could help get into the awkward places on each truck and add the finishing touches. Other teams were set up to service every vehicle before they were shipped out to Saudi Arabia and of course each Driver was responsible for doing the day to day maintenance and prep work just as they did before going on Exercise in BAOR. Light bulbs, coolant levels and tyre pressures all had to be checked and each truck had to be issued with the necessary accoutrements like tool kits, vehicle jacks, First Aid kits, tow bars, slave leads, scrim nets, poles and hessian skirts. George's Section was made up of two UBRE Bedford MK refuelling trucks (one was loaded with Benzine (petrol) and the other diesel). A JCB accompanied them on most of their refuelling missions in the desert. When George requested a new hard type cupola cover for his Bedford MK because the existing canvas one leaked every time it poured with rain, he was told, "You won't need one Corporal Redpath. You'll be operating in a desert environment and it doesn't rain out there," (proving that RCT Troop Staff Sergeant's really don't know everything). As it turned out, just about everyone in the RCT wanted new cupola covers and every other accoutrement that the Royal Army Ordnance Corps (RAOC) couldn't supply simply because there just wasn't enough of everything required. George fixed the leak problem himself using an old green waterproof poncho which he attached to the cupola with several bungees. It became a bit of a pain every time the Section needed Top Cover on a mission because it had to be removed from the outside of the vehicle. None the less, the Heath Robinson contraption worked to a degree.

1 ADTR flew from RAF Gütersloh, West Germany and were accommodated in Al Jubail to give them time to acclimatise to the heat prior to picking up their trucks from the port. Initially the RCT Drivers just drove any vehicle off the ships and collected their own wagon later after everything had been unloaded, before forming up as part of 7 Armoured Brigade (7 Armd Bde). Each crew wanted the vehicle they'd prepped back in Bunde because their own truck held pre-packed home comforts like cigarettes, sweets, favourite tins of food, reading material, and in George's case, rolls of comfy bum toilet paper, rolls of black masking tape, and plenty of batteries for his personal radio and torches. George's Section 2 i/c was a guy called Lance Corporal Bob Robbins who drove and commanded the petrol UBRE in their small detachment. On Christmas Day during the build up to the war, George and Bob had an argument that led to fisticuffs between the pair of them. Even though it was Christmas Day someone still had to cover the sentry duties whilst other troops enjoyed

their dinner. On this particular day even the Senior NCO's and Officers were standing guard. Bob took great umbrage though at the length of time he was left on stag whilst everyone else was enjoying themselves in the Mess Tent. He remonstrated and embarrassed George in front of everyone in the Mess Tent as he shouted and moaned about the way he'd been treated. Bob had to be pulled back into line and George needed to reassert his authority. Punches were thrown and the two were pulled apart before it escalated into a more serious RCT punch-up. This fracas would have a worrying consequence for George with the Special Investigation Branch (SIB) of the RMP's when the war actually started.

During the deployment, Bob and George continued to work happily together as Section Commander and 2i/c but he was given a succession of co-drivers like Driver Eaddie Reeves, Driver 'Arnie' Arnold, Driver Dave Rattery (a man who lived only a couple of miles away from George in Fife) and young Driver 'Squeaky' Hodgkinson who was a particularly nervous lad. 'Squeaky' was given to George because the Squadron Sergeant Major (SSM), WO2 Scotty Traynor, thought that the more mature George would be a nurturing and calming influence on the young lad, a bit of a father figure. The Squadrons' TTF's and UBRE's were parked up a safe distance from the rest of the Troop because if the fuel wagons were hit with tracer ammunition, then all of the Troops vehicles and Drivers could be decimated in one attack. George and his Section made up just part of Zulu Troop which was operating in support of fifty seven Challenger Tanks of the Royal Scots Dragoon Guards (RSDG).

Each wagon had to be a home from home for the RCT Truckies and so George set up a lean-to shelter on the side of his vehicle using some poles, a sheet of canvas, and some bungees. He also asked a REME Mechanic to help him construct an improvised shower system for the Section, using a fire bucket and shower head. Space in the cabs of each wagon was limited because the Drivers had to find space for personal weapons, water, rations, sleeping bags, personal webbing, respirators and radios. They also had to find space for five magazines of ammunition for each soldiers 7.62mm Self Loading Rifle (SLR), several L2 Hand Grenades, hundreds of boxed spare rounds of ammunition and at least two 66mm Light Anti-tank Weapons (LAW's). The cab of an RCT truck wasn't a 'Doctor Who' TARDIS, but the Drivers tried to fill it as if it had the same internal cubic capacity of space. Drivers were ordered to scrim up their wagons every time they parked up, which seemed strange because the US Coalition Forces weren't bothering. And when it came to driving in convoy at night, the lead wagon had only its front side lights switched on and a right angled army torch with a red lens attached to the rear of the truck. Each subsequent truck didn't use any lights at all except for a similar torch secured to the back of each truck. When the convoy set off the Drivers concentrated on following the small dim red light ahead of them. Sounds easy enough, but the concentration levels required were phenomenal because the following drivers had no idea if the wagon ahead was slowing down or had stopped entirely because the brake light system had been switched off for convoy security.

Drivers in 33 Squadron RCT were advised to remove the windscreens from their trucks to avoid facial and eye injuries from shattered glass if they were caught near a bomb blast. George and his Section refused to comply with the order because it just didn't seem to make any sense. Any barrier between them and a bomb blast would be better than trying to deflect debris and shockwaves with just the naked eye or a pair of cheap plastic goggles. On one particular mission to refuel some tanks in the Forward Battle Group, George spoke to a Scottish Tankie called Trooper Tom Strachan as he refuelled his Challenger Tank.

Authors note: I apologise unreservedly for my Scottish style interpretation of two Scotsmen engaged in a conversation.

Tom: "Areeght parl, howse it goowin en'at?"

George: "Aye, noo so bahd en'at. Howse yersell?"

Tom: "Oh aye, ahm noo soo bahd mesell en'at."

George: "Arghhg greet en'at. Listen parl, day yer ken hoo fargh we arrrghe fray the frunt laine en'at?"

Tom: "Aye. Whell whay doont yer get yersell oop here pal awnd hay a wee look fur yersell."

George climbed up onto the turret of the Challenger Tank and stood next to the Trooper who pointed towards the North and over the built up defensive embankment around the Tank.

Tom: "Noow pal, yew see thart wee flag just ower theere?"

George: "Aye."

Tom: "Wheell, thart's wheere the Iraqi Army are camped reet noo parl."

George: "Oooh fuck."

Tom: "Ooh fuck aye pal."

On each mission George's UBRE could refuel about fifteen Challenger Tanks before having to return to the 12,500 litre TTF mother ships to refill the UBRE's storage tanks (the Challenger Tank is a very thirsty beast). George would remain at the front, scrimmed up, and waiting for another re-fill mission. Most RCT UBRE's also accommodated plenty of passing trade because every motorcycle, Land Rover, four and eight ton TM trucks needed to be refuelled time and again. In the very words of Winston Churchill, "War is like a flower, and without transport as its stem, it can never blossom." George's Section even resupplied some American Ground Forces who were desperately short of fuel and they sometimes had to rely on the RCT to keep the wheels and tracks of the United State Army turning.

Coalition Forces started a five week naval and aerial pre-invasion bombardment on the 17th of January 1991. The Ground Assault started on the 24th of February. The night before the liberation of Kuwait began George and his SSM, WO2 'Scotty' Traynor, watched in amazement at the mass of MLRS Multiple Launch Rocket System (MLRS) ammunition being fired off towards the Iraqi Army. George's 2 i/c, Lance Corporal Bob Robbins, was asleep in the cab of his UBRE when the Ground War started and Corporal Alex Gray tried to wake him for an early morning 'replen' mission, whilst giving Bob a shake Alex noticed a pile of vomit next to his friends face. It was obvious he'd been dead for hours because his body was cold and stiff. Assistance was summoned from the nearest Medical unit and an ambulance arrived with two Ghurkha soldiers. The two Ghurkhas gently lifted Bob's lifeless form out of the Bedford MK truck and placed him into a body bag. The RMP's informed 33 Squadron that the vehicle was to be treated as a scene of crime and nothing should be moved until the SIB detectives were on site.

Everyone in the Squadron was questioned about what they knew about Bob and if they had witnessed anything suspicious the previous evening. George went through the following inquisition.

Authors note: I've used the common literary abbreviation for a military detective for no other reason than the fact it is quicker to write this way. I have not used the term 'Dick' to get a cheap laugh:

SIB Dick: "Apparently you and Lance Corporal Robbins didn't always see eye to eye Corporal Redpath."

George: "Bob and I got on alright most of the time I suppose, just like everyone else in the Squadron."

SIB Dick: "Perhaps you'd like to tell us about your fight with him on Christmas Day then, because that doesn't sound like two blokes getting on together."

George: "That was nothing really, he got a bit narked about the time he'd spent on stag before getting his Christmas dinner, just handbags at twenty paces really."

SIB Dick: "He owed you money didn't he?"

George: "Yes, about 100 Saudi Riyals, but I wasn't worried about that because I knew Bob would give it back to me at some stage or other."

SIB Dick: "I've been told you still have his 'Eagles' music tape. Did you refuse to give it back until he repaid the money he owed you?"

George: "No, certainly not."

SIB Dick: "So, let's look at what we know about you and your 'supposed' friend Lance Corporal Bob Robbins. You'd had a fight on Christmas Day, he owed you money, you refused to return his music tape and there are plenty of rumours in the Squadron about you not liking him."

A 19 year old 2nd Lieutenant Troop Commander was in attendance during the entire interview and he didn't give any support to George at all. George turned to the Troop Commander and shouted:

George: "Sir! I'm not taking this shit anymore, it sounds like they're accusing me of murder. Bob and I had our differences but we got on well for the majority of the time. Do me a favour Lieutenant, fuck off and get 'Scotty' Traynor, the SSM, for me."

When the SSM entered the tent George said:

George: "Sir, I could be done for murder at this rate and this little shit isn't giving me any support at all. I need your help sir."

The SIB Dicks continued with their preposterous questioning and 'Scotty' Traynor interjected immediately.

SSM: "Why the hell are you asking such fucking stupid questions? The lads worked together and got on fine, now fuck off and let my blokes get on with their part of the war!"

George went back to his Section and passed through the Burm (a high sand bank that designated the border between the coalition and Iraqi Forces). As he crossed into the Iraq desert he heard a very loud explosion as a Kuwaiti Forces 4X4 Toyota Land Cruiser drove over a small land mine and had its front wheel blown off. Everyone immediately masked up because it may well have been a chemical attack. The convoy had to circumnavigate the now disabled Toyota because the war waited for no man. After driving on for a few more kilometres everyone did a bastardised version of the 'sniff test' before taking their respirators off. Young Driver 'Squeaky' Hodgkinson was driving George's UBRE at the time and he very nearly drove into the only civilian road sign in the desert. After doing an eighteen hour refuelling operation out in the desert, an extremely tired George reported back to 33 Squadrons laager area where he hoped to get some shut eye for a few hours. He was told, "Report to the Command Post (CP) mate, you're on Guard Commander for the next twelve hours".

The First Gulf War only lasted for four days and during that phase George experienced the longest time, apart from cat naps, that he'd ever gone without sleep. He actually stayed awake for forty four straight hours whilst either driving, commanding, or refuelling an assortment of tanks, trucks, Land Rovers and motorcycles. The UBRE Drivers often changed places with their co-drivers without even stopping. The driver would semi stand up and move to the left side of the steering wheel whilst the co-driver would slide underneath him and into the Drivers' seat before taking control of the truck. It was a common practice on Exercises in BAOR and had been done many times before in Land Rovers, Bedford MK's and of course the old AEC Militant ten ton trucks. RASC/RCT Driver's in BAOR had been practicing this sort of drill since 1965, and the RLC are probably still doing it today. Even though George was exhausted through lack of sleep and his constant workload, he still suffered from a common RCT Soldiers' disorder called 'Convoy Cock.' If you combined the endlessly long hours of vehicle vibrations when driving, a bored squaddie mind that easily deviates onto sex, and add these ingredients to the fact that the RCT Drivers hadn't seen their wives/girlfriends (in some cases both) for a while, it would often lead to Drivers being plagued with an irritating penile erection, bulging at the front of their combat trousers. An RCT soldiers' knob has always worked efficiently even under the strain of combat, physical exhaustion and even SIB interrogations.

At the end of hostilities, George's Section was ordered to turn south and head back towards Kuwait because the Iraqi Army had been defeated and its soldiers were now fleeing north to Basra. It was like travelling at night on the journey south because the retreating Iraqi soldiers had set fire to the oil wells and the thick black smoke was blotting out the sunshine. After turning back, George travelled down the now famous six lane 'Basra Highway of Death', the motorway ran all the way from Kuwait City up to Basra in Iraq. Two days earlier an Iraqi Scud missile (a notably inaccurate and unguided ballistic weapon) had by chance hit a US Army barracks in Dhahran killing twenty eight US Army Quartermaster personnel, the explosion also seriously injured one hundred other American soldiers. United States Air Force and Marine Corps aircraft took no pity on the retreating Iraqi Army because of this perceived slaughter of rear-echelon military personnel. The US aircraft destroyed nearly 2000 vehicles and left hundreds of dead Iraqis along Highways 8 and 80. The American pilots initially wiped out the leading and trailing elements of the retreating Iraqi vehicles which boxed the rest of them into concentrated killing zones along the Highways. Unfortunately, a lot of the casualties in the mass vehicle exodus weren't soldiers and the majority of those killed and maimed were reportedly women and children. George was disgusted by some of the scenes he witnessed on Highway 80. There were burnt cadavers and fragmented bits of human wreckage everywhere he looked. It's a cliché often used by actors playing soldiers who have seen death and destruction, but after witnessing the devastation around him, George really did think to himself, 'Why?' Some of his comrades photographed the gruesome scenes around them whilst displaying a façade of cold heartedness about what they were viewing, but for the majority it was exactly that, a façade.

The Highways were littered with burnt out vehicles which meant that maintaining convoy discipline was virtually impossible as each unit weaved in and out of the wreckage. At some point along the journey south each small convoy was told to park up and put out sentries, they then had to 'Wait Out' until given further orders. George's convoy consisted of six vehicles and twelve Drivers so he put two guards out on hour long stags. Whilst on his stag George noticed a slowly moving white mirage on the horizon and it seemed to be walking towards their location. As the illusion got closer and closer, George suddenly realised his apparition consisted of approximately a dozen Iraqi soldiers all walking in arrowhead formation, the one at the front was waving an unfurled toilet roll on the end of a stick. The bedraggled and thoroughly defeated soldiers all had their hands raised in the air. They were dirty, unshaven and clearly traumatised, and some didn't even have boots on their feet. The leading soldier was shouting, "Please, no fight. No shoot…please." As the pathetic soldiers entered George's location an RCT Troop Commander stepped forward shouting, "Right, who saw them first and was a declaration issued to the one in charge? I need to know if anyone from our Troop fired any shots." George was tired and irritated, he turned towards the TC and shouted, "With all due respect Sir, why don't you fuck off! Do they look like they're up for a fight for fucks sake?" The TC was adamant that certain procedures must be adhered to. "A declaration should have been made to the prisoners, Corporal Redpath, and I need to send a detailed report up through the chain of command." George reported to WO2 'Scotty' Traynor and said, "You'd better get a grip of him sir or someone's going to drop him."

George was eventually sent back to Bunde on the Advance Party after hostilities had ended and so he left the clean-up and handover of his UBRE, in the capable hands of his co-driver, Driver 'Squeaky' Hodgkinson RCT. After enjoying a bit of post operational leave George was reinstated as the RP Sergeant for about twelve months. During this time the unit held an auction for Lance Corporal Bob Robbins the 33 Squadron soldier who had died out in Iraq. The deceased soldiers' military equipment was auctioned off and all the money raised was sent to his next of kin. George paid fifty Deutsche Marks for Bob's plastic water bottle and carrier whilst someone else paid a lot of money for his car. The lads who deployed were aggrieved that only the Rear Party could attend Bob's funeral because the Squadron (Main) was still out in Iraq at the time.

Within a year George was to be one of many soldiers selected for the first stage of redundancies to hit the British Army in 1992. He didn't want to leave the army and was given options of transferring into the RAOC, MPSC or RMP. The redundancy offer felt like a kick in the teeth for George even though his Commanding Officer and Squadron Commander both fought to retain him within the Corps. The weekend that the 'Brown Letters' were dished out George got pissed as a rat with his RCT mates. He took the MOD's paltry £5,000 redundancy money and a last six month posting to the Scottish Transport Regiment (STR) in Dunfermline.

Once George's last six months with the STR were finished he stayed with the unit as a TA Corporal and worked full time as the units' civilian REME Storeman. The wages were piss poor and so in 1994 he joined the MOD Police to try and get a secure and worthwhile career that paid well. George was accepted on a 'Modplod' Training Course and on the first day he had to introduce himself to other candidates on the recruit Course. Each applicant had to stand up and give a small talk about specific things they'd done in their life. George related the conversation he'd had with Trooper Tom Strachan of the Scots Dragoon Guards during the Gulf War when he asked how far they were from the front line. Tom Strachan stood up at the back of the class and said, "I thought I recognised you pal, that was my Tank." Small World or what?

After passing the Course, George served in Aldermaston near Aldershot for thirteen years before being posted to Jordan as an instructor. He was attached to an International Police Force and lectured at the Jordanian Police Training Centre on survival skills and permanent vehicle check points (PVC's). During his tenure in the Middle East, Al-Qaeda blew up three hotels in the local area and the Police College was warned that the terrorists had destroyed the wrong lodging house, they'd meant to target a hotel used by UK Police Officers. Special Branch advised all of the British Instructors to get the hell out of the place before one of them was killed. When he got back to the UK, George was posted to Her Majesty's Naval Base Clyde in Faslane Scotland where he looked after Nuclear Submarines and Royal Marine Commandos. George was required to arrest six peace protesters in one day at Faslane, which was more than he'd done in the last thirteen years.

George and Maureen now live in Fife where he works for G4S, a security firm undertaking prisoner escort duties.

24457567 Corporal Ric Spurr
RCT 1977 – 1989

A 20 year old Driver Ric Spurr sitting on the radiator of a Mark 1 Millitant, this antiquated 10 ton truck was affectionatly known as an 'Old Knocker' by all RCT Drivers. Note Ric's puttees and 1970's porn tash.

Ric Spurr joined the Royal Corps of Transport in 1977 just to get away from his girlfriend Catherine. He'd fallen out with her and thought that joining the British Army was the best way to end their relationship. They'd been boyfriend and girlfriend since their days at school in 1970 and after graduating he did a two year engineering apprenticeship and also worked as a carpet fitter, the carpet fitting money was very good but it seemed to be just a dead end job. So at the age of nearly nineteen, Ric headed for the Army Recruiting Office in the hope of cutting the dead wood out of his love, and employment life.

The British Army Selection Centre staff at Sutton Coldfield near Birmingham gave Ric a choice of three career options before he signed on the dotted line. His list of preferences were:

1. Infantry.
2. Royal Tank Regiment (RTR).

3. Royal Electrical and Mechanical Engineers (REME).

The recruiter dealing with Ric was a Sergeant serving with the Royal Engineers and he talked Ric out of joining both the Infantry and the 'Tankies' (Ric only chose the Royal Tank Regiment because his dad had done two years National Service with them). The recruiter tried to encourage him into joining the Royal Engineers (RE) because, apparently, there weren't any vacancies for Recce Mech's in the REME. Ric didn't want to build things though, he just wanted to drive an army truck and carry a 7.62 mm Self Loading Rifle (SLR).The Sergeant relented about the RE choice and instead offered Ric the chance of joining the Royal Corps of Transport, he accepted this opportunity simply because the RCT drove big trucks.

Ric spent his 19th birthday in Basic Training at Buller Barracks where he met his intake Corporal, a man called Charlie Coldwell. "Charlie was a great guy, he was just like my dad and everyone in the Troop looked up to him". Not all of the DS (Directing Staff) at Buller were as noble as Corporal Charlie Coldwell though. After giving out some banter, Ric was beaten up by a Training Corporal and this was witnessed by his Troop Commander. The Lieutenant looked down at a dishevelled Ric and smiled, he then winked at him and walked away without saying a word. The Corporal later apologised to Ric but only to make sure he wasn't reported for the assault. In 1977 Ric's Driver and Trade training were done at Leconfield in Yorkshire and at the time the place was swamped in Green Goddess Fire Engines because of an up and coming fire-man's strike. The Army School of Mechanical Transport (ASMT) was running composite fire courses to train RCT Drivers and Infantry soldiers how to drive and operate the antiquated Green Goddess appliances. Ric passed both of his driving test's first time in a Ford Escort car and a Bedford MK four tonner.

On returning to Buller Barracks at Aldershot, Ric was given the unwelcome news that he was being posted to 17 Squadron RCT, a Squadron that was part of the infamous 10 Regiment RCT. Ric states, "One of the instructors at the Depot told me that 17 Squadron was full of bullies and so I didn't really fancy going there." His fears were unfounded though because he was being put into A Troop and his bosses were none other than Staff Sergeant 'Mac' McKinley and Sergeant Les Gearing, both of these Senior NCO's proved to be wonderful RCT Senior NCO's. No sooner had Ric's boots stamped to attention in the Troop office than he was put on an HGV II driving course; his driving instructor was Lance Corporal Geoff Spate who showed him how to handle the 'beast' that was affectionately referred to as, 'an old knocker.' This six wheeled primitive military 10 ton truck had a crash gearbox, no powered steering, and she was much slower than the average granny trying to climb the stairs in an inner city block of flats. If you could master the old girl you could master any vehicle, anywhere in the world. Geoff must have been a good instructor because Ric passed his HGV II test first time and without any adverse comments from Staff Sergeant 'Mac' McKinley his QTO (Qualified Testing Officer) and Troop Staffie. QTO's usually had at least one negative comment to make about a Driver under test. After passing his HGV II test Ric was moved into C Troop where his bosses were Staff Sergeant Derek 'Windy' Gale (see the first chapter of this book) and 'Scouse' McCarren, another two superb RCT Senior NCO's.

It wasn't long before Ric was given a place on the next available (Transporter, Tanker, Fuel) (TTF) and Unit Bulk Refuelling Equipment (UBRE) Course. He was going to be shown how to drive and operate the British Army's fuel tankers and in hand with that, he would also learn all about the safety aspects of dealing with highly inflammable fuels. Ric loved driving the relatively new 22,500 Litre Foden tankers because they had powered steering, twelve tyres, great brakes, lots of Gucci switches, and because of fire risks he didn't have to, "Camouflage the fucking thing when I went out on Exercise!" Authors note: Every RCT Driver hated scrimming up on Exercise. There were times when Ric also had to take a turn on the Bedford MK 4 ton UBRE Petrol, Oil and Diesel (POD) vehicles. These smaller, slower, but very reliable and robust vehicles were less comfortable and they weren't the sort of military vehicle an RCT soldier wanted to be seen out with either. Mainly because they looked a bit like an old girlfriend who had gone to seed, you just didn't want to be seen hanging around with her because you know your RCT mates would take the piss. A mixture of POD Tanks could be loaded onto the back of these trucks so that both petrol and diesel could be distributed from the same tanker vehicle. The truck also carried quantities of oils and greases so that Drivers could properly maintain their Squadron vehicles whilst out in the field. Things looked to be going well for Ric, he was by now an established and respected Tanker Driver within 17 Squadron and he could possibly get promoted if he kept his nose clean and did a Junior Military Qualification Certificate (JMQC) Course. But, after one night's drinking at the 'Old Crow' nightclub in Bielefeld, Ric saw his military career take a sudden and drastic nose-dive.

Ric's friend, Driver Don Samson, was on an operational tour of Northern Ireland at the time and he'd lent his car to Ric for the duration. Ric drove the car down to the 'Old Crow' where he had a 'couple of beers' and then drove through the town on the return journey to camp. As he slowly manoeuvred through the precinct in Bielefeld a German gentleman banged rather heavily on the top of Ric/Don's car. Somewhat put out at this aggressive and needless ambush, Ric stopped the car, got out of the vehicle, and proceeded to 'slap' the German gentleman a couple of times. The next morning whilst Ric was working on the vehicle park a runner came up to him and said, "Ric! The Special Investigation Branch (SIB) would like to have a word with you down in the Squadron office." Ric made no bones about the incident and admitted to the assault but only because the German gentleman had been rather aggressive towards him and his friends car. On Commanding Officers Orders the CO told Ric he was referring the Actual Bodily Harm (ABH) case for Court Martial. Apparently if you bruise someone in an assault it is ABH, but if you break a bone or the skin it's considered to be Grievous Bodily Harm (GBH).

During the trial Ric was shouted and screamed at by a Sergeant from 17 Squadron every time he was marched in or out of the Courtroom. "It was all part of the game really" says Ric, "The Sergeant was a great bloke who sympathised with me entirely but he had to play the nasty bastard for the sake of the Senior Officers commanding the Court Martial". All of the evidence presented to the Court Martial was documentary and by the end of the very short trial, Ric was found guilty as charged and sentenced to 112 days incarceration at the Military Correction Training Centre (MCTC) in Colchester. Ric was marched out of the Courtroom without his hat and belt and was then locked up in an 8 foot cell in the Guardroom where the Provost Sergeant told him to remove his boot laces so he wouldn't have the means to hang himself in his cell. When the cell door was slammed shut Ric looked around the cell and thought, 'What the fucking hell have I done.' With time off for good behaviour Ric eventually did five weeks of 'Porridge' at Colchester.

On arrival at the 'Training Centre' Ric had every single bit of kit that wasn't of military issue taken from him, inmates weren't even allowed to have civilian underwear. The Warrant Officer and Sergeant Warders were cold and severe with every prisoner without exception. The doom and gloom atmosphere enveloped Ric like a plague because his own life was now out of his control and he had no idea what was going to happen next. On the plus side, he was re-issued with some bootlaces, but only because he was going to be doing some of the most extreme physical training he'd ever experienced so far in the army. In Stage One of his sentence Ric and the other prisoners did hour long periods of drill and log races, this went on every day for the next few weeks. The funny thing was that Ric really started to enjoy his time at Colchester because he learned things that he'd never covered in training at Buller Barracks. He especially looked forward to the drill lessons because he learned how to change arms on the march, how to Slow March and how to Reverse Arms when taking part in a military funeral. He also did weapon training to a standard above even that taught to the Infantry serving in the British Army. He re-learned about the 9mm Browning pistol and Sterling Sub Machinegun (SMG), the 7.62 mm Self Loading Rifle (SLR) and Light Machine Gun (LMG) and even covered lessons on the 84mm Charlie G (Carl Gustav) Anti-Tank recoilless Rifle and hand grenades. Stage Two of his sentence was considered a promotion within the prison system and every day Ric was thinking, 'God I hope it'll be today,' "At

Colchester the MCTC Staff broke you down to the lowest possible level before re-building you back up so you become a useful and extremely skilled soldier. You learnt from the very start that the only way out is to behave and do exactly as you're told."

On release from his 'time-served' at 'Collie,' Ric was sent to Buller Barracks in Aldershot so he could be processed back into the Corps. WO2 'Taff' Maher was the Squadron Sergeant Major at the Depot and he asked Ric where he wanted to be posted. Ric asked to go back to 17 Squadron. He got the impression that no-one was going to fuck with him in 10 Regiment because he'd done time at 'Collie.' It's an aura that bad boy soldiers have and one that they don't mind using to boost their own status and reputation. Unfortunately, when he arrived back in 17 Squadron Ric felt that the old place was now like serving in a slum army, compared to the discipline at Colchester. He felt his fellow RCT Drivers dress and behaviour was border-line slovenly. When he was offered the chance to do his JMQC Course he grabbed it with both hands because he missed all of the bullshit and intense learning curve that life in a military prison gave him. He passed the Course with flying colours and Ric was subsequently promoted to Lance Corporal and made a Section 2i/c within the Squadron. Life was changing for Ric because he was starting to make the right decisions in his life. In 1977 he'd done a runner from his girlfriend Catherine because he felt they were getting too comfortable and complacent with each other. Well, in 1980 he'd had a change of heart and married the very same Catherine he'd done a runner from only three years earlier. They married at Lightcliffe Church in Halifax, West Yorkshire with Driver Tom Hair RCT as his Best Man at the wedding. A year later Catherine gave birth to their son Reece at the British Military Hospital in Rinteln.

Ric also got involved in 10 Regiment's boxing competitions where he boxed at both Squadron and Regimental level. His first inter-squadron fight was against Driver Twigg of 9 Squadron and the fight only lasted for 22 seconds because Ric chinned him and knocked the poor bloke out. The 22 seconds included the official 10 second knock-out countdown. Ric's fight was followed by a REME Craftsman from the Workshops who was up against a Driver from 36 Squadron. Both boxers were eventually disqualified because they fought with the aggression of two Girl Guides taking part in a flower arranging competition. This proved a problem for the inter-squadron competition because Ric now didn't have anyone to fight in the final. Sergeant Les Gearing RCT was Ric's first Troop Sergeant in A Troop and a unit Physical Training Instructor (PTI) and he came up with an idea. Les suggested that Ric take part in an exhibition fight against Corporal Lionel Braithwaite RCT who was a black, regimental and Corps boxer of notoriety. Ric agreed to the slightly unequal match and the fight went ahead, but in the end Ric was unequivocally beaten. The Regimental

Sergeant Major, WO 1 RSM Bob Card commented after the fight saying that Ric had, "Put more leather on Corporal Braithwaite than he was letting on," which Ric took to be a fantastic compliment. On his interview Ric told the author, "Lionel might have won the fight that night but at least I came second." Ric came off second best again sometime later when he was the passenger in Corporal Dave Sherwood's car.

Driver Ric Spurr slogs it out against Corporal Lionel Braithwaite in their exhibition fight during the 10 Regiment RCT inter-squadron boxing competition, Ric says, "Lionel won the fight but I came second."

Corporal Dave Sherwood RCT was the TTF and POD Operator/Instructor within the regiment and he and Ric were very good friends. They both shared a passion for fishing and one night after a competition Dave was driving back to his Married Quarter in Asemissen. After overtaking a German civilian car Dave was dazzled by his rear-view mirror because the car he'd just overtaken still had its headlights on full beam. Dave flashed his rear fog light to let the driver know and he subsequently lost control on a bend and crashed into a ditch before hitting a tree. Ric wasn't wearing his seat belt at the time and his face hit the windscreen which smashed both the glass, and his cheekbone. The German Fire Brigade attended the scene and extracted a comparatively uninjured Dave from the car but they left Ric in the motor because one of the firemen said, "Der andere Mann ist todt" ("The other man is dead"). As this was happening, a British civilian man and his girlfriend had stopped to see if they could be of any assistance. The young man got into the crashed car, cleared Ric's airway and got him breathing again. Ric of course knew nothing about this and he only remembers waking up in the local German Krankenhaus (hospital) where he recognised Catherine and his OC, Major Baker sitting at his bedside. After twenty four hours Ric refused to stay in the German hospital any longer. He took the drip out of his arm himself and went home but he at least had the good sense to report sick to the Dental Centre on Monday morning. The Dental Officer took one look at Ric and told him he needed to go to BMH Rinteln immediately for an emergency operation. Ric's zygomatic arch (Cheek bone) had been broken and it had to be repaired, a wick dressing was applied after the operation which had to be regularly replaced until the wound healed.

In 1985 Ric was posted to 41 Squadron RCT in Bordon, but Catherine had had enough of living in army Married Quarters, so they decided to invest in their own bricks and mortar and bought a house in Halifax so that Reece would have the benefit of a good stable education. With perfect timing and a lot of good luck they bought a house for £15,000 and sold it two years later for £26,000. Ric's new job at 41 Squadron RCT was comparable to a civilian job and he hated every minute of being there. Another RCT Lance Corporal at 63 (Parachute) Squadron RCT in Aldershot was equally unhappy in his posting and so to rectify the problems both OC's arranged for them to simply swap their jobs. Ric threw all of his kit into the car and drove to the Airborne Squadron which was based at Montgomery Lines opposite Depot Para, "I was still a 'Hat' (Crap Hat – a derogatory term used by Paratroopers to describe non -Airborne soldiers) at this time and so I worked in 63 Squadrons support troop." In a couple of weeks Ric started doing some training tabs (Tactical Advance to Battle - where Paratroopers run and force march to a designated point as a squad) and on sports afternoons he was carrying 35lb of weight in his webbing every time he went for a run. Ric also joined in with the Squadron when they went on a ten miler, during which he was never at the front of the runners, but also never at the back either. The lad's from 63 Para assisted the Hat's on the run and encouraged them all the way round the route, "Get a move on you fat fucker! Move your fat lazy fucking arse, tubby or I'm going to stick my boot up it." There's nothing quite like a 63 Squadron RCT paratrooper for dishing out a shed load of encouragement.

After the Squadron came back off Block Leave, Ric was promoted to full Corporal and he applied to do the All Arms P Company Course at Browning Barracks. Soldiers from the RCT, Royal Engineers (RE), RHA (Royal Horse Artillery), Royal Army Ordnance Corps (RAOC), Royal Electrical and Mechanical Engineers (REME), and the Royal Signals (R Sigs) were all put together on the same course. Infantry soldiers destined for 1 Para, 2 Para and 3 Para all attended a different course. Prior to P Company they had to complete a three week 'Beat Up' Course called Pre Para, every day involved the candidates doing hard physical training like stretcher and log races and extensive Tabs (runs) carrying heavy Bergen's on their backs. Anyone who passed the 'Beat Up' then progressed onto P Company which incorporated another torturous two weeks of physical training, and again, if they were successful they then went onto test week. Part of the Airborne test week begins with 'milling' where each candidate is put up against a soldier of equal size and they have to fight for a full one minute. The fighters wear 16oz boxing gloves but they don't actually box, they just have to try and pummel the other bloke with as many punches as possible within sixty seconds of controlled aggression. Pausing, posing and prancing are definitely frowned upon. Ric was put up against Sapper Graham Hill and when the bell rang the Royal Engineer ran towards Ric whilst screaming like a banshee. After ten seconds of punching, the Sapper's gloves started to drop because he tired very quickly, the next fifty seconds belonged to Corporal Ric Spurr RCT. In Ric's own words he says, "I splatted the fuck out of him." His end of course report commented that 'Corporal Spurr struggled to maintain a position with the front runners at the start of P Company but he was particularly commendable during the milling. 'Recommended for service with the Airborne Forces.' It had never been known for a complete Course to pass P Company in one attempt, but bizarrely there were 83 candidates on Ric's Course of which 63 made it to test week. All 63 candidates passed test week and Ric remembers it so clearly because 63 (Parachute) Squadron RCT was where he would now be heading. At the end of their six weeks of hell the candidates paraded in the gymnasium and when their names were called out they had to stand to attention and say, "Sir." The Course OC then said either "Pass" or "Fail" to which the soldier had to say, "Sir" and then sit back down. An incongruous culmination to one of the most gruelling tests in the world of soldiering. Ric was presented with his airborne issued maroon lid but he immediately went down to Victor's shop in Aldershot to buy a much better quality beret that had a soft leather band. After enjoying the weekend off he reported back to 63 Para and within a week he was sent on his three week parachuting course down at RAF Brize Norton.

After finishing their Ground Training the candidates had to complete one mandatory balloon jump (which is usually the first), six day jumps and a final night jump made from an RAF C130 Hercules aircraft. Paratroopers openly admit to being extremely nervous of the balloon jump. Because of its very nature, the gondola cage used to carry the jumpers constantly and silently sways about in the wind giving a gut wrenching experience. Both the jostling movement and the accompanying sound of the wind as it whistles through the balloon's cables, tend to make the balloon jump an eerie and bowel moving occurrence. After having parachutes strapped onto them, the four very nervous candidates and an RAF Flight Sergeant Dispatcher climb into the metal gondola suspended underneath a large barrage balloon, (the Dispatcher checks everyone's equipment and makes sure all static lines are clipped onto the bar above the cage). After these checks have been made, the whole contraption is winched up to 800 feet above the ground ready for the jumps to begin. The first jumper is called forward and he has to stand in the exit of the cage and when the Dispatcher shouts, **"RED LIGHT ON"** the candidate has to put his right hand across his reserve parachute, when he then shouts, **"GREEN LIGHT ON"** the jumper has to let go of the static line and put his left arm across his reserve chute, and when the Dispatcher screams **"GO"** the jumper has to step out of the cage and trust to luck and his parachute. Whilst plummeting to earth the jumper has to shout, **"ONE THOUSAND, TWO THOUSAND, THREE THOUSAND, and CHECK CANOPY!"** If his parachute does open he then has to look at the airspace around him to make sure there aren't any other paratroopers in his airspace that he might collide with. On operational jumps a paratrooper will then release his equipment container that is strapped to his leg and let it drop on a cord secured to his harness. When the container hits the ground on a night jump the paratrooper knows he has seconds to prepare for his own landing.

The morning after completing their jump training all of the candidates were presented with their wings whilst on parade but Ric never sewed his on any of his uniforms. His printed name was on the back of his presented wings and he still has them at home. Ric had an edge on his comrades on the parachuting course because he was already an experienced sky diver, he'd already accomplished thirty two skydiving jumps before even attempting P Company. Having said that, military parachuting is an entirely different experience from skydiving. Ric considers Para trooping a means to achieving a mission at work whereas skydiving is more of a social pleasure. His civilian parachuting career started when his wife Catherine was a cleaner at Headquarters 1 (BR) Corps at Ripon Barracks in Bielefeld. There was a space on the next BAOR course and

Catherine was asked if her husband would be interested in filling the vacancy. She asked and he jumped (pardon the pun) at the chance.

Captain Bob Card RCT was in charge of the British Army sky diving courses held at Bad Lippspringe RAPA (Rhine Army Parachute Association) and more importantly he'd previously been Ric's Regimental Sergeant Major at 10 Regiment RCT, which ultimately made him Ric's God like boss. Bob was the sort of man you wouldn't argue with because he was as tough as old boots having previously served with 63 Para Squadron RCT. Setting aside his authoritative position he was also a very approachable man, the sort of man's man who would inspire you to follow him into battle. Bob later recruited Ric into the 'Silver Stars RCT Freefall Parachute Team' and he travelled all over the world doing freefall displays. His time at 63 Para and with the Silver Stars gave Ric the chance to travel extensively, doing Exercises and displays in the United States and Norway to name but a few. On one trip he deployed to Washington State for six weeks and worked alongside the US Airborne Forces. Ric was working in support of 1 Para who were taking part in a collaborated US/British Airborne Exercise. Ric also became qualified to wear the US Airborne wings whilst out in America, "It was a courtesy thing really, all we had to do was complete two jumps from a Chinook helicopter at 1,800 feet whilst wearing one of their steerable parachutes. Once we'd done the two jumps we were allowed to wear their wings above the left breast pocket of our Para Smocks. To be honest there's no fucking way they'd be presented with our wings, not without doing the whole of P Company and completing every part of the jump training. British Airborne Forces are very strict about awarding our wings."

Whilst in 63 Para Ric also went on Exercise with 42 Squadron RCT who were based at Bulford in Wiltshire. 42 Squadron was part of Ace Mobile Forces Land (AMF (L)) which often Exercised out in Norway in preparation for a possible Soviet attack on the NATO Northern flank. After competing in a Norway Arctic Warfare/Survival course, Ric played the part of a Ninja (Airborne nickname for enemy soldier) against the soldiers of 2 Para who were playing the good guys. The temperature in Norway during the Exercise fell to minus 30 degrees Celsius and whilst hiding in a snow hole Ric and his Section had a problem thrust upon them, Ric explains, "A fucking 'Hat' Lance Corporal fell asleep whilst on stag (sentry duty) and he failed to wake up the soldier due to take over from him. As a result our Ninja unit was surrounded by a platoon from 2 Para, some of us made a break for it and we managed to escape in a BV 202 Volvo Snow Cat". They were eventually stopped at an enemy checkpoint and the Troop Commander bluffed his way out of the situation using some great bullshit and a stolen 'Friendly Forces' armband. Whilst the TC was bullshitting the Paras for all he was worth, the 'Hat' Lance Corporal alighted from the rear of the Snow Cat to have a piss and before he had a chance to get back in they deliberately drove off and left him there. He was ultimately captured by the 2 Para platoon who gave him a hard time and a really good going over. Oh well, 'C'est la guerre.'

Ric's final military parachute jump with 63 (Parachute) Squadron RCT was on **Exercise Purple Warrior** in Scotland, he parachuted from an RAF C130 Hercules aircraft that was supposedly flying at a height of 800 feet. Ric jumped from the aircraft, felt his chute deploy and steered into clean air, he then lowered his container but had less than two seconds to prepare for his landing after feeling the container hit the DZ (Drop Zone). "I reckon the RAF got it wrong that night because I think we jumped from about 500 feet, it was definitely the lowest military jump I've ever done in my career in the British Airborne Forces".

By 1989 Ric was pining for his family because he was either on Exercise with 63 Para or away with the Silver Stars doing displays, and even when he was in the UK he was more often than not in Aldershot while his family were all the way up in Yorkshire in their family home. He applied for a posting to the Army School of Mechanical Transport (ASMT) at Leconfield in Yorkshire so that he could drive to work every day from his own house. Ric's boss at Normandy Barracks was a Warrant Officer who didn't like Paras and tried to knock Ric's Airborne attitude out of him, it didn't work. During an annual Nuclear Biological and Chemical (NBC) training session, Ric was ordered to remove his respirator in the CS gas chamber and recite his number rank and name. After doing this all soldiers should be allowed to exit the chamber because their eyes are streaming and they're usually coughing their guts up. This sort of training session is only supposed to be done once during a recruits' training so that rookies understand the effects of a riot control agent, after that CS gas is also used to test whether a soldier's respirator is fitted properly and trained soldiers are not made to fully remove their respirators. When Ric didn't react to the irritant in the chamber (that's the gas not the Warrant Officer) his boss told him to start doing some press ups and then asked him further questions. Again Ric showed none of the usual signs and symptoms of CS poisoning and after doing yet another twenty push ups he stood to attention in front of his boss who was wearing a respirator throughout the test, and said, "Do you want me to do it again…**Sir**?"

The treatment by his boss was bad enough but one day Ric's world imploded when he spotted a trainee Driver walking into the NAAFI with his beret on the back of his head, even worse was the fact that the same Driver was holding his girlfriend's hand like a love sick puppy. That was the defining moment for Ric and he thought to himself, 'Nope! This is toy town soldiering. I can't do this sort of shit for a living' and so he signed off at the 11 year point of his career. The transition from Airborne soldier to 'Crap Hat' was just too much for Ric and he says of his time with 63 (Parachute) Squadron RCT, "63 Para Drivers were much better than the Privates in the Parachute Regiment, we could do everything they were capable of doing but we also had extra responsibilities, they would've had to do a lot more training to be able to cover our jobs on a Drop Zone (DZ)."

In September 1989 Ric was discharged from the British Army and given a resettlement grant of £4000. Since leaving, he has done agency driving, worked as a self-employed gardener, qualified as a Corgi registered gas installer and is currently employed by Flogas to travel all over the country as a Health and Safety Audit and Controls Officer. When not working he lives an idyllic life on the East Yorkshire coast near Withernsea, the beach is a mere 1,000 yards from his house and he has a golf course at the bottom of his garden, perfect.

Ric's wife Catherine and his son Reece have both completed tandem skydiving parachute jumps.

Staff Sergeant Les Reed
RCT and RLC 1983 - 2005

Corporal Les Reed

The Reed family have always done their bit when it came to serving within the British Armed Forces. Les Reed's Grandparents served in the Royal Artillery and the Women's Auxiliary Air Force (WAAF) throughout the Second World War. His dad, William, also signed up and served with the Royal Navy in the late 1950's before transferring into the Merchant Navy as a Chief Engineer. Les and his two younger brothers also served, Les joined the RCT in 1983 and William Kenneth, who was the youngest, joined the Royal Marines in 1991. His half-brother, Rob Campbell, went into the Royal Signals in 1987 and became a Junior Regimental Sergeant Major (J/RSM) and is still currently serving as a Major. Living in an area of high unemployment in the North East may have had some influence on the lads joining up, because in Percy Main near Newcastle most school leavers either worked on the railways or in the coal industry. Les Reed didn't fancy doing either of those mundane and rudimentary jobs and so became a trainee butcher. It was friends who persuaded him to join them in the Territorial Army (TA). He went along to 216 Squadron which was part of 150 (Volunteer) Transport Regiment RCT based in Tynemouth. He joined in the hope of getting some Heavy Goods Vehicle (HGV) licences and improving his employment opportunities.

Staff Sergeant Terry Rook RCT was the Permanent Staff Instructor (PSI) in 216 Squadron who took Les under his wing, introducing him to what it was like on Military Field Exercises. Before actually joining the unit, Les went on a Squadron weekend Exercise to experience what the lads did out in the field and see whether or not he would enjoy life as a soldier, albeit as a Territorial one. Les had a great time and fell in love with the military way of life. In October 1981 he headed off to the Territorial Army Training Camp at Grantham for two weeks of army Basic Training, at the age of 19. Having always lived at home, he initially found it strange living in a room with twenty four other recruits but soon became accustomed to it. On the recruits first Nuclear, Biological and Chemical Warfare (NBC) lesson, Corporal 'Bloggs' RCT, a Regular Army soldier, strode into the classroom and asked if anyone had any O' Levels. Les put his hand up and the Corporal said, "Good, plug in the overhead projector for me!" At the end of the Course, Les was presented with the best recruit award (and not just because he knew how to operate a plug). He then headed back to 216 Squadron to fulfil his goal of gaining some driving licences.

Les sailed through his Driver Training because he already held a motorbike licence, his previous road experience, comprehension of clutch control, and excellent knowledge of the Highway Code made the whole Driver Training program relatively easy for him. After passing his car test in a Ford Escort he progressed onto his HGV driving training in a TA Bedford RL which had a petrol engine. To do his test though he was assigned a Bedford MK four tonner that had a diesel engine. The Bedford MK and RL are completely different vehicles to drive because they have distinct driving characteristics, for instance, the Bedford MK's brakes slammed on no matter how gently you pressed the brake pedal, which could lead to an initial brick shitting experience. Staff Sergeant Tommy Appleby RCT had seen service in the Aden conflict with the (Royal Army Service Corps (RASC). He was the Qualified Testing Officer (QTO) who took Les on his HGV III Test. Tommy was so impressed with Les Reed's driving ability that he urged him to take his HGV II and Group B Class II driver training as soon as possible. Within a year Les had passed his HGV II driving test, driving a Foden 16 wheeler.

Les was by now a Group B Class II Driver, a qualified motorcycle instructor, and had also been recommended for promotion to Lance Corporal. During his two years with the TA Les had worked alongside Regular Army soldiers which prompted him to try and enlist into the Regular Army as a Royal Military Policeman. Every Driver who has ever served within the ranks of the RCT will now be booing, hissing and shouting, "He's behind you." At Ridley Place Army Recruiting Office in Newcastle a Royal Artillery Sergeant Recruiter gave Les some advice, "Listen son, you're only five foot four inches in height and at the age of nearly 21 years old I really don't think you're going to get any taller. You're too short to get in as a military copper! You need to be at least five foot seven inches to get into the RMP's. What's your second choice?" When Les told him the Royal Signals, the Sergeant looked perplexed, "Why the hell do you want to go into the Signals?" Les was, and still is today, a motorcycle freak and he fancied getting into the Royal Signals White Helmets motorcycle display team. The recruiter told Les a little white lie to try and throw him off the scent. "Well son, you'll have to do at least nine years as a Signalman before they will even consider giving you a place on the team. What's your third choice?" The RCT was third choice for Les, which was strange if you think about it, he was already a fully trained and well qualified RCT Driver and so after completing Basic Training he wouldn't even need to do any Trade Training, it would surely be a breeze. The Sergeant accepted the RCT option, which was a no brainer really because Les had already read the book and acted in the play, and all before even setting off to do his Regular Army RCT Basic Training.

On arrival at Aldershot Railway Station Les already had a crew-cut hair style was wearing a granddad shirt, tank top, tight jeans and 'Dessie boots' which were in vogue with soldiers at the time. He also had the attitude, demeanour, confidence, and swagger of a 22 year old experienced soldier. He approached the RCT Driver who was standing next to a minibus and asked, "Are you the transport for Buller Barracks?" The Driver snapped to attention and quickly replied, "Yes Corporal, we can't go just yet though because there are some recruits due in on the next train." After watching the Driver load his suitcase into the minibus Les then climbed into the front seat to await the short drive to the RCT Depot. When the Driver pulled up outside the Guardroom at Buller Barracks an RCT Provost Sergeant immediately started screaming and shouting at the newly arrived recruits as they climbed out of the minibus. He then noticed Les and said to him, "Alright mate, where are you going?" Les truthfully told him he was going to 64 Training Squadron but failed to tell him he was there as a recruit, not as an instructor. The Sergeant turned towards the alarmed young lads bumping into each other at the back of the minibus and shouted at one of them, "Oy scrote! Pick up his case and take it up to 64 Squadron! Come on, fucking move yourself!" After walking round the corner Les reclaimed his case off the petrified recruit and said, "It's alright mate, I can take it from here. You get back to the Sergeant." He then thought to himself

"Oh my God, what the fuck am I going to do now, one of my fellow recruits has been carrying my bags for me and the Permanent Staff all think I'm a fucking instructor… SHIT!" Two days later the Provost Sergeant recognised Les and he made him polish the Guardroom ceiling using a heavy hand powered bumper, the punishment was for pulling the wool over his eyes.

Les found the accommodation block and reported to a Sergeant Farquharson who was going to be the recruits Drill Sergeant and he directed him to wait in one of the rooms. Intake 150 was going to be the biggest recruit training course the Depot had ever accommodated and Les had been warned back at 216 Squadron, "For fuck sake don't tell them you've been in the TA because you will get a whole world of shit dumped on you." The new Course recruits paraded in the corridor and they were called into the Squadron Office one by one where they had to attempt to march in, halt, and then recite their number rank and name. Les heard his name called:

Sergeant: "Reed!"

Les: "Sergeant!"

Sergeant: "Get your arse in here, NOW!"

Les: "Yes Sergeant!"

Les marched into the office and smartly halted in front of the Sergeants' desk.

Sergeant: "Why have you got a different service number to everyone else?"

Service numbers are dished out in batches and of course Les had retained the TA service number that he'd received two years earlier.

Les: "I don't know Sergeant!"

Sergeant: "Where did you learn to march?"

Thinking on his feet Les gave what he thought was a plausible excuse. To be honest Les would rather have told the Sergeant he'd just been shagging his youngest daughter up against the corridor wall than have to admit he'd served in the Territorial Army.

Les: "I was in the cadets many years ago Sergeant."

Sergeant: "Right, get out!"

As Les marched back into the corridor he heard the same voice bellowing from behind him.

Sergeant: "Reed! Get your fucking arse back in here!"

Les: "Yes Sergeant!"

Sergeant: "Are you an ex Regular Soldier?"

Les: "No Sergeant."

Sergeant: "Hmmn. Ok, get away!"

Les marched out and then heard the Sergeant call him back yet again.

Sergeant: "Get back in here Reed!"

Les: "Yes Sergeant."

Sergeant: "Is it because you live near Scotland? Sometimes those Jocks get a different number to everyone else!"

Les: "It could be that Sergeant, but I'm not really sure."

Sergeant: "Right, that must be it then, go on, fuck off!"

Les: "Yes Sergeant!"

Again Les marched out into the corridor and again he heard the same ear-splitting voice calling him back.

Sergeant: "I've fucking worked it out Reed, you were a fucking stab weren't you?"

Les: "I don't know what a stab is Sergeant."

Sergeant: "The letters stand for **S**tupid **T**erritorial **A**rmy **B**astard, were you ever in the fucking TA, Reed?"

Les: "Errrm…well…now you come to mention it Sergeant. Yes I was, but only for two years, honest."

The Sergeant then told Les his fortune.

Sergeant: "Right! Listen to me Reed. No matter if you come top in every lesson, run faster than every other recruit, and even if you are the smartest Driver ever to have marched in these hallowed halls, you will never, I repeat never, be made Best Recruit. Now fuck off out of my office!"

The stage was set and Les did get some grief off the Permanent Staff for being ex TA but with his tough 'Geordie' attitude, he just shrugged it off. After Basic Training the recruits, including the already qualified Les, were sent up to Leconfield in East Yorkshire to do their HGV Driver Training. The Buller instructors decreed that none of his previous training and qualifications counted because they were of a TA standard. Within twenty four hours Les was back in Aldershot because the Driver Training Wing in Leconfield declared he was more qualified and competent than some of their own Instructors. For the sake of historical accuracy, Driver Les Reed wasn't awarded Best Recruit of Course 150, but we think that you the reader already knew that was going to happen. After four days in Holding Troop, Les was given a posting order to B Troop 6 (Artillery Support) Squadron RCT at Glamorgan Barracks in Duisburg, West Germany. When Driver Les Reed, '**Regular Army**', arrived there on 1st March 1984, 6 Squadron was at that time an independent unit that came under the umbrella of Headquarters 4 Division in Minden. After being interviewed by the OC Major Hutt Les was told to report to B Troop where his Troop Sergeant would deal with the rest of his administration. After knocking on the Troop door his new Troop Sergeant looked him up and down and said, "I know you, what's your name?" Les introduced himself and realised that the Sergeant sitting behind the desk was none other than the arrogant Corporal 'Bloggs', his NBC instructor at Grantham. The Corporal had obviously been promoted to Sergeant but his attitude towards anyone who'd been in the TA hadn't improved a jot. After informing the Troop Sergeant of his driving qualifications, Sergeant 'Bloggs' declared, "Well none of that counts here, it's all TA crap so you'll have to start from the beginning and do it all again." Les was gutted because he constantly seemed to be coming up against aggressive Senior NCO's within his own Corps, and they appeared to dislike him purely because of his time served with the TA.

Corporal Les Reed Don R

It wasn't just the senior NCO's that Les came up against either. There was an unwritten law in the RCT world that Nig's (New In Germany) were not allowed to enter the NAAFI Bar unless invited by a seasoned Driver. Les didn't know about this common-law regulation and after being threatened by three Drivers he headed for the toilets without finishing his beer. Whilst standing at a urinal Les heard the Drivers come into the toilet and menacingly stood behind him. Without turning round Les said, "I can't believe you three are going to assault me from behind while I've still got me dick in me hand". One of the Drivers replied that they would wait for him to finish his piss before they started dishing out his punishment. Les thought to himself, 'How long can I make this fucking piss last for.' When the violence started Les was pushed onto a very hot radiator which burned the skin on his back, his instinct made him push back and he crashed into a toilet cubicle with his hands around the throat of one of the thugs. Les knew he was in for a good kicking and decided he was going to take out at least one of the bully's before that happened. He relentlessly punched the guy in the cubicle over and over again in his face before the other two finally pulled him off and pinned him up against the wall. The one he'd punched had blood all over his face and it didn't look like their new relationship was going to improve much and so Les said to them, "Alright then, let my arms go and at least have the guts to take me on one at a time." The bloodied Driver then surprised Les when he said, "No no, that's it, you're done. You've stood your ground and we're happy with that, now go back in the bar and finish your beer." It later transpired that Sergeant 'Bloggs' had put the word out that Les was an overqualified know it all ex-stab who needed taking down a peg or two.

Karma is a wonderful thing if you believe in it. Sometime later Sergeant 'Bloggs' was Court Martialled for a disturbing sexual crime, if they'd collared him in the NAAFI toilets he'd have earned himself the ultimate kicking from hell by every decent British soldier. Within nine months of arriving at B Troop 6 (Artillery Support) Squadron RCT, Les had re-done his Group B Class II Course, completed his Group B Class I course and also come top on a Junior Military Qualifications Course (JMQC) (promotion course) which resulted in him being promoted to Acting Lance Corporal. Things were definitely looking up for Les until he was admitted to RAF Hospital Wegberg for an operation that necessitated him having to take life at a slower pace for a while.

In November 1987 Les was back to full fitness when he was seconded for a six month roulement tour of Northern Ireland with 35 Squadron RCT at Moscow Camp in Belfast. During the tour Les was tasked to command a Bedford MK with a protective cage around its cab. He had to take it to the Royal Navy camp in Belfast docks and pick up an outboard engine and a Pacific 2000 SBS (Special Boat Squadron) high powered patrol boat. The engine was in a metal scaffold cage and had to be strapped down onto the back of the truck before the boat, which weighed 3 ½ tons, was then secured onto the trucks trailer which weighed in at 1 ½ tons. The towed weight alone was a hefty five tons and once loaded it then had to be delivered to an Ulster Defence Regiment (UDR) barracks in Warrenpoint. Les was allocated a Driver for the four tonner and an armed escort, provided by some Royal Artillery Gunners who were based at the Maze Prison.

The convoy arrived in Warrenpoint at 2200 hours and was met at the barracks by some Royal Ulster Constabulary (RUC) policemen and members of the Royal Marines/Special Boat Squadron (RM/SBS). They briefed Les on what was going to happen and told him exactly what they wanted him to do. He had to wait until 0200 hours before quietly driving through a golf course and down to a slipway where everyone would rendezvous with an incoming SBS patrol boat. He then had to reverse the truck and trailer down to the water's edge so that the new boat could be safely launched at high tide. The old boat was then to be loaded onto the trailer and taken back to Belfast docks before Les and his Driver could return to Moscow Camp. All this was to be done in complete darkness and any instructions had to be given in whispered voices. Les murmured to the Royal Marines that they should take the engine off the back of the truck whilst waiting for the incoming boat to arrive. After unhitching the trailer, Les guided the Driver into the area where the engine had to be delivered. Twelve muscle-bound Marines waited at the tailboard while Les and the Driver slid the very heavy engine towards the rear of the truck. Then, as the crated engine pivoted over the edge the Marines grunted as they took the strain and took the full weight of the very heavy consignment. Unfortunately, the heavy engine shifted within its metal cage and trapped Les's hand, breaking his knuckles. Les only whimpered at the pain because he didn't want to break the noise discipline and appear to be an RCT mincing faggot in front of a dozen butch Royal Marines. He was dragged out of the truck along with the engine and his still trapped hand, falling on top of the metal crate as the Marines lowered it to the ground. A more sympathetic Commando whispered, "What the fuck do you think you're doing Pongo?"

At high tide the SBS boat duly arrived at the slipway and the changeover was completed with the RM/SBS doing the majority of the handling. The returning boat was swiftly loaded onto the trailer because its engine would remain attached to the boat during the return journey and didn't have to be loaded separately onto the truck. Les was in agony during the journey back to Belfast. He was surprised when the front escorting Land Rover pulled up at the side of the road just after crossing a roundabout somewhere in Antrim. The Bombardier climbed out of his vehicle and approached Les on the passenger side of the four tonner. He'd been unsuccessfully trying to contact Les using the green spot and red spot cougar net communication which was notoriously unreliable. The Bombardier smirked as he asked:

Bombardier: "Where's your fucking boat?"

Les: "It's on the fucking trailer, where do you fucking think it is?"

Bombardier: "No it isn't mate."

Les: "Fuck off and stop pissing about will you, my fucking hand is killing me."

Bombardier: "I'm telling you it ain't there."

Les: "And I'm telling you it's round the back, it can't fucking go anywhere without this fucking truck pulling it."

Bombardier: "Come with me mate and take a look."

After painfully climbing out of the truck Les and the Bombardier went round to the rear of the vehicle where Les shouted,

Les: "FUCK ME!!! WHERE'S THE FUCKING BOAT GONE?"

The escorting rear Land Rover was also missing and its soldiers couldn't be raised on the radio. Les then noticed that the whole towing hook on the Bedford had completely snapped off and he thought, 'Thank fuck for that, it's not our fault.' The convoy turned around and headed back up the Duel Carriageway to look for the missing trailer, boat and escorting Land Rover. After a couple of miles Les saw his escorting Land Rover on the other side of the road with its four way flashers blinking. After crossing the road they parked up behind it. The escorting Gunners were still pissing themselves with laughter as they tried to explain what had happened to the trailer and boat. The triple-axled trailer with its leading bogey wheel had suddenly become detached and the Gunners saw it veer to the left and actually start to overtake the four tonner, on the inside. Because of the protective mesh around the cab of the truck, Les hadn't noticed it undertaking him on the grass verge. The trailer eventually hit a tree which split into two and the five ton renegade trailer then somersaulted down the embankment, ploughing through a barbed wire fence before finally coming to rest on the 14th hole of a golf course. During the recovery operation Les found his towing hook and noticed that the REME had repaired a previous break by welding it back onto the truck. Over the next few years, rain and dirt had got inside the repair, causing it to rust and significantly weaken. Les presented the tow hook as evidence to the OC of 35 Squadron RCT who submitted his own findings on the incident who then declared that his soldiers were not at fault.

After the tour in Belfast Les got married and stayed with 35 Squadron who wanted to retain him. 35 Squadron was also based in Duisburg, West Germany and Les happily worked in the Squadron motorbike bay and completed his Senior Military Qualifications Certificate (SMQC) – (promotion course) at Buller Barracks in Aldershot. Les was promoted to full Corporal in time for his second tour of Northern Ireland, but this time he went as the RCT Detachment Commander at Woodburn RUC Police Station in West Belfast; the Squadron took over from 21 Squadron RCT and operated in support of 3 Para. The Squadron had a good working relationship and successful tour with 3 Para but Les was about to learn some devastating news when he got back to Duisburg.

Les was a 31 years old full Corporal with two tours of Northern Ireland under his belt and was waiting to be promoted to Sergeant at that time. Whilst at home one day he was reading the BBC's CEEFAX reports and noticed a headline that read, 'TWO ROYAL MARINES DIE IN A TRAGIC ACCIDENT WHILST ON EXERCISE IN NORWAY.' Les clicked on the story and read that the two Commandos were from 42 Commando and felt a sense of relief because his Royal Marine younger brother was serving in 45 Commando. Les knew 45 Commando, who were based in Arbroath, weren't in Norway at that time. The report went on to state pretty much what was printed in the Independent newspaper the following day:

'TWO Royal Marines died yesterday after being found unconscious in a tent while on an Arctic warfare training exercise in Norway. A third man was revived after being airlifted with them to hospital in Gjorvik, southern Norway.

The Ministry of Defence named the dead last night as Marines Philip Yates, 22, from Norfolk and William Reed, 19, from Tyne and Wear. It said they did not die from cold or exposure and may have been suffocated by fumes from a stove.

The news came as Malcolm Rifkind, the Secretary of State for Defence, began a three-day visit to Norway, which will include a visit to the brigade to which the dead men belonged today.

'The deaths are obviously very tragic and there will be a full and thorough investigation into the circumstances, an MoD official said.

The men, from 45 Commando based in Arbroath, were among 2,000 Marines from the 3,500- strong 3 Commando Brigade who were on the exercise, 'Winter Deployment '93', which included live firing in the Valdres Valley in central southern Norway.

Sources said they seem to have settled down to sleep last night in a four-man Arctic tent near the firing ranges but did not wake up. The stoves in use are similar to primus stoves and fuelled by naphtha.

Although temperatures in southern Norway last night were just above freezing near sea level, the valley floor is over 1,000 metres above sea level. Officers with the Commando brigade headquarters in the adjacent Hallingdal valley said it was very windy in the mountain valleys, with the resultant chill factor forcing temperatures well below zero'

Les initially thought 'Bloody hell, that Marine's got the same name as my brother.' What Les didn't know was that his brother had been seconded to 42 Commando for the Winter Warfare Exercise. Within minutes of reading the CEEFAX report, Captain Adrian Batley RCT an ex-Air Dispatch Officer, knocked on Les's front door and confirmed that it was indeed his brother who had died in the tragic incident. This catastrophic occurrence was exacerbated by the fact that a cousin of Les's German wife had only recently been murdered. The British Army usually steps up a gear when these heart-breaking events happen and the Quartermaster at 38 Squadron was no different. He orchestrated a flight from RAF Bruggen to RAF Odiham where Les was met by a military staff car that took him all the way home to Newcastle so that he could be with his grieving family.

Marine William Kenneth Reed's wake was held on a retired Sealink ferry called Tuxedo Princess. Until 2007 the ship was permanently moored under the Tyne Bridge in Newcastle and used as a floating nightclub. Les celebrated Williams' life in the usual military fashion by drinking copious pints of beer, telling taller and taller stories about William, and then dancing in the disco with nearly two hundred and fifty Royal Marine Commandos from 42 and 45 Commando. The Board of Inquiry findings reported that P049009U Marine William K Reed and P050421S Marine Philip Yates had died from carbon monoxide poisoning. It also stated the cause of their deaths was because they were using primus stoves in a confined area to try and keep warm in the intense winter conditions. The Commandos who were on the Exercise with William told Les an alleged different story at the wake. It involved a Warrant Officer sitting in the cab of a Volvo BV 209 Snowcat in which he kept the engine running to keep warm. The Warrant Officer hadn't used an exhaust extension hose to take the Carbon Monoxide fumes away from the bivouac area. He allegedly also died in the same incident but for some reason his actions weren't included in the report.

Within a year of completing the tour in Northern Ireland, 35 Squadron was disbanded and Les spent six months with 75 Squadron RCT before being posted to 38 Squadron in Mulheim, West Germany as an Admin Sergeant. Whilst with 38 Squadron, Les was sent to the British Army Training Unit Suffield (BATUS) in Canada for eight months during which time he rebadged into the Royal Logistic Corps (RLC). To this day Les states, "I enlisted into the Royal Corps of Transport in 1981 and in March 1993 the Royal Logistic Corps joined me. I've had some great times in the RLC but I still consider myself to have been an RCT soldier, not a Loggie." Les was responsible for the G1098 stores in BATUS and each unit that deployed on an Exercise Med Man was issued with the necessary equipment to feed their men in the field, everything from vehicles, tents and pots and pans were signed for by the army chefs and it all had to returned in good order. During the Exercise Les would also deploy with the Exercising unit to give advice on safety issues and would co-ordinate communications with the red topped safety vehicles and staff.

There isn't an MOT test for civilian vehicles in Canada and if anyone was stopped by the Mounties and a fault was found on any sort of vehicle, they would simply recommend to the driver that the fault be checked out by a mechanic at some time in the future. But the British Army being what it is, any soldier who bought a cheap run-around car for their Rest and Recuperation (R&R) leave would have to take it into the REME Workshops for a simple brakes and steering check before being allowed to take it onto the open road. Any detected faults on the car could then be put right by the inspecting REME

Mechanics, for a modest fee, which would then make the vehicle 'British Army' roadworthy. An enterprising Warrant Officer Master Chef who closely worked with Les at BATUS bought half a dozen cheap motors which he then tarted up a bit, then put the vehicles through the REME mini MOT system to have them declared fit to drive on the Canadian highways. 'The Batus Bangers' could then be rented out to a group of soldiers going on their R&R leave without them having to go through the hassle of buying a motor and risking it failing the REME inspection. A soldier could buy a car off the Master Chef at a reasonable price…he wasn't asking for 1200 Canadian Dollars…he wasn't even asking for 1000 Dollars…the Master Chef was cutting his own arm off and virtually giving away the cars for a miserly 800 Canadian Dollars. At that price, to have the freedom to drive anywhere they wanted go, well…it was like the Master Chef was doing them a personal favour at his own expense. And when the soldier came back to camp a week later, the Master Chef would buy the car back off them for the extortionate price of 200 Dollars (well he did have unseen overheads). One wonders how the Master Chef ever made a profit.

Les also took full advantage of this private car hire enterprise when he went on Rest and Recuperation (R&R) in a 1972 Ford Country Squire Station Wagon. This old beast of a car would travel approximately 300 miles using 60 litres of petrol that cost less than £15, however, he also had to buy 1 litre of oil for the leaky engine every time he filled up the petrol tank. This massive American car drove like a Sperm Whale and was so big that when parked next to a Volvo estate it made the Swedish car look more like a Mini Clubman Estate. Les chipped in 200 Dollars with his Troop Commander, Lieutenant Beck, Staff Sergeant Mal Dobinson and a REME Lance Corporal Vehicle Mechanic. The VM and his tool box were graciously allowed to accompany them on the R&R trip just in case they had any mechanical problems. The foursome went to Calgary, Edmonton, Niagara Falls and they even drove south and headed for Venice Beach in California.

After his eight month tour in BATUS came to an end, Les returned to 38 Squadron and was given three sequential postings to units that all closed down shortly after he arrived (Authors note: Perhaps it was your personal hygiene Les). He was posted in and out of 3 Battalion REME in Detmold and 16 Air Defence Regiment in Dortmund in quick succession before being posted to 14 Support Battalion RLC ARRC (Allied Rapid Reaction Corps) in Rheindahlen. Within four weeks of arriving at 14 Battalion, Les deployed to Bosnia with them as part of the Implementation Force (IFOR), this was a North Atlantic

Treaty Organisation (NATO) led multinational peace enforcement force. The United Nations (UN) had originally moved into the area in 1992 but had failed to control the situation in Bosnia and so IFOR was the next 'step up' phase in December 1995. 14 Support Battalions' vehicles were taken to Hamburg and shipped out to Bosnia and the unit personnel were flown out to Split in Croatia on 14th November 1995. The unit was accommodated in Dalma Warehouse transit accommodation for a few days. The complex had been taken over by the army and had been fenced off and reinforced for their own Ordnance use to resupply IFOR troops based in Bosnia. When 14 Battalion had collected their trucks from the docks they moved in a 50 Kilometre long convoy carrying ammunition and rations, through the French Sector in Mostar, and up to Sarajevo which was where 14 Support Battalion RLC was going to be based.

Les was based in a small town called Visoko which was located about twenty miles North West of Sarajevo where his Troop lived in tents that had been erected in an old bombed out warehouse. On Christmas Day morning the Officers and Senior NCO's carried on with the British Army tradition of serving their Drivers 'Gunfire' (Tea laced with rum) in bed. A Belgian unit called the Belugers took over from Les's Troop who moved to an old abandoned brick factory in Kiseljak which they shared with the Special Air Service (SAS), Special Boat Service (SBS), and US Special Forces. The small secluded location was guarded by a Company of Ghurkha Infantrymen and Les had never felt safer in his entire life. During this phase of the Operation, Les and some of the other troop members often flew back to JHQ in Rheindahlen to pick up some brand new 4x4 Mitsubishi Pajero's. The drive back to Sarajevo took about three days and was completed working in two man teams wearing civilian clothing until they reached the Bosnian border, everyone then got back into uniform before finishing the last part of the journey.

During the tour in Bosnia Les also flew back to RAF Bruggen in BAOR to play for the British Army as a striker in a hockey match against the RAF. In the second half of the game Les moved in towards the opponent's goal and was caught on the left side of his head and face as the Goal Keeper swung his hockey stick. Les wasn't knocked out and he simply shook his head and continued on with the game, they do breed them tough up in Newcastle. The following day he flew back to Sarajevo and re-joined his Troop in the Brick Factory. Ten days later Les attended an early 'Prayers' (Orders Group) for an operation that was being carried out later that morning, at the end of the briefing everyone went down to the G10 wagon for a full on British Army breakfast.

After loading up his mess tin with sausages, bacon, eggs fried bread, beans and tinned tomato's, Les sat down opposite one of the SAS medics and started troughing. The medic looked quizzically at Les and said, "Geordie, have you been hit on the head recently?" Les had forgotten about the minor hockey incident and he replied, "No, not as far as I can recall. Why?" The SAS Trooper stated, "Well your eyes are telling me something different, your left pupil is totally dilated and you need to go and see the MO (Medical Officer) Stat immediately. Les was examined by a French Military doctor in the main Headquarters in Kiseljak which was about one mile away from the Brick Factory. The MO couldn't speak a word of English and Les spoke even less French. This resulted in the two of them behaving like Una Stubbs and Lionel Blair in 'Give us a Clue.' During the examination, there was plenty of arm waving, posturing and when they couldn't explain what they wanted to say, they simply shouted in their own native language.

A French armoured vehicle took a very confused Les down 'Sniper Alley' and delivered him to an underground multi-national military hospital which was located beneath a destroyed multi-storey car park. On arrival at the hospitals' location Les noticed some Royal Signal Ptarmigan vehicles were co-located on the same site. The nurses allocated Les a bed and then took his Blood Pressure (BP) and Temperature, Pulse and Respiration (TPR's) recording them on a clip board, he was then examined by more doctors who also couldn't speak any English. An injured French Foreign Legionnaire who spoke a bit of Pigeon English was in the bed opposite Les and he explained that the medical staff were going to send Les to a German/French hospital in Croatia for an operation. Les had to get in touch with his own location because he still had his rifle, bayonet and ammunition and it all had to be returned to his unit before he went on to Croatia. With plenty of arm waving and gesturing Les found out from the Legionnaire where the Royal Signal's Ptarmigan box bodied vehicle was situated and he set off to get in touch with his unit. It was a bitterly cold night outside and when Les spotted the British Army truck he was looking for, he climbed the steps at the back of the vehicle and knocked on the door. A small Royal Signalman opened the door and said, "Fuck me a Brit! Come in and have a cup of tea mate!" The Signalman put Les in contact with Staff Sergeant Kevin Miller back in the Troop location who arranged for Les's weaponry to be collected in exchange for some clean knickers and socks. The Commanding Officer and Squadron Sergeant Major, John Roskelly (Later Lieutenant Colonel), both came down to visit Les before he was put on a German C130 Hercules aircraft and flown to a German hospital in Croatia.

Les understood everything the Bundeswehr medics told him because he spoke fluent German, which is just one of the benefits of having a German wife. They explained that they were going to do an exploratory operation in which they took Les's left eye out and thoroughly examined it. They discovered that the rear of the eye had been ruptured after Les had been hit on the head by the RAF Goal Keepers hockey stick. Unfortunately, over the following two weeks the wound had started to heal itself because it had gone untreated and there was nothing else the ophthalmic surgical team could do. As a result of the injury Les now has to wear glasses and sunglasses when outside in any bright sunshine and he has been warned that by the time he reaches the age of sixty he'll probably be blind in that eye. After four days recuperating in the hospital bed, Les returned to his Troop and completed the tour. You the reader, might be wondering why Les hadn't noticed the loss of vision in his eye and that his eye was dilated after flying back from RAF Bruggen. A lot of soldiers, Les included, shave by feel and don't use a mirror so he never saw his own face (lucky him), and because he was in Sarajevo during the winter months the lads in the Troop were allowed to wear sunglasses because of the sun reflecting off the snow, and at night it was dark and so Les wouldn't have noticed any slight change.

The troop was ultimately moved from the brick factory and into the Ice Rink in the centre of Sarajevo which the RLC lads shared with 7 Signal Regiment. The arena was the location of the 1984 Winter Olympics where Jayne Torvill and Christopher Dean won a Gold Medal for Team GB. Gloomily, the arena had been severely bombed and desecrated and the grassy areas outside had all been turned into mass graveyards. Beneath the Ice Rink were some rifle ranges that some vigilante group had used on live targets during the ethnic cleansing. IFOR troops had the grim task of helping the Bosnian Police and local undertakers in removing the cadavers. During the tour, six RLC Drivers had been shot and wounded by snipers in 'Sniper Alley' which was a road running through the centre of Sarajevo. The snipers consistently fired from bombed out blocks of flats at any army vehicle driving along the street. Les's Troop Commander Steve Jermey (later an RLC Full Colonel), was shot through the nose and the bullet ended up in the arm of his Driver, Lance Corporal 'Windy' Miller RE. The TC may well have been killed if he hadn't moved his head a split second before the bullet hit him. Tragically one soldier from the unit died on the last night when he choked on his own vomit after a heavy drinking session during the units' leaving party.

Les stayed at 14 Support Battalion for another two and a half years before being posted to 68 Squadron RLC in Dulmen, West Germany where he worked as an Admin Sergeant before doing another tour of Bosnia running a Mechanical Transport (MT) Section. On return to BAOR he was promoted to Staff Sergeant before being posted to 1 Armoured Field Ambulance (AFA) as their MT 'Staffie.' Les was divorced from his German wife by this stage of his career and got re-married to an RAMC Corporal in the unit, called Diane. 1 AFA was disbanded a short while later and amalgamated with both 2 AFA and 3 AFA to become 1 Close Support (CS) Medical Regiment RAMC and Les was absorbed into the new unit as their Evacuation Squadron Quartermaster Sergeant (SQMS). During his three years with the Medics, Les was lucky enough to be sent on tours of Kenya and an Exercise in Cyprus. During his time in the RCT Les has played hockey for the Corps, the British Army and also played for the Combined Services teams against the Welsh National team which the Welsh won 3 – 2.

In September 2002 Les was posted to the Defence School of Transport (DST) at Leconfield in East Yorkshire, as the Accommodation Stores SQMS. He unhappily worked mainly with civilians, who didn't want to change their way of doing things. The Bedding Senior Storekeeper Nigel Innes, an ex RAMC WO1 (RSM) (who has since sadly passed away) once told Les, "You're only here for a couple of years and we'll change everything back to how we like it when you've gone, so save yourself a lot of work and frustration and let us run everything the way we like it." In 2005 Les left the army and moved to Portsmouth with his wife Diane who was still serving in the RAMC and he became a house husband to their two children. The Reed family moved to York a couple of years later when Diane was posted as a Warrant Officer to 34 Field Hospital which was based in Strensall. At the same time Les went back into uniform and served in the RLC at DST Leconfield on the Full Time Reserve Service (FTRS). He taught soldiers how to operate the Weapons Mount Installation Kit (WMIK) a weapon mounted platform, used on most military vehicles, Roll Over Drills Egress Trainer (RODET), the Ridgeback and Mastiff vehicles. Whilst out on a night training Exercise, Les was catapulted out of his Ridgeback vehicle observation hatch whilst travelling over a hillock on the training area. His knee was so badly damaged that he had to have an operation that resulted in him having a titanium and plastic knee replacement. He was compulsorily discharged from the FTRS and granted compensation and a pension for his injury.

Since leaving the FTRS, Les has divorced his second wife Diane and now lives in Market Weighton where he runs Forklift, First Aid, and Health and Safety Courses and LGV Training.

24588230 Warrant Officer Class 1 (RSM) Bob Alexander QCVS RCT and RLC 1981 – to date

Lance Corporal Bob Alexander brewing and bivvying up whilst on patrol with the Royal Marine Commando's in Belize. (Note: Bob's personal weapon is an M16 Assault Rifle.)

Bob Alexander simply wanted to drive trucks for a living when he left school, but UK law decreed that he must be at least 21 years old to hold a Heavy Goods Vehicle (HGV) Licence. The only way around this annoying piece of legislation was to join the Royal Corps of Transport (RCT) for a few years, that way he could gain and hold HGV licences in the British Army as an 18 year old, and then get out after completing his three years' service. There was an army advert on the television in the 1970's which Bob was impressed with; an RCT Corporal climbed into the cab of his army truck and said, "Hi, I'm off to Düsseldorf, do you fancy coming along for the drive?" Bob was born in Dumfries and raised in Kirkkcowan in Scotland, and he was the first person in his family history to join the British Army, so his influence to join up came purely and simply from this advert and his desire to hold an HGV licence.

In 1981 Bob travelled by sleeper train from his home town in Scotland to the Junior Soldiers Battalion (JSB) in Taunton, Somerset. On arrival at 34 Squadron he was met by Sergeant Bonness his Recruit Training Sergeant. Sergeant Bonness wasn't an archetypal sort of British Army senior NCO, he didn't spend most of his days shouting at recruits just because he liked the sound of his own voice. He was the silent but deadly type of Warrior. Sensible soldiers recognised the fact that he was a quiet bear that really shouldn't be poked with a stick. Sergeant Bonness was an ex Paratrooper who'd transferred into the RCT because of an injury he'd sustained whilst soldiering in his Battalion. Putting aside his injury he was still a very fit and tough man. Just before taking his recruits on a Basic Fitness Test (a three mile run) Sergeant Bonness finished his cigarette and then stamped it out on the road. He then turned towards his raw recruits and said, "OK, let's get going. Turn to your right, by the left…double march!" and he was always the first to cross the finish line.

Bob didn't request any particular posting after he'd finished his training because he didn't know where any of the RCT units were located, so when told he was being posted to 2 Squadron in 1 ADTR (1st Armoured Division Transport Regiment) at Munsterlager, he simply accepted it with the nonchalant attitude of, "One place is as good as another." The two new arrivals were picked up by minibus from Hanover airport on Friday afternoon and they were then unceremoniously dumped at the camp gates of their new unit. Whilst the 'rookies' unloaded their kit from the back of the minibus, the driver shouted at the sentry guarding the camp gates, "Two Nig's for 1 ADTR!" The word Nig was a derogatory term for any soldier who was considered to be 'New In Germany.' Bob was eventually put into C Troop, 2 Squadron and went through the usual Nig bashing initiation ceremony. Nig's had to parade in the Squadron cellar bar, remove all of their clothes and perform a 'Dance of the flaming arseholes.' This ceremony involved a length of toilet tissue being stuffed in between the unfortunate victims bum cheeks which was then set alight. The prey had to dance around until the burning paper had extinguished itself. It was nigh on impossible not to suffer from a small amount of first degree burns. Because the entire Squadron audience became a bit bored with the traditional routine, Driver Stan Baxter was made to perform his turn whilst running around the Main Square. The ritual also included each Driver drinking the contents of a bottle of Pernod, throwing up or wimping out of this rite of passage was severely frowned upon and slaps around the head ensued as a result. Oh those halcyon days! Both extremely drunk Nig's were then taken down town to see if they could meet the drinking standard required in order for them to become a proper RCT Driver.

Some of the Drivers in 2 Squadron had formed a clique called the 'Slack Pack' and their members were constantly pushing the boundaries of military discipline. The representatives all had long hair that was stuffed under their berets whilst wearing army uniform, they firmly believed that, "What's under the beret is mine." After the initiation ceremony had been completed, the 'Slack Pack' coerced Bob and his mate into joining them down town to continue with the festivities. The ¾ of a mile walk from the accommodation block down to the camp gates took the delegation past the Squadron Headquarters. A senior 'Slack Pack' member had been bad mouthing the OC of their Squadron and he snatched Bob's nearly empty bottle of Pernod out of his hand then threw it in the general direction of the headquarters building. Unfortunately the bottle crashed through the OC's window and smashed against the office wall. The next morning the Squadron Sergeant Major went ballistic when he saw the broken glass all over the OC's office. He knew that the 'Slack Pack' were to blame for this heinous crime and so rounded them all up, because Bob had booked out of the guardroom at the same time, he was also in the frame. It wasn't a good start for Bob, he'd only been in the unit for four days and was already on OC's Orders for causing criminal damage to the Squadron Headquarters, but because he was only a Nig the OC admonished him with a warning, "Driver Alexander! If you mix with these degenerates you'll get absolutely nowhere in this man's army." Bob continued to mix with plenty of degenerates in the RCT and he actually had a very successful career within the Corps.

Over the next three years with 1 ADTR Bob did an Exercise in Canada at British Army Training Unit Suffield (BATUS), an Operational tour in McRory Park in Northern Ireland, and on leaving 1ADTR was posted to Airport Camp in Belize. The Exercise in Canada involved 1 ADTR resupplying 3rd Battalion the Queens Regiment who were also deployed out on the prairies. Bob was the co-driver on a UBRE POD (Unit Bulk Refuelling Equipment, Petrol Oil Diesel) even though he hadn't been trained how to operate the refuelling equipment. It would be a year later before Bob eventually completed his TTF (Tanker Truck Fuel) and UBRE Course, until then he could legally drive the UBRE MK truck - but that's where his responsibilities should have ended. However, Lance Corporal Moby was in charge of the vehicle and he gave Bob some on the job training and then proceeded to snooze in the cab of the truck (Moby was a member of the 'Slack Pack') whilst Bob did most of the refuelling duties. The Queens Regiments' Armoured Personnel Carriers (FV 432) divided into three lines and an RCT UBRE travelled down each row, refuelling the parked vehicles. Prior to starting a refuel, the RCT fuel team had to put an earthing spike into the ground and place two fire extinguishers at the front and rear of the truck. They also had to adhere to all of the safety rules and only use their assigned non-spark tools. The Fire Extinguishers and earthing spike would have to be moved and replaced every time the UBRE moved onto the next APC. With forty APC's to refuel, the safety procedures took time and were in essence a bit of a pain in the arse for the team. For the sake of expediency Bob simply didn't carry out these safety procedures mainly because he was working on his own. Lance Corporal Moby was snoozing in the driving seat of the truck most of the time and only woke up when Bob tapped on the roof of the cab and told him to drive forward to the next APC.

After connecting the fuel line into the next APC, Bob noticed that the legs of his overalls were on fire and suddenly the back of the UBRE erupted into flames. After jumping off the truck, Bob beat out the flames on his legs with his leather gauntlets and screamed for Moby to get out of the truck. Moby hadn't noticed he'd locked the door locking button with his elbow whilst snoozing, and when he saw the flames in his rear view mirror he went into a serious panic mode. He started kicking his driver side locked door because the fire had already engulfed the truck's passenger side door. After a couple of seconds he realised his mistake, unlocked the door and jumped down from the truck before legging it towards Bob. He shouted, "Fucking hell Bob, what the fuck happened!" Bob hadn't a clue what had happened, there hadn't been an electrical storm and he was fairly sure he didn't cause the fuel to ignite, it would take a military board of inquiry to solve the conundrum. When the UBRE burst into flames the parked APC crews carried out their Unit Standard Operating Procedures (SOP's) and immediately drove to a safe distance from the fire. The APC that Bob was refuelling had, unfortunately, also caught fire. The Infantry crew started yelling, "MORTARS! THERE'S LIVE MORTARS IN THE APC!" Everyone either drove or ran to a safe distance and the two vehicles weren't approached until the fire had burned itself out and the mortars had stopped exploding. Bizarrely, when Bob returned to his wrecked UBRE the next day he astonishingly found the Bedford MK's diesel engine was still running. The write off bill for this minor Training Exercise incident included 1x APC, 1x Bedford MK UBRE, 1 x General Purpose Machine Gun (GPMG), numerous Self Loading Rifles (SLR's), Mortar rounds and some Small Arms Ammunition (SAA), all this and a long list of other minor equipment. God bless the British Tax Payer. When the Squadron returned to BAOR Bob and Moby had to remain in Canada for another two months until the Board of Enquiry had concluded their findings. To pass the time the unfortunate RCT lads had to take part in some Adventure Training in the Rocky Mountains. The Board of Enquiry worked out that whilst Bob was refuelling the APC some diesel fuel and vapours had trickled through a hole in their drip tray and it had run down a slope at the side of the UBRE. Further down the slope a soldier had decided to get some hot food organised for the troops and he lit up a number 2 burner. The kerosene operated military catering equipment is like an oversized Bunsen burner lying on its side, once fired up the burner ignited the trickling diesel fuel which then back tracked up to the UBRE and caused the catastrophic damage.

Driver Bob Alexandra's burnt out UBRE (Unit Bulk Refuelling Equipment) in BATUS (British Army Training Unit Suffield) Canada. (Note: The fuel tanks and pumping system on the back of the MK have been totally destroyed after the explosion.)

On return to Munsterlager Bob was posted to Bunde where he was selected to box for the Regiment against the Queens Regiment. Wullie McMillan, an old school mate who was serving in the Kings Own Scottish Borderers Regiment (KOSB), warned him about the boxer he was going to fight in the forthcoming competition. He was up against Private Vickers who was supposed to be a bit of an animal when he stepped inside a boxing ring. Bob states that, "Private Vickers won the fight fair and square on a majority decision, but I think he won it mainly because he showed much more aggression in the ring than I did." After the fight, Private Vickers did the gentlemanly thing and held open the ropes for Bob to step out of the ring. Bob refused and offered him the same compliment on his side of the ring, neither boxer wanted to accept but Vickers was the one who gave way and he stepped out of the ring whilst Bob held open the side ropes for him. The Regiment lost the competition by seven bouts to two but the RCT boxers had put up a great display in front of 1st British Corps, 1 (BR) Corps, Brigadier. At the post-fight party Bob got pissed very quickly because he hadn't had any alcohol during the preceding months, he'd been on a strict diet and training regime that was accompanied by total abstinence from alcohol. He woke up the following morning with his Squadron Sergeant Major and Troop Staff Sergeant screaming at him to get out of his pit. "Driver Alexander! Get your fucking arse out of bed, the OC wants you tapping the boards in front of his desk in less than five minutes, come on, fucking move yourself!" Bob thought the worst because he had no recollections about what

218

he'd got up to during the previous evenings high jinks, he thought, 'What the fuck did I do last night?'

After putting on his tracksuit and splashing some water on his face he was verbally bounced across to the Headquarters where he was confronted by a stern looking OC.

Bob: "Good morning sir."

OC: "What were you up to last night Alexander?"

Bob: "I was boxing for the regiment sir."

OC: "And?"

Bob: "Well unfortunately I got beat sir."

OC: "What else did you do Alexander?"

Bob: "We had a few drinks and then I went straight to bed sir."

OC: "You must have done something else last night or why else would you be up in front of me this morning?"

Bob: "I'm sorry but I haven't got a clue what I've done sir?"

OC: "Well, 1 (BR) Corps Commander came into our Officers' Mess after the fight last night and told everyone how impressed he was with your leadership skills."

Bob: "Sorry sir, I don't understand, what do you mean by my leadership skills?"

OC: "You made another soldier do something that he didn't want to do. You made Private Vickers climb through your ropes and he believes that is a good display of your leadership qualities. On the authority of the Brigade Commander you are hereby promoted to Local Lance Corporal. Congratulations and well done."

The OC took a Lance Corporal's tape out of his drawer, presented it to Bob and then shook his hand. Bob had the rank on his arm but he now had to gain the qualifications to justify it. Over the next six months Bob did his B2 Course and HGV II followed by a Junior Military Qualification (JMQC) and finally his TTF and UBRE POD Course. Bob wasn't quite 18 years old by the time he'd completed all of these Courses and he was soon promoted to substantive Lance Corporal and he completed his tour of Northern Ireland as a Section 2i/c.

A year after returning from the Province, Bob was sent on a six month detachment to Belize in Central America. It was a long flight out to Belize and Bob was feeling very tired, so when some of the RCT Section tried to talk him into going down to Raul's Rose Garden, he politely declined. Raul's Rose Garden was a den of iniquity that really should have been called, 'Raul's knob rotting whore house.' This Belizean establishment proudly displayed its business philosophy on an exterior wall of the building, '**Raul's Rose Garden, where every customer comes first.**' This iconic erection (sorry but I couldn't resist that one) burned down in 2011. On Bob's first day he was given an orientation tour of Airport Camp which involved a visit to the Camp Medical Reception Station (MRS). On one particular ward the beds were occupied by eight 'casualties' who had all seen action at Raul's place. One soldier's testicles had swollen to the size of coconuts (probably an Orchitis infection) and others had pus oozing from various disgusting venereal sores. The other patients were suffering from lesser diseases like scabies and pubic lice. The Medical Sergeant waved a condom at Bob and the other new arrivals and told them, "If you do go down town for the night, we've got plenty of these available and they won't cost you a penny, just pick them up from the guardroom on your way out." Bob never frequented the Rose Garden after seeing the results of what one drunken night could achieve.

A Driver in the Squadron had put in a written application to marry his girlfriend who was a prostitute working in Raul's Rose Garden. The OC and SSM were deeply concerned, but no matter how hard they tried, they couldn't persuade the soldier to change his mind about getting married to a Belizean whore. One day he was detailed to drive the baggage truck that was going to meet a flight returning to the UK. After unloading the returning soldiers' suitcases from his vehicle and making sure they were then all safely loaded onto the RAF VC10, he drove back to the airport terminal. An RAF serviceman told him to report to the pilot on the aircraft because they'd discovered a problem with one of the suitcases. Once on board the plane he was asked to produce his Identity Card and a Flight Sergeant checked his details. When the crew were happy they'd got the right man he was told to take a seat and put on his seat belt because he was flying back to the UK with them. He pleaded, "You've got to be joking, I can't go back to the UK, I'm getting married to a local girl next week." his pleas fell on totally deaf ears. The OC and SSM had pre-arranged the deception with the RAF's help just so they could get him out of Belize. The Driver hadn't even noticed that he'd loaded his own secretly packed kit onto the plane.

Bob drove the camp rubbish truck for his first two weeks at Airport Camp. After emptying the bins into his truck he'd drive down to the local rubbish dump which stank to high heaven, the stench on the site was almost overpowering. On his first trip to the rubbish dump he spotted plenty of local vagrants with plastic bags sifting through the rubbish in the hope of finding anything remotely useful. The arrival of the British Army rubbish truck seemed to cause a flurry of interest and even before Bob had had the chance to park up the scavengers swamped over his vehicle. They dragged the black plastic bags out of the back and immediately ripped them open in the hope of finding some treasure that a British Serviceman deemed to be worthless. Bob found his two weeks on the rubbish truck quite disturbing because some of the Belizean people were living in abject poverty.

Whilst Bob was at Airport Camp, the Royal Marines were carrying out a campaign to find and destroy some of the illegal marijuana fields that were hidden in the jungle. He volunteered to join them on a two week patrol in the unforgiving tropical rain forest. Being attached to the Royal Marines gave him a first-hand opportunity to see how the Commandos operated in the field. He also gained some valuable experience on how to live and survive in a jungle environment. Bob drove one of the vehicles to the Commandos drop off point and then accompanied the Green Berets on their patrol. In the evening it gets dark very quickly in the tropical forest and therefore it's important that a soldier can quickly and competently set up an SAS style A-frame shelter. Once his shelter was constructed a soldier must then cook and eat an evening meal before last light because any fire in the jungle would betray the harbour area to possible enemy forces. Bob went through the same routine every night for two weeks. Everything the Commandos did, he followed suit and that included slogging through the hot and steamy wilderness. He loved every minute of it.

One thing he noticed about the Royal Marines was the fact they could win an Olympic Gold Medal in the eating discipline. Their workload on the patrol was so strenuous that each Marine was given two 24 hour ration packs, every day, to sustain them whilst in the Ulu (Jungle). They even tried to scrounge any leftovers that Bob didn't want. Several days into the patrol one of the Marines got bored and he chopped down a tree whilst waiting for his food to heat up, the tree was rotten and it fell down without using up too much energy. After last light Bob couldn't see his hand in front of his face because it was so dark, the moonlight simply couldn't penetrate the jungle canopy and whilst lying in his shelter, wearing nothing but his gungies, Bob could feel things crawling all over his face and body. The Marine who had felled the tree was responsible for disturbing an ant's nest and the whole area became covered in the damned things, not even the soldiers mosquito nets could keep them out. It was an unnerving and unpleasant experience. Bob spent the last two weeks of his tour in Belize driving the ration truck down to the Belize Keys. He was solely responsible for delivering the daily rations from Airport Camp to a beautiful facility where soldiers enjoyed some hard earned Rest and Recuperation (R&R). Once his truck was unloaded, Bob spent the rest of the day either sunbathing or swimming. Bob was posted to 22 Signal Regiment in BAOR for a year after leaving Belize and his time with the 'Bleeps' wasn't exactly scintillating. He was put back on the UBRE's and spent the next six months, on and off, on Exercise. Bob describes what it was like working with 22 Signal Regiment. "They called it being on Exercise but they remained static in one location for the whole period of the Exercise and the only military practice they performed was camouflaging their trucks. I drove to 10 Regiment RCT in Bielefeld every day to replenish my UBRE and then drove to the same location to top up their vehicles and Jerry Cans, it was really boring."

In 1986 Bob was posted to C Troop, 17 Squadron, 10 Regiment RCT and was promoted to full Corporal at the same time. There he was put in Command of a Section of 10 tonners. During his time at 10 Regiment he was given the option of joining the regimental boxing team or going with 17 Squadron to Northern Ireland. Because he was new to the boxing team and hadn't got a firm placement in the team, he chose to go to Belfast instead. Regardless of what job a soldier would be doing on the tour everyone still had to take part in all aspects of the Northern Ireland training, which included Driver Training on the 'Pig' APC. At the time the weather in Germany was bitterly cold, so driving a 'Pig' that didn't have any form of heating for the driver or passengers was a miserable experience. Some of the Section Commanders got their heads together and decided to meet up at RAF Gutersloh Camp during that nights Driver Training. The latest film 'Top Gun' was being shown at the Services Sound and Vision Corporation (SSVC) Cinema so they could all watch the film whilst keeping out of the cold at the same time.

Next day on the Squadron Working Parade, WO2 (SSM) Stevie Hearn seemed particularly pissed off. He shouted at everyone on parade, "It has been bought to my attention that a number of Sections went to the cinema in Gutersloh last night instead of carrying out their Driver Training duties. Those who were at the cinema last night take one step forward now!" No-one moved a muscle for fear of it being taken as a sign of being guilty, and so the SSM upped his game, "I want to know which of you fuckers was watching 'Top Gun' last night and if you don't step forward then I'm going to punish the whole Squadron." Bob, Corporal Lionel Braithwaite and Corporal Eddie Smith all looked at each other and stepped forward, the three of them took full responsibility for the jolly boys evening. That afternoon they were put on Commanding Officers Orders where he awarded them a £200 fine each with a severe reprimand to be noted on their records, they would also be kicked off the Northern Ireland tour. As it turned

222

out there weren't enough Section Commanders available to cover the tour so the last bit was quietly forgotten about. Bob subsequently found out that it was Lieutenant James Craig, a Troop Commander from 9 Squadron, who'd put in the bubble on the guys from 17 Squadron. When a Troop Commander sneakily drops men in the shit with their Squadron Commander, it breeds a lot of resentment.

On arrival in Belfast, Bob was put in charge of various civilian style petrol tankers that might as well have had, 'WE ARE SQUADDIE'S' printed on their sides. At the time the IRA was threatening British Petroleum (BP) that if they continued supplying the British Army with fuel they would execute any of their tanker drivers and or their families. To resolve the problem, Bob and his Section drove their tankers all over the province supplying army locations with the fuel needed for their vehicles. After making a delivery at a very small outpost in Aughnacloy on the border of Southern Ireland, Bob headed back to Moscow Camp. Drivers had to vary their routes so that the IRA couldn't anticipate their movements and this involved driving along some of the very narrow B and C Class roads in South Armagh. Whichever route they took was always ripe for an ambush because the tankers always travelled without an escort. In the event of being bushwhacked, each tanker crew was tooled up with two 9mm High Powered Browning pistols and a couple of Colt Armalite rifles so that they could defend themselves. Bob was driving the tanker up a hill on a very narrow road when in the distance he saw some armed men step into the road and they held up their arms to indicate that they wanted him to stop. Bob couldn't reverse the tanker to get away and there weren't any side roads where he could escape. He immediately stopped and applied the handbrake whilst they were still quite a distance from the blockade. His co-driver said, "Here we go," and they both pulled out and cocked their pistols ready for a shoot-out. As they prepared to do a Butch Cassidy and the Sundance kid final scene, an Ulster Defence Regiment (UDR) Land Rover pulled into view and parked up next to the armed men, the potential terrorists were in fact UDR soldiers.

After completing their tour in Belfast, the Squadron returned to Bielefeld and Bob was included in the 10 Regiment RCT Boxing team that won the 4th Division (4th Div) finals. 10 Regiment and the Queens were tied at four wins each just before the final bout of the evening was about to commence, Bob had won his bout on a unanimous decision. 10 Regiment placed their faith in a Glaswegian Driver called 'Mel' to finally win the competition for them. Both sides of supporting soldiers were going ballistic on the night and as the event was held in 10 Regiment's gymnasium the RCT supporters were desperate to win on their home ground. In Round One, 'Mel' battered his opposite number all around the ring, but his enthusiasm seemed to have sapped his energy and in Round Two he was on the receiving end of some very good punches. It was

'Even Stevens' between the two boxers. The result of the whole competition was going to be decided in the very last round. Both boxers went toe to toe at full pelt because the honour of their Regiments' was at stake. In the last minute of the Third Round it looked like the bout was going to end in a draw when the referee shouted, **"STOP"** to both boxers. The Queens boxer caught 'Mel' with one more punch and he dropped to the canvas. 'Mel' was completely unconscious and an RAMC doctor who was officiating at the fight stepped into the ring to treat him. It was absolute pandemonium in the gymnasium as the Queens Regiment soldiers rose to their feet and cheered with delight. Only those soldiers who have attended an army boxing competition can understand what the noise and passion was like on that night. When 'Mel' started to come round, the referee tried to help him stand up but 'Mel' looked and behaved like an intoxicated prize fighter suffering with Muscular Dystrophy. In the ensuing noise and confusion the referee finally got through to the judges that the last punch was illegal and that he was disqualifying the Queens boxer, 10 Regiment RCT were the 4 Div boxing champions.

Bob had won all of his fights in the 4 Div competition and as a result he was entered into the Army Individual Championships in Berlin. During the competition Bob was caught with a magnificent left hook which caused him to collapse onto the canvas. He felt pain in his legs and back but was unable to get to his feet because of a sensation of paralysis. Bob was stretchered out of the ring and taken to BMH Berlin were an army surgeon diagnosed that he had a trapped nerve and a slipped disc in his back. He was put on traction and remained in the hospital for the next three weeks before being taken to BMH Rinteln in West Germany. It took Bob several months to get back to full fitness which was when he went on his Senior Military Qualification Certificate (SMQC) Course at Buller Barracks in Aldershot. He blitzed the promotion course and on return to 10 Regiment he was transferred into the Regimental Training Wing as a Junior Military Qualification Certificate (JMQC) instructor. Bob was so good at instructing that he was recommended for a post as an Instructor at the Corps' Depot, Buller Barracks in Aldershot where he'd be teaching the RCT recruits on their Basic Training courses. In 1990 Bob was also used at the Depot to help train some of the Battle Casualty Replacement (BCR) soldiers who were deploying out on the First Gulf War. Although disappointed that he couldn't go himself Bob says, "With hindsight that was probably a good thing for me, especially when you see some of the medical and psychological problems those veterans are suffering today."

After instructing recruits at the Depot for three years, Bob was then posted to the Princess Marina College at Arborfield as an Acting Sergeant where he would be a Troop Sergeant at the REME (Royal Electrical and Mechanical Engineers) Depot for the next eighteen months. Because the college at

Arborfield was primarily a REME establishment, Bob was the only RCT soldier on the camp. When he visited his old RCT mates at Buller Barracks he was surprised to see them all wearing a different style stable belt and cap badge. The Royal Corps of Transport had been disbanded six weeks previously and had now trans-morphed into the Royal Logistics Corps (RLC). No-one in the Corps had thought to inform Bob.

By 1993 the conflict and violence in Northern Ireland had been vastly reduced in comparison to the 'Troubles' of the 1970's, and as a result the amount of military boots on the ground was reduced accordingly. The British Army's' roulement tours were expensive to maintain because it was costly to fly whole Battalions and Regiments into and out of Northern Ireland every 4 - 6 months. So the military 'Heads of Sheds' at the MOD decided to abandon the practice and install a permanent answer to the problem. 26 Squadron RCT/RLC was and is a permanent fixture in Northern Ireland but now it was being expanded with the addition of E Troop. These supplementary troops were posted to Kinnegar in County Down as part of 21 Logistic Support Regiment and Bob was the Troops' Admin Sergeant for the next three years. He was heavily involved in setting up the new unit and was responsible for the administration of seventy to eighty RLC soldiers. Bob left E Troop after six months to set up another new post in 21 Log Sup HQ and within eighteen months he was promoted to Staff Sergeant. His promotion came with a posting to 77 Squadron in 27 Regiment RLC at Aldershot where his job would be Squadron Quartermaster Sergeant (SQMS). He arrived on Saturday and reported to Captain Roger Cass, who was the QM (Tech), on Monday morning. The QM Tech is a Quartermaster in charge of a units technical stores, like vehicles, radios, and weapons. The moment Captain Cass spotted Bob in the corridor he called him into his office:

Captain Cass: "Good morning Staff, congratulations on your promotion by the way and welcome to 27 Regiment."

Bob: "Thank you sir."

Captain Cass: "Do you have your passport available?"

Bob: "Why sir?"

Captain Cass: "You're going to Bosnia on Tuesday."

Bob: "What! You don't mean next week do you sir?"

Captain Cass: "No …..I mean tomorrow."

Bob: "Oh shit. I'll have to go home and find it sir."

Bob went straight back to his Married Quarter where his wife was busy emptying the packing boxes. His passport was out of date and so two days later he went to the passport office in London to get a new one. Bob flew out to Bosnia within seven days of arriving at his new unit, which only goes to prove that life never stands still for long in the British Army. The tour in Bosnia was challenging for the whole Squadron because of the overwhelming amount of snow that fell in their area of Operations in the mountains. The units' tents and Portakabin accommodation collapsed under the sheer weight of snow and ice and as a result the unit was ultimately moved back to Split. After eight months operating as an SQMS Bob then served within 27 Regiment as their TQMS (Technical Quartermaster Sergeant) before being posted back to 10 Regiment RLC which was now based in Colchester. He went on promotion to WO2 (SSM) and took charge of the soldiers of 66 Fuel Tanker Squadron RLC. Bob was surprised and somewhat downhearted to find out that his new OC was Major James Craig RLC, the same Officer who was responsible for getting him a £200 fine for watching Top Gun. Over the next 2 ½ years Bob had to endure Major Craig telling him how wonderful his previous SSM was, luckily Bob eventually picked up a posting to the Scottish Transport Regiment in Glasgow before he did something he really would have regretted. He reported for duty in Glasgow as a WO 2 because Major Craig had only given him a mediocre Confidential Report and Bob thought that he was being put out to grass for his last four years in the army.

The last years of his army service can hardly be equated to being put out to grass. After a couple of years, Bob was posted back to NICSS (Northern Ireland Combat Service Support) Regiment in Kinnegar as the WO 1 (RSM). He and his wife were divorced by this time and he had a request to put to his female Commanding Officer, Lieutenant Colonel Gardner after they'd dealt with the usual aspects of Monday morning Regimental life.

Bob: "Ma'm, I've got a personal request I'd like to put to you if you don't mind."

CO: "What is it you want RSM?"

Bob: "I'd like permission to date one of your Squadron WO2's Ma'am."

The CO looked quite startled at the request/announcement and asked,

CO: "Which one?"

Bob realised what his boss was wondering and quickly put her right.

Bob: "Oh no, nothing like that Ma'am! She's one of the female ones."

CO: "Hmmn, thank goodness for that. These days one has to ask, RSM."

 Bob: "Yes Ma'am."

The request was immediately turned down and so Bob saluted and marched out of the office. As he reached the door the CO called him back because she'd changed her mind (typical woman – sorry, cheap shot). As long as they were both discreet, Lieutenant Colonel Gardner would allow their relationship to continue. Bob describes his boss, who later became a Brigadier, as being one of the best Officers in the Corps. He says of his brief interview, "It felt like I was asking my Mum if I could go out to play." During his tenure at NICSS Bob took part in a Carrington Drum challenge and helped to raise £15,000 in aid of the Army Benevolent Fund (ABF) and was subsequently awarded a Queens Commendation for Valuable Service (QCVS).

As he approached his discharge from the army, Bob applied to join Lothian Border Police but instead took a job on the Long Service List (LSL) at Defence Equipment Support (DE&S) in Andover. He was then posted to APC Glasgow as WO1 Operational Commitments for soldiers for the next six years and he then extended to become the Regimental Sergeant Major (RSM).

Life at APC became a little bit too mundane for Bob. He was in his late 40's and had come to the conclusion that he'd like to do something a bit more challenging. "For the sake of my own sanity I assigned myself to go on one of my Operational Posts and deployed on a four month tour of Afghanistan in 2012. I was working with Media Ops in Lashkar Gah and provided Close Protection to any journalists visiting the British Area of Operations. I felt like a young Corporal again because I was tooled up and got to work with the Royal Marines and Parachute Regiment." This is how the journalist Adam Cornell described Warrant Officer Class One Bob Alexander RLC:

"He was to be my escort. I liked him from the moment I heard his name. Bob is a good name, a safe name – you can rely on Bob. Luckily my instincts turned out to be right. From getting me breakfast on the first morning - after I had managed to rack up a massive five hours sleep in two days - to looking after me throughout the first part of the tour, he never let me down. I decided to stick

closer to him than loved up teenagers at a school disco. Part security blanket and part actual armed protection he proved invaluable."

Bob was the first member of his family to join the British Army and he may have started a trend, his son Lance Corporal Grant Alexander is currently serving in the Corps of Royal Military Police in Aldershot.

Epilogue

Joining up into any branch of the Armed Forces can be an intimidating, and yet wonderful experience. You need to be both mentally and physically tough in the Forces because at some stage you are going to end up in a violent situation, albeit in a pub or on a battlefield somewhere in the world. It's the nature of the beast I'm afraid. On the other hand you will make friends with other servicemen who will risk their own lives to pull you out of the shit, buy you a beer when you've already spent your last penny and those same people will also make you laugh when you really feel like crying. And yes, soldiers do cry. This happens every day in all branches of the British Army, Royal Navy, Royal Marines and the Royal Air Force. The same can be said of old comrades who are no longer serving but are still prepared to travel great distances just to call in for an hour or so to have a brew and a catch up. Steve Tong and Keith 'Hank' Antcliffe are just two of many old friends that popped in to see me this year, and for no other reason than we hadn't seen each other for many years. That bond of friendship can never be broken.

Whilst writing 'Rickshaws Camels and Taxis' I travelled all over the country to interview old comrades and record their experiences. I hadn't seen some of those interviewee's in over thirty five years and yet the conversations continued as if I'd only just walked out of the room for a couple of minutes. Some looked as fit as they did all those years ago, albeit a little greyer on top, others had piled on a few pounds (and yes that includes the author) but the one thing that remained resolute in absolutely every one of them was a cheeky smile, a firm handshake, and a very warm welcome into their homes. I met some of these ex-RCT soldiers for the first time when I conducted their interviews for this book and yet they treated me like a long lost brother, which only goes to prove that our Corps really was, and still is, a 'Band of Brothers.'

When I started writing 'Rickshaws Camels and Taxis' (Rogues, Ruffians and Officers of the Royal Corps of Transport) in 2013, I wanted to show the diversity of Trades that soldiers of the Royal Corps of Transport covered and I also wanted to show exactly what sort of characters they were. Courageous but sometimes flawed is, I think, one way of describing them, and tough but complex has to be added into this mix. I pretty much wanted to do the same in 'Most Roads Led to 10 Regt' and I think I've achieved my aim. Soldiers of the RCT were, in general, very tough men who were extremely proud of their Corps. I would like to take this opportunity of thanking everyone who graciously invited me (and on occasions my wife Nicky) into their homes and extended us such a generous and courteous welcome. Without your time, patience and effort, the biographies in both of these books would never have been written and all of that personal and Corps history would have been lost forever.

Thank you

Brian (Harry) Clacy

BIBLIOGRAPHY

Gallant and Distinguished Service (The Royal Army Service Corps and Royal Corps of Transport Medal Collection 1794 – 1993). Published in 2006 by the Trustees of the Royal Army Service Corps and Riyal Corps of Transport Institution.

My War on Wheels. Farthings Publishing September 2012, 8/1 Avenue Victoria Scarborough YO11 2QB.

Red Ball Express. Ian Allan Publishing August 2007.

The Story of the RASC and RCT 1945 – 1982. Brigadier John Sutton. Leo Cooper in association with Secker and Warburg, London 1983.

Wait for the Waggon. The Story of Royal Corps of Transport and its Predecessors. Brigadier John Sutton. Pen and Sword Books Ltd, Barnsley 1998.

TWO MEDICS, ONE NURSE AND A GOB DOCTOR

Two wars in Iraq without fighting

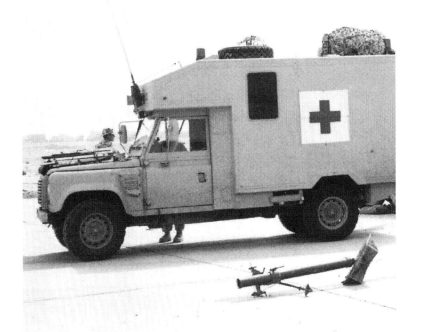

Brian (Harry) Clacy

always
HARRY^WAS
A CRAP HAT

Brian (Harry) Clacy

RICKSHAWS, CAMELS AND TAXIS

Rogues, Ruffians and Officers of the
Royal Corps of Transport

Written by **Brian (Harry) Clacy**

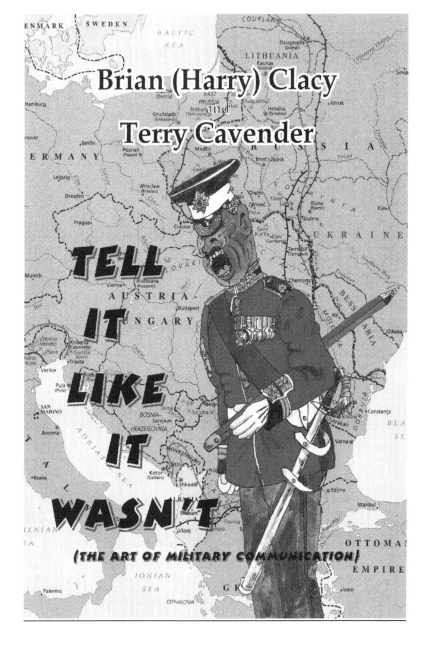

Brian (Harry) Clacy
Terry Cavender

TELL IT LIKE IT WASN'T

(THE ART OF MILITARY COMMUNICATION)